PERSONALITY FACTORS ON THE COLLEGE CAMPUS
Review of a Symposium

Editors: ROBERT L. SUTHERLAND
WAYNE H. HOLTZMAN
EARL A. KOILE
BERT KRUGER SMITH

Contributors:
NEVITT SANFORD
T. R. MCCONNELL
C. ROBERT PACE
ERNEST R. HILGARD
THEODORE M. NEWCOMB
DANA L. FARNSWORTH
FILLMORE SANFORD
ROBERT F. PECK
MARTIN TROW

D1517514

Published by: THE HOGG FOUNDATION FOR MENTAL HEALTH
THE UNIVERSITY OF TEXAS
AUSTIN, TEXAS 78712

PRINTED IN THE UNITED STATES OF AMERICA
BY THE PRINTING DIVISION OF THE UNIVERSITY OF TEXAS

the **Hogg Foundation** for Mental Health

THE UNIVERSITY OF TEXAS • AUSTIN 12, TEXAS

Dear Reader:

Social scientists have studied communities from Samoa to Iceland to Outer Mongolia. They have also examined nearer at hand subcultures such as hobohemia in a metropolis; suburbia on the fringe; and Elmtown in the country. Investigators have gone out from the colleges to make these studies.

Now the trend includes something new. The college community itself has been discovered by its own social scientists, who have found that the subcultures and the processes of informal communication have much to do with the educative goal of the college.

The question of who the student is and what constitutes the total culture in which he lives has been looked at intensively in recent years by R. Nevitt Sanford in his psychological work at Vassar, by C. Robert Pace in his psychological-culture studies at Syracuse, and by Martin Trow in his sociological inquiry at the University of California. These and similar efforts were reported in 1960 and 1961 at meetings in Berkeley sponsored by the Western Interstate Commission on Higher Education. Colleges in the South also have responded through conferences called by the Southern Regional Education Board. Behavioral science departments and the Hogg Foundation for Mental Health at The University of Texas had a part in this trend.

Planning for the symposium here reported, "Personality Factors on the College Campus," began in the offices of the college presidents or deans on 30 campuses. Personal visits, a bit new in conference technique, were made by Earl A. Koile, Department of Educational Psychology, The University of Texas; Lucile Allen, Consultant to the Hogg Foundation and now Dean of Women, Stanford University; and William E. Truax, Director of Student Personnel and Guidance, East Texas State College. From these interviews grew a list of problems which were to be reflected in the agenda of the conference.

Contributors to the conference, in addition to the leaders already mentioned, included T. R. McConnell, University of California; Ernest R. Hilgard, Stanford University; Theodore M. Newcomb, The University of Michigan; and Dana L. Farnsworth, Harvard University. Papers were given by staff members of The University of Texas and of other colleges of the state.

Wayne H. Holtzman, in charge of research at the Hogg Foundation, moderated the session which reviewed studies on local campuses. He has edited and commented on the papers thus assembled.

Bert Kruger Smith, head of the Foundation's Professional Information Division, performed the complicated task of editing and integrating the entire volume. Fillmore H. Sanford, Professor of Psychology, The University of Texas, reacted to the papers as he read them, putting down in by-play fashion his query or comment. Earl A. Koile listened to the yards of tape recordings to salvage ideas from the discussions.

In this publication the term "conference" is stretched a bit because two papers were added after it was over. One, an attempt to classify students according to their mental health, written by Robert F. Peck, Professor of Educational Psychology, is based on four years of inquiry. The other, Part III, was given by Martin Trow, Professor of Sociology, University of California, at the Southern Regional Education Board Conference in Austin, Texas in July, 1961. He and they generously let us fill an important gap in the November meeting with this concluding paper.

The conference has already lived beyond its adjournment. More people are beginning to think about the way social science can help the educator, the parent, and the community worker understand the subculture known as the campus. Because this view of the student in his culture has mental health implications, the Foundation staff was pleased to join the social scientists on the campus to sponsor the meeting and to facilitate the printing of this report.

ROBERT L. SUTHERLAND, *Director*

The education of a college student cannot be understood adequately just in terms of the courses he takes or the professors with whom he comes in contact. A student learns and develops in a complex environment, being influenced by and influencing the student groups of which he is a member, the friendships he forms, and the roles he plays in college affairs. He also is influenced by his teachers, advisors, and the somewhat intangible climate of the college.

During the past ten years, an increasing number of colleges have begun to recognize the need for greater understanding of the learning and developmental processes taking place on their campuses. This knowledge could provide a basis for more intelligent planning of college programs and for more effective teaching and guidance of students than has been the case. At the same time, social scientists have begun to appreciate the fact that the college campus is an excellent laboratory for the study of social processes.

As these two interests in student development and education on the college campus became known, the Social Science Research Council appointed a Committee on Personality Development in Youth, one purpose of which is to encourage and assist social scientists in investigating social processes on the campus. In the Spring of 1959 the Committee sponsored the Andover Conference to which were invited 75 social scientists conducting studies of college students. At this conference, reports were made on the progress of studies under way, and arrangements were worked out for continuing exchange of information among the colleges and research workers involved. The Committee has identified more than 100 colleges and universities where studies of this sort are going on. Ultimately they will provide not only knowledge useful to each campus but more widely a broader and deeper understanding of the problems and processes involved in the development of educating American youth.

RALPH W. TYLER, *Director*
Center for Advanced Study in the Behavioral
    Sciences
Stanford, California

the *Hogg Foundation* for Mental Health

THE UNIVERSITY OF TEXAS • AUSTIN 12, TEXAS

MEMORANDUM

The publication program of the Hogg Foundation is based partly on trial efforts to communicate mental health information in new ways. These efforts have been directed especially at describing pilot projects in community mental health and in translating the findings of basic research.

Other innovations have been added. One is an "Air Force Blue" series from the Foundation-sponsored seminars for chaplains. The second is a quick preview of research published in summary fashion while the findings are still fresh.

Personality Factors on the College Campus represents the third innovation, which began in 1960 with the appearance of a report on an aging conference. The publication at hand also communicates to many people who did not attend the meeting what was new and underlined. It is our hope that still more high-level conferences may be reported in like manner. Special thanks for painstaking assistance with this book go to J. Louise Chatham of the Foundation staff.

BERT KRUGER SMITH
Professional Information Division

STEERING COMMITTEE

Dr. Ira Iscoe
Associate Professor of Psychology
The University of Texas

Dr. Earl A. Koile
Associate Professor of Educational Psychology;
Coordinator of Counseling, Testing and Counseling Center
The University of Texas

Dr. Reece McGee
Associate Professor of Sociology
The University of Texas

Dr. Robert F. Peck
Professor of Educational Psychology
The University of Texas

Dr. Robert L. Sutherland
Professor of Sociology;
Director, The Hogg Foundation for Mental Health
The University of Texas

EVALUATION COMMITTEE

Dr. William C. Adamson, Director
The Woods Schools
Langhorne, Pennsylvania

Dr. Joseph Bobbitt
Assistant Director
National Institute of Mental Health

Dr. John K. Folger
Dean of the Graduate School
Florida State University

Dr. Lorrin Kennamer
Associate Dean, College of Arts and Sciences
The University of Texas

Dr. William E. Truax
Director of Student Personnel and Guidance
East Texas State College

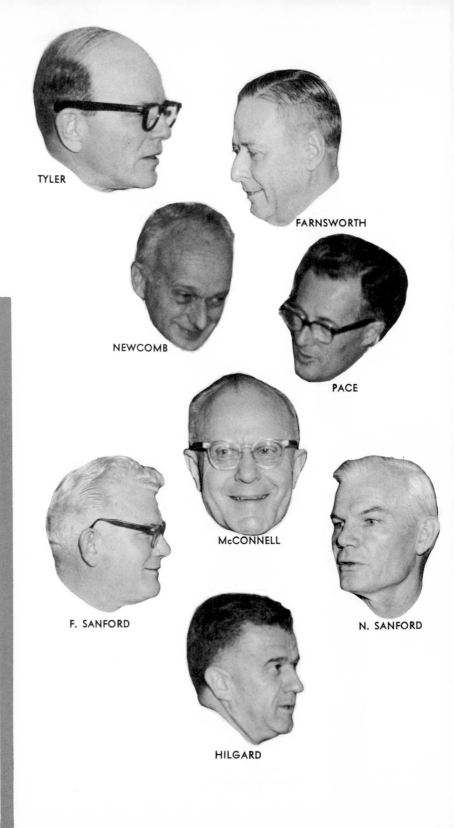

TYLER

FARNSWORTH

NEWCOMB

PACE

McCONNELL

F. SANFORD

N. SANFORD

HILGARD

CONTENTS

Some Questions Submitted in Advance of the Symposium

Dr. McConnell's research points to the belief that students categorize the college—make it a certain type. What process would be necessary to alter college type? In what ways does college type relate to mortality rate of students?

In view of present world conditions, what effective steps may be taken in institutions of higher learning to develop attitudes, skills, and knowledge which will improve the impact of educated Americans on world ideologies?

An area which appears to be of major concern is the use of peers to work with students in academic and educational advising and in activities in the college dormitory. It would be helpful to know more about successful practices and research findings that would shed light on the subject of dormitory counseling as well as the use of dormitories as an educational medium.

PART I

Ed. Note: The interpolations identified by italics represent remarks from the discussions held after the talk. Speakers are not identified because, in many cases, the remarks are a composite of statements made by several people.

Remarks identified by bold face paragraphs are those of Fillmore H. Sanford, Professor of Psychology, The University of Texas, who was invited to comment on each paper.

KOILE
SUTHERLAND
RANSOM
HOLTZMAN

F. SANFORD
N. SANFORD

FOLGER
SMITH
HOBBS

Chapter I

IMPLICATIONS OF PERSONALITY STUDIES
for curriculum and personnel planning

Liberal education has as its aim the fullest possible development of the individual personality. The limits of human potentiality are unknown, and there is no generally agreed way of describing the fully developed individual; but it seems that one may set forth the essence of much psychological theory and include the explicit aims of many educators by saying that the highly developed personality is characterized chiefly by complexity and by wholeness.

In such a personality the processes of perceiving, thinking, feeling, and willing are sufficiently differentiated so that the individual is uniquely responsive to multitudinous aspects of his natural, social, and cultural environments; the largeness of his world is matched by the diversity of his interrelated sensibilities and capacities; he has breadth of understanding, subtlety of appreciation, and freedom in judgment and action.

At the same time, all these different parts and processes of the person are organized; communication among them is sufficient so that the person is capable of acting as a unit, calling upon such of his resources as are needed for the solution of new problems; the judging and controlling parts of the personality are in touch with the deeper sources of emotion and will; there is freedom of imagination and an enduring capacity to be fully alive.

The organization of personality has a fundamental stability, which is expressed in consistency of behavior over time; this durable structure underlies the individual's sense of direction, his independence of thought and action, his capacity to make and to carry out commitments to others and to himself. But the structure of the highly developed person is not fixed once and for all, nor is the consistency of behavior total or absolute; the individual is always open to experience, capable of further learning; his stability is fundamental in the sense that he can go on developing while remaining essentially himself.

A moment's thought should convince us that it would be quite impossible to give young people specific training for all the kinds of activities they will be called upon to engage in; nor is it fair to them to ignore their general development, their chance to realize their full potential, by preparing them only for particular roles, as now conceived; and, of course, it does not do us much good to say that they need to have knowledge of Western civilization and Western society and Western culture. Of course they do, but they could not be expected to learn more than a few fragments of this vast complexity in four years of college. More than this, there is no question but that the facts and principles learned in college courses are almost completely forgotten by the time three or four years have elapsed after graduation. Thus, we have to accent not what a students knows, but rather his inclination to go on trying to know. We cannot accent what is remembered; we have to be concerned instead with what remains after all specific contents have been forgotten. The student can be prepared for his diverse roles and functions in life only through the development of his qualities as a person. These have to be conceived as general in nature—things which are brought into play in all of the kinds of situations and tasks that confront him.

Dr. Sanford rightly reminds us that since students cannot acquire all the knowledge and training they need and since they forget so much, we must concentrate on what remains when specific information is forgotten. This does not deny the need for specific subject content. When he talks of the lack of evidence that a particular curriculum or a particular course has a great impact on the student beyond graduation, he is forcibly raising for me such disquieting questions as: are we wasting endless hours and priceless energies on our campuses when we engage in continuing arguments on the minute details of requirements for each degree? How much are we neglecting the major experiences, the overall progress, the identification of factors that do have impact on the lives of students?

NEVITT SANFORD

Every course in the liberal curriculum has to be evaluated in terms of what it contributes to the development of the person. Other kinds of education, although they are undertaken without deliberate consideration of such individual development, nonetheless have an impact upon the developing personality. It is not only that certain kinds of vocational and professional education may restrict the outlook of the individual by not permitting him a variety of experiences, but what happens in the course of such education is that individuals come to identify themselves with the vocation or profession in question, limiting their self-conceptions in this way, and restricting their performances in social roles to those that would be consistent with membership in the chosen occupation.

I am somewhat impatient with claims that ascribe to the curriculum effects that really should be ascribed to the way teaching is organized. But when all is said and done, we still have to face the question: What should we teach?

The central question that our speaker confronts is that of what we should teach. Each teacher has some freedom to answer such a question for himself within the limits of his own course in his own subject matter. Few courses are so prescribed that the teacher does not have fairly wide choice as to how he will spend his time and his effort with his own students. Once we focus on the individual and his development, what happens to our existing convictions about the worthwhileness of representing the area of knowledge at its best and about the matter of coverage? If we really take this paper seriously, many of us will need to re-examine our implicit assumptions about what we should do in class.

I think the notion that general education developed the whole person has been fundamental in education since the Middle Ages at least.

General education seems to be staging a comeback at the present time. One might hope that now it may find support in a sound psychology of individual development.

I must introduce, in however sketchy a way, a conception of the personality as a whole, and say something about how it is organized and how it develops. I want particularly to stress the view that the person functions as a unit and that we cannot make any categorical separation of the "intellect" and the rest of the person. Changes in what might be called the intellect, changes in knowledge and in modes of thought, if they amount to anything, would bring with them changes in the rest of the personality, just as changes in the rest of the personality leave the individual in a different state of receptivity to knowledge and ideas.

The conception which I shall present derives from the psychoanalytic one according to which the personality is constituted of three major systems: impulse life, the system of control, and the system representing the internalized demands of sociey. The major organizing principle in personality is that all of the person's resources, abilities, mechanisms, and so on are brought into the service of his needs—his needs to survive, to grow, to maintain himself. The major task of the personality is to find ways to satisfy basic needs (impulses) in ways that are sufficiently in accord with the requirements of reality and the demands of society.

The development of the personality can be thought of in terms of expansion, differentiation, and integration. Each of the major systems of the person exhibits, in time, all of these characteristic developmental processes, and so does the personality system as a whole. The highly developed person is thus one who is complex in the sense that he is possessed of many parts or elements having different functions and standing in different relations one to another, and he is integrated in the sense that all of the parts have the possibility of communication with all the others. In the face of some adaptive requirement the highly developed individual can bring to bear all of the resources that he needs, but no more than he needs, thus meeting fresh situations in ways that will develop him further while permitting him to go on being himself.

The fundamental principle of development is that of challenge and response. The individual develops when he is placed in situations that require the making of new responses, provided that these situations are not so threatening as to cause the individual to fall back upon earlier, primitive reactions.

Given this framework, what is the role of knowledge and of thinking? According to the point of view just expressed, knowledge and thinking are in the service of needs. But the beginnings of cognitive functions are present from the beginning, and after some development has occurred, knowing and thinking may be motives in their own right. More than this, the particular needs that a person will come to have depend upon what is known or thought.

Learning in the Academic Situation

This brings us to the difficult problem of how to formulate the kinds of learning that occur in response to the college curriculum.

In the first place, a great deal of the knowledge of facts and of principles that is acquired in college remains fairly peripheral to the personality structure. I should say that anything that a student knows is a part of his personality at the time that he knows it, but I would have to say that much of this remains in the outer regions of the personality and that much more remains peripheral in the sense that it never becomes integrated with the major or central processes of the person. Students may learn a great deal—in order to pass examinations and to get through college, or in order to please parents and teachers, or in order to maintain a role in a certain kind of academic community—without changing their personalities in any important way. Much knowledge is quickly forgotten, and the person does not change for the forgetting any more than he changed from the learning. It is interesting to consider, too, that a great deal of knowledge and, one might say, knowledgeable modes of functioning, may be quite persistent but at the same time superficial in the sense that they are not utilized in the interests of the individual's inner needs. There are people who can take the role of "intellectual" and carry on in their social relations with the use of symbols that could only have been acquired through contact with high culture, without this "education" being related in any functional way with those needs of the personality that determine the individual's attitudes and orientation with respect to values.

I suppose the general statement to be made here is that education in the sense of acquiring knowledge and skills may go forward without any change in the individual's structure. He may perfectly well assimilate vast amounts of knowledge to the structures that he already has, including quite infantile ones. It is a great advantage to be able to deal with one's problems at the level of symbols rather than at the level of overt action. The person who cannot read or find satisfaction in the diverse art forms, is reduced to action or sensation as the means for satisfying his needs and knowing that he is alive. This is the road to delinquency and the general primitivization of life.

One of our functions in the colleges is to help persons discover the means of continued learning, of continued increase in capacity to deal with and to understand more and more complex things. If this can be done more effectively through better curriculum adaptation, a valuable contribution will have been made to the common life and to the professional life as well.

What I am trying to do here is dramatize the point that the kind of learning in college that we really want is the kind that involves a change in the individual's structure. And of course the kind of change that we want is that which involves development—that is, expansion, differentiation, and integration. I want to argue now that

NEVITT SANFORD

education in college can and does develop the individual in this way, and that it will do so more often once we have discovered what are the conditions and processes of this development.

One thing that can and does happen, and that can be encouraged to happen more often, might be described as the expansion of the "primary process" (the process by which tension gives rise to wish-fulfilling images) or, one could say, the freeing of the imagination. Where this is our aim, the point to be stressed is that the teacher's best ally is not conscience but the impulse life. The best way to manage impulses is to offer them outlets in fantasy, in dreams, in poetry, and in art; or, to put this the other way around, if we are interested in freeing the imagination, opening the individual to experience, encouraging creativity and spontaneity, we have no recourse but to free the individual's impulse life. Much education in schools, and perhaps even in the colleges, is concerned with suppressing the impulse life, building up to the highest possible degree the controlling functions. Much of this is, of course, necessary, but one could put the major problem of college education in this way: how can one undo or set aside the restrictions upon the imagination that have been abuilding for years. What we try to do, I think, is to show the student that the world of literature and drama and art, and creativity in the sciences, offers not only the best but the only means by which the impulses of childhood may now find gratification.

The development of reality-oriented thinking seems to pose somewhat less of a problem. Here our procedure is to confront the individual with problems the solutions to which require that he make new responses, that he find new ways of adapting. This of course is what the curriculum is designed to do. The question is how to involve the student enough so that he feels that the problem being set is his problem.

Dr. Sanford takes the position that the individual develops when he is challenged, when he is required to makes new responses. Of course, if the new responses are too demanding, then he gets defensive and falls apart. But there must be some dissonance, or behavior will not change.

How do we create adaptive dissonance, then, in class? How much time do we spend trying to create the adaptive amount of dissonance? To stretch minds, to create the kind of confusions out of which a student, by his own resources, must learn his way? Ideally, of course, the student should be inspired in a need to learn the essentials by creating the dissonance which can be resolved only through a knowledge of the essentials. But we don't know how to do this.*

I think we may put it down as a safe assumption that if the individual can be involved in certain purposes, the achievement of which depends upon his actually utilizing what he has learned in school, then these new responses become a part of himself, and his structure is thereby changed. This, I take it, is why we regard it as so important that students have the experience of pursuing truth, as in individual projects. We have good reason to believe that the resources that become utilized in this activity are likely to become firmly integrated with the student's personality.

Of course the clearest examples of how information is remembered when it is put into the service of purposes, is to be found in the life of a scholar or researcher, or in the life of a person who is preparing for a professional role. It should be accented here that the intellectual worker is able to find in the carrying on of his work means for gratifying a great variety of personal needs, needs which range from the lowest to the highest. The excitement generated by the hot pursuit of truth can be as great as that accompanying any human activity. The scholar or researcher so involved can bring to bear upon his problems information acquired in a great variety of contexts in the past, and in this case there is no question but that knowledge and modes of thought become in-

* If a bit of familial flavor creeps into comments on this particular manuscript, it is not unexpected, since the two Sanfords are brothers.

NEVITT SANFORD

tegral parts of the person. This is the basis for the belief on the part of so many educators that knowledge must be tested and utilized in action. But often it is very difficult to make arrangements for this.

Although I would regard it as fundamental that the student learns, in a restructuring way, when knowledge and thought become integral with his purpose, I would at the same time give much attention to the possibility that knowledge of facts may be acquired now, without its being relevant to any central purpose of the person, and that it may be, as it were, stored, later to find a place in some fresh insight or in some creative achievement of the individual. I think that much of our college education is based on the assumption that this acquiring without change of structure may eventually serve the individual. I certainly think that this happens, but I also think that we may easily over-estimate its frequency.

It may be doubted that such storing will occur unless the information has relevance to some need of the individual, but, happily, in people of college age the variety of needs may be enough to lead to the registration and retention of much factual knowledge. And then, college students have the possibility at least of reaching that type of integration of personality that I have described, that is, a state of affairs in which there is communication among the various subsystems or substructures of the person, so that knowledge acquired and stored, because of its relevance to one purpose, however superficial or temporary that purpose might have been, may now be utilized in the interest of some fresh purpose such as the solution of a new and vexing problem. Such knowledge, having been stored, may also make possible fresh insight into relationships existing in the world, once such relationships are presented to the student at times when he is suitably receptive.

Dr. Sanford develops the idea that there seem to be two levels of education. There is one level at which a great deal of knowledge is acquired in the interest of passing examinations or making adjustments to a particular college environment; all of this is peripheral to the deeper needs of personality. By contrast, there is a level of education that hits more centrally to the organized integral core of personality. One wonders if in a lot of "super-intellectual" colleges and universities there is a great pressure for every individual, ready or not, to do a good deal of learning that will enable him to play the skilled but superficial role of egghead or intellectual. The yen of some parents to send bright children to the most prestigious institutions of higher learning may indicate a response at the superficial level. Maybe we are interested in having our children acquire a rather slick "high culture" veneer, and at times we may put too much evaluation on this surface aspect of education. It is likely that if we could discriminate more intelligently about the needs and potentialities and developments of an inner personality, our choice of educational institutions for our children would be more discriminating. Perhaps the gifted college student will find true quality, for his deeper self, in a year at some less visible college. How does one tell? Perhaps there are discriminations here that ought to be made or attempted more often.

The Curriculum

I shall speak briefly of some of the major types of curricula, considering them in relation to the general theory which I have sought to outline. I have the impression that these curricula make implicit assumptions concerning the developmental status of the students for whom they are designed, although they are not usually defended on this basis. One conception of the entering college student is that of a mature person whose value-orientation has already been established. We expect him to make choices in accordance with his predilections and his conceptions of what he expects to do or be. We assume that he is already an independent person or, if he is not, that he will develop independence more rapidly if he is allowed or encouraged to do independent work. Where this conception of the entering student prevails, we are likely to have accent on free electives, and are not put out if a student chooses courses in accordance with plans for a future vocation. The opposite conception is that the student is by no means ready to make such fundamental decisions, that far from permitting him to make choices in accord with the values that he already has, we should be concerned with teaching him what are the values that he ought to consider. The

NEVITT SANFORD

more common *distribution* type of curriculum, the type that seeks to achieve breadth of education through distribution requirements, and depth of education through a chosen area of concentration, seems to be something of a compromise.

We know little enough about development in the college age-ranges, but there seems to be reason to believe that in general the student's readiness for a core program is achieved before there emerges readiness for independent or individualized work,

I would bring the function of developing the individual and the intellectual heritage together. You cannot really have an intellectual life in the freshman year or at any other time unless you have some common core of ideas and materials to talk about. Essentially the reason the intellectual heritage is so important is that this is our common intellectual material; this is where we start and what we can communicate about. *

If we want to have the best of both worlds, then it would seem best to arrange for the common experience of learning within a supporting community first, and the experience of independent work later. This seems to be in accord with what we know about development. On the other hand, if we offer first the core curriculum and the community of experience, we should be sure to arrange later for independent work.

Of course the great difficulty is presented by the fact that different students mature at different rates. Within the same institution, at the same time, there are undoubtedly students who would benefit most from one type of curriculum and other students who would benefit most from a different type, and yet that institution offers and defends as universally good a single curriculum. A revolt against this practice has taken the form of individual education, as in the early days of Sarah Lawrence and Bennington Colleges. Everyone knows how difficult and expensive this kind of education is, and

* Nevitt Sanford in discussion.

NEVITT SANFORD

I believe that experience has shown that many students entering these colleges were not ready to take advantage of the opportunities for individualized programs. I can only make a plea for further research, aimed at telling us what are the common developmental statuses of entering students, and how these entail different kinds and degrees of receptivity to curricula. And I would urge that we recognize in our debates about types of curricula that there is probably no one curriculum that is best for all students at all times, but that curricula have to be devised with attention to multiple criteria.

Just as education has other aims besides the development of the individual, so does the curriculum—even the curriculum of the liberal college—have other functions besides the purely liberal one. Preparation to meet the requirements of graduate schools, preparation for a vocation, preparation for citizenship, are legitimate aims that undoubtedly help to govern the choice of what is taught in colleges. I am not quarreling with the general aim of preserving culture and offering it to students, whether or not they are prepared to receive it. What I want to say is that insofar as we propose to utilize the curriculum in promoting the development of the individual, we have to think again, and virtually from the beginning, about what we are doing. I submit, for example, that we know almost nothing about when students should be introduced to particular ideas. We know just as little about what sequences of experience would be optimum for purposes of the student's development. It is in the absence of such knowledge that the curriculum is likely to be determined by the interests of the departments rather than by consideration of the student's welfare.

The Freshman Curriculum

Let us take up the point of view being developed here in considering, for a moment, the curriculum of the freshman year. It is here, in my opinion, that the greatest failure occurs. I don't mean failure of the students, but

NEVITT SANFORD

rather failure of the college. Typically, freshmen arrive on the campus filled with enthusiasm, with eager anticipation of the intellectual experiences they are about to have. By the end of the year 10 per cent have dropped out and a large proportion of the remainder are ready for what in the eastern colleges is known as the "sophomore slump."

The point is sometimes made that existing arrangements serve well to "weed out" inferior students. At some state universities indeed there is weeding out with a bulldozer. Nobody knows how many potential scholars go out along with the unable and the indifferent; nor do we know to what extent remaining in college is a matter of gamesmanship or capacity to adapt oneself to conventional pressures.

Existing programs are easy to criticize. What are we to do? I would suggest that where our foremost concern is with the development of the personality, the major aim of the freshman year should be to win the student to the intellectual enterprise; with full recognition of the fact that for many it is now or never, we should make every effort to capture the student's imagination, to give him a sense of what it means to become deeply involved in a discipline or subject, to learn things that make a difference in his life, to be a member of a community that is devoted to the pursuit of truth. Most essentially we must show the student that college education is a means for the expression of his impulse life, an opportunity for the gratification of his natural curiosity, and not merely a set of painful tests designed to make him more appreciative of his college degree.

There is one current approach to the freshman curriculum that is in keeping with the point of view expressed here. The entering student is allowed to indulge to the full any interest that he already has, the assumption being that if the interest is genuine, he will soon be led into the study of various subjects that are related to it, and that if the interest is superficial, or if the object of interest is essentially insubstantial, it will be supplanted by others without loss in motivation. The trouble, of course, is that not many students have interests that are sufficiently developed so that they can serve as guides to protracted courses of study. More than this, according to the theory of development outlined above, college freshmen are capable of enormous expansion and development in their interests, values, and modes of thought; we should be wary of proceedings that indulge their natural inclination to confirm themselves as they are.

The president of Colby College has spoken about his orientation program which consists of sending all of the new freshmen at the beginning of the summer a required list of readings which included the *Book of Job,* MacLeish's play, *"J.B."* and several other items. Some students are shocked, but they read and arrive at the college loaded for bear. The intellectual discussion among the freshmen is rife. Some of the faculty are terrorized, for they have not read these materials recently. The important point is that the freshmen arrive with a background of recent reading and are in a position to carry on some intellectual life.

The curriculum as it exists in so many places has been evolved without much attention to the developmental needs of students. Perhaps the curriculum is better understood as a kind of treaty of peace among the warring departments of the university, accenting the professional and preprofessional elements in all disciplines. If we want seriously to talk about the development of the student, we probably have to begin with an attack on the way we arrive at a curriculum. I am not really hopeful of any radical change in the circumstances of today. I don't believe we are in a revolutionary mood.

It takes a considerable gift to make very complex things sound simple. This is what Nevitt Sanford has been able to do. One example of a learning situation which seems quite consistent with what Dr. Sanford is talking about is found in a freshman seminar at Harvard. It is given by a cultural anthropologist, but the process could apply to almost any field. The seminar has no set content. Two concepts, culture and the psychoanalytic view of man, are the jumping off points. The students work simultaneously as members of a group and as individuals. During the course of a discussion certain students discover that particular as-

NEVITT SANFORD

pects of a topic are of concern to them. The enormous bibliography that is spun off during any single session by professor and students is then selectively drawn upon by each individual according to his special interest. Similarly, the papers which students write, though several may be inspired by a single discussion, are likely to deal with quite different aspects of a common topic.

For some students, the principal path is toward discovery of themselves in relation to the world of the intellect. Many of them have gone through school and have come to college because parents and society say this is the thing to do. They have worked hard and succeeded thus far because our culture reinforces such behavior with immediate rewards. For those for whom these assumptions are true, it becomes particularly important that they discover reasons of their own for pursuing knowledge. There are at least two possible results of a failure to do so. First, they may never attain any degree of selfhood as they go through life performing successfully the tasks which someone else imposes and rewards, or second, they gradually awaken to a feeling of dissatisfaction with themselves and the world and rebel against performing for others without ever realizing that it might be possible to start using the same instruments for purposes of their own.

I would hope that the studies reported on at this conference and various other studies may help us to find ways and means of altering the attitudes of faculty members and to improve generally the quality of the contacts that faculty and students have toward the end of helping students in this achievement of selfhood or inner motivation.

Dr. Sanford talks about alternative conceptions of students on the part of college instructors and administrators. Such a point inclines the individual teacher to examine his own conception or his own general "theory" of college students. One can be fairly sure that the teacher's theory of his students is consonant with his general way of relating with them in class. If he regards them as callow, unformed, half-civilized beings, then he will drill them and coach them and work on their superegos and set firm requirements for their behavior. If he views them as adults, as responsible, as already possessed—or not—of functioning consciences, then he behaves quite differently. Perhaps we can say that whole institutions are characterized by the prevailing view of what a freshman is like. Perhaps we could do some fruitful exploring, not only by looking inward at our individual theories of students, but by collecting systematic data on the prevailing theory on a campus or among teachers of college students. Certainly, the way any teacher sees students has a determining hand in his behavior toward them. And of course the

reciprocal is true. What is the freshman "theory" of a professor? The student's view of the professor, at least a moderately sensitive professor, has a determining hand in the professor's behavior too. Few of us can go far against prevailing expectancies. Perhaps some explicit examination of a truly tenable view of freshmen—a view based as much as it can be on psychological assessment of freshmen—would have great bearing not only on our behavior in class but on the larger considerations of curriculum, of disciplinary rules, and of the general organization of the academic institution. Certainly one can, in looking at any given institution, begin to get impressions as to how that institution conceptualizes a student. Perhaps the pointing out to an institution of the prevailing view of a freshman could serve a useful purpose. Often the mere process of making the implicit explicit leads to the examination and revision of behavior.

Nevitt Sanford makes a good deal of the problem of involving the student in his own education, and points out that the "hot pursuit of truth" can carry with it great excitement when the whole person is involved in that pursuit. Certainly youngsters do occasionally involve themselves deeply in the educational process. Would it be useful to devote time early in the college career of the student to his own exploration—explicit, soul-searching exploration—of what college is for and how it can affect him as a person? The idea that college can help the student implement and express and enjoy his impulse life is a notion relatively novel to many teachers. It is probably a notion even more novel to students. What would happen if students were made early in their college careers to face this notion, to examine it for themselves? I have the impression that many students go through college without ever formulating for themselves a workable theory of knowledge, a workable overview of what these four years are for and what should be derived from them.

My main argument is that we ought to ignore conceptions of what freshmen "ought to know," whether the concern be with their preparation for more advanced courses or with a suitable sampling of organized knowledge, and that we ought to concentrate instead on giving these students experiences that set in motion the developmental changes in which we are interested. Each course should be conceived as an end in itself; it should be designed with first attention to developmental objectives—and to the developmental status of the freshman. Subject matter has a crucial role to play, but the outcomes that we seek will have little to do with "how

NEVITT SANFORD

much is covered." There is irony in the fact that when we teach elementary courses, we tend to look ahead to the advanced ones, asking ourselves what information is likely to be required, and supposing that we can impress the teachers of these advanced courses with how much our students know; but if we teach advanced courses, we are likely to assume that very little has been learned in the elementary ones, and to make sure of "proper coverage" we proceed to teach what all the students have had before.

We are justified in looking elsewhere, and in making any kind of break with tradition, in our search of materials that will excite, involve challenge, or win the commitment of freshmen.

I'm really agreeing with Nevitt Sanford's larger point that we need to know more about the development stage of our freshman—with development conceived in the psychological terms—before we really begin planning his curriculum for him. If we can add to our present knowledge of a freshman more knowledge about his conception of himself, his attitudinal readiness to join the intellectual enterprise, his history of wrestling with *Weltanschauung*, then we are in a much better position to plan not only for his sequences of academic hurdles but for his sequences of personal experience.

We might use what is now offered in an upper division anthropology course, a whole course devoted to a single English poet, the latest decision of the Supreme Court, an integrated course in 17th century England, a course in economics taught as if this were the only exposure to this subject that the students would ever have. Or we might use another judicious selection from the traditional liberal arts curriculum. We might well choose more specific contents from areas such as those just mentioned, whatever we thought might reach into the student's life, and provide genuine experience because it connected with experiences that he had already had or was having. We should in each case be guided by some hypothesis stating just how the content influenced development in people who had reached the freshman's level.

Certain aspects of psychology, sociology, and anthropology are very well calculated to involve students by offering them light on problems with which they are already preoccupied. When all else fails, there might be resort to these "sure-fire" disciplines. Yet, consideration of the freshman's stage of development leaves me extremely reluctant to start them off with this very rich diet. We know far too little about the matter, but it does seem that the introduction of these subjects so early in the student's career might, by taking up too much of his time, make it impossible for him to have certain kinds of experience to which he is entitled and which would be important to his over-all development. For example, a student ought to have the experience of passionate devotion to an over-all religious or philosophical scheme which seems to him to explain everything. He will in time analyze such experiences, using the categories of psychology and social science, and come eventually, one might hope, to some truly useful scheme; such analysis will be far more educational if he has first had the experience himself than it will be if he has to utilize the reputed experience of others. This holds for those course materials, chiefly literature and the arts, which may be used to educate—to refine and to help organize—the feelings or affective life.

On the matter of a learned curiosity motive we can make the case that the motivated individual who is reinforced for his exploration, directly and naturally through the attainment of satisfaction, may acquire an insatiable need to know. Certainly it ought to be at least as easy to learn a need to know as it is to learn a need to achieve. We probably ought to be able to spell out the conditions under which such a mechanism becomes a drive. We need certain schedules of reinforcement, we need to catch the child at a time where generalization is most likely to occur, we need to arrange the non-duplicability of the experimental conditions, and perhaps we can teach a young human organism an everlasting, nonextinguishable yen for knowledge.

There may be many occasions on which the teacher, through reliance on vocational carrots or other extrinsic rewards for learning, simply drives the curious student away. The bright and curious student may

NEVITT SANFORD

feel that learning literature or algebra is not going to be of any particular good for him if he's headed into pharmacy or veterinary medicine. But if the teacher has worked to arouse a strong autonomous need to know, then he is not caught in the falsehood of holding out maladaptive carrots. In addition, he is devoting his energies to arranging his subject matter in a manner that can constitute an incentive to a potentially powerful motive for learning.

Some Specific Content Areas

To carry the theory further and to illustrate in somewhat more concrete fashion the kinds of changes which can and sometimes do come about, I shall now consider some of the particular content areas. Literature, and the other arts—drama, painting, music—it seems to me, offer one of the best means for freeing the impulse life. The student's natural inclination, of course, is to judge characters in literature, as well as elsewhere, according to the values and attitudes that he brings with him to college. If his anxiety is so great that he cannot tolerate any change in these structures, he will of course not be good in literature. But if he gets the point, if he discovers that anything may be done in the imagination and that everything that he has so far imagined has been done by somebody, and that those who did things can be understood, then he is bound to admit into his scheme of things a broader range of human potentialities. These he can see as present in himself as well as in other people. The thing about literature, as I understand it, is not that it simply releases fundamental impulses to be expressed in their original fundamental form—this could hardly be called freedom; instead, it gives to the individual something of the very thing which made the creation of that literature possible in the first place, and that is the means for transforming the impulse life in such a way that it meets the requirements of reality and of conscience—but just barely. Now I should argue that if this kind of change in the individual is brought about through the study of literature, it will affect the individual's performance in all of his other courses, as indeed in his life generally. A change brought about by education in one discipline ramifies throughout the personality and affects ways of responding to any discipline.

The appeal of what we call good literature and art is fundamentally the same, with several big differences. As people develop, new needs are generated, and hence there is the possibility of more kinds of conflict among these needs. There is, as we have seen, more complexity of personality, and in these circumstances a person can derive benefit from literature and art only when what is presented is sufficiently subtle and complicated to match the development of the person. As a person becomes more differentiated, he cannot identify himself with gross over-simplified emotional expressions, nor can he learn anything from childish material about how to express his adult feelings. Nevertheless, and perhaps most important, that which we value most highly in literature and the arts is typically in very close touch with the impulse life. It is far from being an accident that most of what is great in these areas, comes at one time or another into conflict with the authorities and is subject to being banned, though I hasten to add that not everything that is banned is good.

The study of language seems to contribute very little to the development of the individual unless this study leads to enough mastery so that the individual may have some grasp, some appreciation, of the culture that language expresses. If much appreciation is achieved, the individual is bound to take a different view of his own culture, and hence of himself, and once this process is set in motion the individual is not only free from a parochial outlook but finds it difficult ever to restrict himself to such an outlook again. It may be that the study of a foreign language gives the individual something of the same thing that can be derived from living in a foreign culture for so long a period of time. There is the chance, at any rate, that the sense of the other culture will, as it were, creep up on one, that it will become somehow internalized and begin to affect one's thinking without its ever being ordered to those intellectual categories which, after all, were supplied by one's own culture.

NEVITT SANFORD

We can build up a picture of how teaching would progress if we really concentrated our efforts on the arousal of the need to know or the arousal of native curiosity rather than on any of the other kinds of appeals we make to students. Good teachers probably already do this, from the first grade on up. Maybe we need to say that many motives are operating simultaneously. We probably should arouse them all and unless we have procedures by which we can trigger off the curiosity motive or the derived need to know, we may be missing the motivational boat. Somehow the college environment needs to be structured in such a way that intellectual needs have a fair chance of reaching arousal.

We have spoken earlier about the necessity for challenging the cognitive structures—the conception of one's self and of the world, the ethical principles—with which the student enters college. These structures undoubtedly derive in the main from the family and the community: many have been taken over automatically and have not been derived from the subject's own thought and experiences. It would seem that the study of philosophy and religion and the history of ideas is nicely calculated to provide the necessary challenge. It is tempting to say that everything depends upon the way in which the subjects are taught, that it is up to the instructor to see to it that the student is challenged, and not allow him to avoid issues in the way that students are wont to do. But however effective the teaching, the teacher must certainly have something to teach. He can only challenge ideas and conceptions with other ideas and conceptions, and it seems that he might as well use the heritage that is at hand.

It is to be recognized, of course, that the values and beliefs with which students leave college are not always, as the Jacob Report has shown, very different from the values and beliefs with which they enter college. There is, however, the possibility that the values and beliefs are now held in a different way, that they have a firmer basis in the subject's own experience and thought, and hence a different relation to other processes of the personality. One might also hope that regardless of the content of one's values and beliefs at the moment, one has available to him the means for improving his decisions in this area as time goes on. Once again we must remind ourselves that how the individual functions in this area depends on many potent factors that have nothing to do with the content of the curriculum. But it remains our task to replace the half-baked ideas of the student with ideas that are intrinsically good.

Faculty members representing different specialities do differ in the extent and depth of their interest in students beyond imparting information. I am puzzled about whether such differences stem from the nature of the disciplines, from the nature of the faculty member's personality, or from other factors. Then the question arises: to what extent are faculty attitudes toward students and their interests in them influenced by the academic climate on the campus, by the educational philosophy that pervades the curriculum, by the policies of the administration and trustees, and by the beliefs and values of the community and region it serves? These are questions to which research may address itself.

There does seem to be a strong hint here that mathematics and science, as these subjects are often taught today, favor the maintenance of defensive structures, that they play into the hands of the conventional, the restricting, the suppressing functions of the personality. The study of these disciplines may very well support the aim of being a well-disciplined, well-controlled, well-behaved young lady or young man who grimly accepts the formulae, memorizes a mass of factual material, and hands in meticulous laboratory reports. But we know that things do not have to be this way, that it is possible to teach science in a way that conveys its spirit as well as its facts or its precise techniques, a way that introduces the student to its wayward aspects as well as to its discipline. Science, after all, tends to upset the existing order of things. It is essentially daring and unconventional. Its rules, its discipline, derive from its own processes and needs, and have nothing to do with conventional morality. Many young people who choose science hope thereby to capitalize upon their prematurely organized consciences. When science is chosen in this way, and its discipline is used to support the suppressing and

NEVITT SANFORD

controlling functions of the personality, it is difficult to see how instruction in these disciplines will later free the individual. Would it not be better to recruit for science, students who are passionate and curious and out to discover and to change the world and then to undertake to teach the necessary discipline?

I think I hardly need to elaborate the point that if natural science is taught in the right way, or if the student discovers for himself what the subject is about, there is nothing that can be more instructive in how to think. I have often been struck by what an enormous difference proper training in scientific thinking can make when it comes to dealing with practical problems or problems in human affairs.

Dr. Sanford states that science is not to be treated as so much knowledge which the student should memorize. Rather, it should be a means by which the student can be helped to appreciate how the scientist carried on the inquiry. The student needs to learn how to think in scientific terms. Or in the social studies, he should become more able to carry on inquiries on his own about social issues. In literature, music, the arts, and humanities, it is not enough to know that there is great literature. He learns the disciplines of interpretation, of examining, appraising, and of judging the illusion of reality that is being created. He develops criteria by which he can discover for himself what art, music, and literature mean and how significant they can be for him.

There is no question but that training in science can put powerful tools or, one might say, weapons of this kind in one's hands. But it is obvious that our natural science teachers, given the vast array of facts and principles which they feel they must somehow cover, often neglect to assure themselves that the students have grasped the fundamental modes of scientific thought. It may very well be that for the time being, until training in the natural sciences has been reformed, psychology and social science might be the better instruments for teaching students how to think.

Mathematics, of course, offers one of the best means for training in thinking. Here Frank Pinner has pointed to the most essential fact. Mathematics, he says, can exhibit the processes of thought and of feeling by which truth is discovered. The student may here learn that the maxims and theorems are not unalterable, that they do not have an objective existence but are creations of the human mind that aid the pursuit of truth. Pinner also points out that in mathematics one may learn of the close affinity between beauty and truth, how it is that an elegant solution or the demonstrated generality of a truth may be a cause for joy. When one looks at the matter in this light, it becomes sad to contemplate how many young people are deprived of a great and inexhaustible source of joy by kinds of teaching that leave them either terrified of anything involving mathematics, or else fixed in the notion that mathematics involves nothing more than a set of devices for manipulating numbers. It is easy indeed to criticize much of the teaching of mathematics and of science, but if one knew how to teach something in the right way, it is hard to know what might be better to teach.

SUMMARY

My main point is that anything that is taught in a liberal college ought to be justified on the ground that it contributes to the development of the individual. Usually what is taught can be so justified, assuming that it is taught in the "right way"—a way that increases self-control, self-understanding, self-development. This may hold even for vocational courses, which may contribute in unexpected ways. Such courses may give the young person his first recognition of the fact that knowledge may be relevant to his real needs; they may contribute crucially to his sense of worth and to his independence and, hence, to his capacity and his willingness to learn something more substantial. I am inclined to believe, however, that as instruments for the development of the personality the basic liberal studies have the most to offer. Their great strength is their inexhaustibility; and their great flexibility. That great teachers and great faculties who were concerned primarily with the development of the personality have through the years stayed with the liberal studies is not an accident, nor merely an expression of a stubborn tradition; they had good reason to believe that these studies were the best means for the general development of the personality and this, as I said in the beginning, is the aim of liberal education.

I also argue that Nevitt Sanford may not be placing enough emphasis on the importance for the individual of highly developed skills, of personal mastery of a technical field. Maybe skill does more than therapy can to make the youth into a man. I don't really believe that, but it's a hypothesis that should not be ignored.

Dr. Sanford leaves us with some serious ideas to ponder insofar as our teaching goes. One wonders what might happen in a classroom if all of us as teachers devoted our skills of attention to the stimulation of flights of fancy, to the increase of skill in entertaining hypotheses contrary to fact. Certainly the thrill of creative research is often close to the thrill of the spinning out of an inventive fantasy. Eventually, of course, it has to be a fantasy tied inexorably to reality. Maybe science and poetry have more in common than we often admit. And perhaps if we taught science a little more poetically, we could tie it into the impulse life of the individual and break it loose from any unnecessary regimens. Eventually, of course, the declarative sentences in science must be hard and rigorous and logical and testable and communicable. Perhaps if we encouraged more flights of fancy in our science courses, we could begin to create sciences in which the declarative sentences were about the more significant and inventive matters.

Other questions teased at our consciousness after we listened to Dr. Sanford. For example, how do we win the student to the intellectual enterprise? Some join it, some battle it. What is the role of identification with the teacher who obviously has enthusiasm for the intellectual life? What are the conditions under which identification can occur? How do we help students to see and to feel the unique role of the university in the overall pattern of our organized existence? Why don't we assign our best, most versatile and most mature teachers to the freshman year? Is there a period of imprinting in the first year in college? Is general personal dissonance here at some kind of height so that the models the freshman adopts and his responses during that period take on a greater importance than in any other semester? What circumstances can we create so that the intellectual needs have a chance to burst through the plethora of other and perhaps stronger and more primitive needs? Many questions, few answers . . .

Certainly the view of the educated man as one possessed of extensive relevant knowledge, of a variety of alternative intellectual responses available to him in any situation, of many concepts in terms of which he can make precise discriminations, is still a pretty good view. We want that kind of person walking through democratic life. But to ask a college freshman to sit still and absorb vast arrays of coldly impersonal knowledge on the off-chance that he will need it in the future seems a hopeless motivational strategy. The problem is to arouse needs now. Perhaps again we need to examine critically the motivational reality of knowledge for its own sweet savor.

We were sold on the idea of discarding the old orations delivered to the students during orientation week and on getting some thinking started. I have talked to the freshmen at Harvard for six years now, and I have been making a systematic survey to see how many of the juniors and seniors remember my talk. A total of three students out of a potential 7,000 remembered that I had talked to them for half an hour. I gave them a good speech too!

The moral? Dr. Sanford may have an all-important point: How students learn is more important than what they remember. Our task is to look anew at the college to see what the four-year experience does to the development of the student as a person. That is the problem on which this discussion has centered.

Chapter 2

DIFFERENCES IN STUDENT ATTITUDES
toward civil liberties*

The Center for the Study of Higher Education of the University of California, Berkeley, is engaged in two investigations of student development during the college years. One of them is a study of the college careers of some 900 young men and women who received scholarships or certificates of merit from the National Merit Scholarship Corporation in 1956 and who entered colleges and universities that fall. These students fell within the upper two or three per cent of the population in academic aptitude. The other investigation is concerned with the impact of different college cultures on students of both similar and varied characteristics.

In both investigations, extensive information has been secured about students either just before or soon after they entered college, including data on their social, cultural, and educational backgrounds; their attitudes, values, or beliefs about a variety of important matters; their educational and vocational aspirations; and their psychological characteristics, including those measured by what is called the Omnibus Personality Inventory, a research instrument which touches primarily, although not exclusively, intellectual interests and dispositions.

Unfortunately, longitudinal data are for the most part either unavailable or unanalyzed as yet, but we do know a good deal about the characteristics of students at entrance. We have information about their attitudes toward civil liberties and academic freedom at the beginning or the end of their freshmen year, and we have some data on changes in attitudes toward civil liberties between the freshman and junior years. We also have data from a cross section of freshmen, sophomores, and seniors in four of our cooperating colleges.

* Assisted by Martin Trow, Austin Frank, and Kenneth Walker.

T. R. McCONNELL

First, let us consider students' attitudes toward civil liberties. The inquiry on this subject was not exhaustive; students were simply asked to respond to questions covering a limited number of issues. We shall be concerned, first, with the responses of the National Merit Scholarship students. The questions were asked toward the end of their freshman year.

A quarter of these students (men and women together) said "yes" to the question, "Should congressional committees investigate the political views and affiliations of college faculty members?" and 63 per cent gave a negative answer.

How much one year of college experience may have affected their reactions to this question is unknown, but some inkling may be secured from the responses of freshmen at the beginning of the year in three highly selective liberal arts colleges, which we shall identify as A, B, and C. Although the average scholastic aptitude of the NMSC students would be higher than the average of the freshmen at the three colleges in question, these institutions have student bodies of high intellectual quality. At the beginning of their freshman year, students in the three colleges were asked essentially the same question as the NMSC students, except that the statement was put in the negative form, "Legislative committees should not investigate the political beliefs of university faculty members."

Thirty-two per cent of College A freshmen, and 22 and 23 per cent of college B and C freshmen, respectively, took the position that legislative committees should investigate faculty members' political beliefs. On other questions pertaining to civil liberties, the B and C students were also somewhat more liberal than those at A. The responses of the B and C freshmen to the item under discussion were not greatly different from the NMSC group. Neither were the responses of 894 students on the Berkeley campus of the University of California whose attitudes toward principles of the

T. R. McCONNELL

Bill of Rights were studied by Selvin and Hagstrom in 1957. Twenty-nine per cent of this group favored congressional investigation of faculty members' political views.[1]

The NMSC students were asked to react to the question, "Is it in the public interest to allow scientists to explore whatever they wish without restraint?" The responses were overwhelmingly favorable; 85 per cent of the entire group said "yes." This support for freedom of scientific investigation may not only reflect the high prestige which science now enjoys but also an assumption that scientific research lies outside sensitive areas of social and political beliefs.

The students also were asked, "Is it in the public interest for boards of censorship to suppress the sale of books or the showing of movies?"[2] More than a third—nearly 37 per cent—replied "yes." This is a substantial vote for censorship, and one wonders whether students change their attitudes toward it appreciably during college. The Center has data on changes in NMSC students' responses between the end of the freshman and the junior years for approximately 700 students. The change was not great; 35.5 of the freshmen favored censorship and 32.3 of the juniors took the same position. There seems to be a hard core of exceptionally able students who condone suppression of books and movies.

There was considerably more change in attitude toward congressional investigation of the political views of faculty members. Although 25 per cent of the NMSC freshmen were favorable, only 14 per cent of the juniors reacted positively.

---

[1] Selvin, H. C., and Hagstrom, W. O., "Determinants of Support for Civil Liberties." *British Journal of Sociology*, 11:51–73, March, 1960.

[2] Some persons may object to the form of this and other questions or statements on the ground that they should be qualified. For example, it may be said that publication should be subject to laws on libel. But to cast a statement in its extreme form may reveal sharper differences of opinion than to qualify it in one way or another; furthermore, to add many qualifications would emasculate the principle involved. Such emasculation is often the purpose of laws curbing freedom of expression.

In its study of the effect of different college cultures on students of similar or dissimilar characteristics, the Center for the Study of Higher Education has secured extensive information on the characteristics of entering students at the three colleges already mentioned and at a state college, D.[3] Students' responses to six questions bearing on civil liberties will be summarized below.

The students were asked to agree or disagree (or check "don't know enough to decide") with the following statement: "A former member of the Communist party who refuses to reveal the names of party members he had known should not be allowed to teach in a college or university." The percentages of agreement of freshmen (men and women together) at the four colleges were as follows: A, 18; B, 12; C, 13; and D, 45.

The percentages of agreement among the sophomores were A, 10; B, 6; C, 7; and D, 36. Among the seniors, the following percentages agreed with the statement: A, 7; B, 0; C, 7; and D, 25.

Low proportions in all three classes at the three "elite" liberal arts colleges agreed with the statement. In all three schools there was a decline in agreement, even from low beginning levels, between freshmen and seniors. (Here, as in the case of the five other statements to be discussed, the increase in "permissiveness" may be due to actual changes in students over time, or to a disproportionate drop-out of the more "less permissive" students, or both. This we cannot determine until we have the longitudinal data.)

As with almost all the other items, the College D students were markedly less liberal in every class than students in the other three colleges. In fact, more of the College D freshmen agreed than disagreed with the statement. The percentage of agreement declined from freshmen to seniors, as in the three elite schools, until

---

[3] The longitudinal data from this study will not be available until later; the students being studied have just finished their junior years. Supplementary cross-sectional data were secured by querying sophomores and seniors at the time information was secured from freshmen.

T. R. McCONNELL

twice as many seniors as freshmen disagreed with the statement, although a quarter still agreed as compared with no more than seven per cent in any of the other colleges.

The second statement was that "present members of the Communist party should not be allowed to teach in colleges and universities." This statement evoked much more agreement in all the colleges than the one concerning a former communist who refused to reveal names of party members, but there was still a large difference between the three liberal arts colleges and the state college.

The percentages of agreement among the freshmen were as follows: A, 46; B, 32; C, 41; and D, 77. Among the seniors, the percentages of agreement were: A, 16; B, 20; C, 23; and D, 61. Although there was greater agreement among the College A freshmen than among the freshmen at Colleges B and C, particularly B, there was less among the A seniors than among the seniors at the other two liberal arts colleges.

In all four institutions, the percentage of agreement dropped from freshman to seniors, and very markedly in the "elite" schools, especially at College A. The drop was smaller at D, from 77 to 61 per cent.

The statement that "a high school teacher who 'pleads the Fifth Amendment' while being questioned by a congressional committee should be fired at once" proved to represent the least popular infringement on civil liberties in any of the four colleges—fewer than 10 per cent of the students supported this statement in any of the liberal arts colleges and not many more in College D. Furthermore, this item provoked the least difference between the liberal arts colleges and the state college of any of the statements under discussion.

The freshman percentages of agreement were A, 8; B, 6; C, 9; and D, 13. For seniors, they were: A, 2; B, 0; C, 7; and D, 11.

The percentage among 894 Berkeley students in the Selvin and Hagstrom study was 11.[4]

[4] *Ibid.*

The next statement was that "the government is acting properly in refusing a passport to a socialist." There was very little support for this proposition in any class in any of the institutions. The percentages of agreement in the three liberal arts colleges ranged from 2 to 7 among freshmen and seniors—the senior percentages being somewhat smaller in each college. Even in College D, the percentage fell from 19 among the freshmen to 6 among the seniors. It should be noted, however, that there was a high proportion of "don't knows" at the state college—47 per cent of the freshmen and 30 per cent of the seniors. This was much higher than on any other item. Those who professed not to know ranged from 17 to 21 per cent of the freshmen at the other three colleges, although the percentages were quite small among the seniors.

The last statement to be discussed here is that "the government should have the right to withhold relevant FBI files from defendants in criminal cases, when opening the files to them might reveal the names of confidential informants."

There was considerable support for this statement in all four institutions. The percentages for freshmen were: A, 42; B, 33; C, 37; and D, 47. There was less agreement among the seniors: A, 27; B, 21; C, 36; and D, 42. In this case, the difference between freshmen and seniors at College C was only one percentage point.

The Berkeley students were more conservative concerning this statement than either freshmen or seniors in the four other institutions; 56 per cent of the University of California sample agreed with the proposition.[5]

Right to Confrontation

Certainly one of the most fundamental rights in a free society is the one guaranteed the defendant in a criminal case by the Sixth Amendment, the right "to be confronted with the witnesses against him." The right of confrontation presumably includes the right of the ac-

[5] *Ibid.*

T. R. McCONNELL

cused to a full and accurate statement of the charges against him, and the right to cross examine his accusers.[6] It is true that the latest decision of the Supreme Court bearing on this right did not support it without qualification. It took the position that each case is to be treated individually.

Again, however, we asked the students to agree or disagree with an unqualified statement with respect to confrontation. But this statement, we would contend, incorporates the fundamental principle, and the individual's response to it is a fair representation of his basic attitude toward one of the essential civil liberties. That so many students in all the colleges agreed that the government should have the right to withold relevant FBI files from a defendant in a criminal suit is, to me, a cause for serious concern.

The permissive attitudes toward issues involving certain civil liberties or guarantees in the Bill of Rights on the part of the students at Colleges A, B, and C—and especially at College B, for students there were nearly always somewhat more liberal than at the other two colleges—is noteworthy. The Center has no data on the attitudes of the faculties of these colleges on the same issues, but it is probable that they, too, are predominantly permissive. At least this is the expectation that could be derived from reading the Lazarsfeld and Thielens report on *The Academic Mind*.[7]

The authors of this volume constructed a scale of "permissiveness" for the assessment of faculty attitudes, and they also devised a method of rating the quality of colleges and universities.

Their ratings of the quality of the participating colleges were based on an index which involved the total number of volumes in the library, the ratio of library books to the number of students, the ratio of the annual budget to the number of students, the proportion of

[6] See Cushman, R. E., *Civil Liberties in the United States*. Ithaca, Cornell University Press, 1956, pp. 115–156; 192–194.

[7] Lazarsfeld, P. F., and Thielens, W., *The Academic Mind*. Glencoe, The Free Press, 1958.

Ph.D.'s on the faculty, the production of scholars, and the amount of tuition charged.[8]

The data showed that "the better a college, the larger the proportion of permissive scientists included in its faculty."[9]

Suppose the teacher with a mission does not allow himself the luxury of preaching but instead hews to a line of scholarly and scientific examination of issues. Attitudes have human histories—in the culture and in the individual. Attitudes have consequences, for the individual and for the culture. One can teach these histories and these consequences without ever stooping to any departure from the scholarly and analytical stance. In the best of all societies, the best of all values are functionally rooted, are intertwined with other values, are espoused not blindly but in thorough understanding of histories and consequences.

Attitudes Toward Academic Freedom

Although "academic freedom is not a civil liberty in the orthodox sense," it is closely related to civil liberties and to intellectual freedom in society at large. An atmosphere of intellectual restraint in a college or university is inimical to the purpose and validity of the whole educational enterprise.[10]

One of the most articulate spokesmen for academic freedom, and one of its most courageous defenders—I can find no evidence that he ever made the slightest compromise with his ideals—was Dr. Samuel P. Capen, long the chancellor of the University of Buffalo. It is appropriate to quote here his forthright definition of academic freedom:

"The university must be an institution without intellectual boundaries. It is and must be wholly free to prosecute the search for truth. Any aspect of nature, any work of man, any accepted idea, any respectable prejudice, any institution of society must be open to its inspection, must be subject to evaluation by it, must be for

---

[8] *Ibid.*, p. 411.
[9] *Ibid.*, p. 161.
[10] Cushman, R. E., *Op. cit.*, p. 70.

T. R. McCONNELL

it a fair field for new discovery. There must be no restraint upon the publication of its findings and interpretations, whether these happen to be popular or unpopular. Those who pursue the truth under the sponsorship of the university cannot walk in jeopardy of their careers, should they chance to offend a board, or a board member, or an administrative official, or even an important segment of the general public....

"Acceptance by an institution of the principle of academic freedom implies that teachers .... are free to differ with their colleagues and to present the grounds of their difference in their classes or elsewhere; that they are free as citizens to take part in any public controversy outside the institution; that no repressive measures, direct or indirect, will be applied to them no matter how unpopular they may become through opposing powerful interests or jostling established prejudices, and no matter how mistaken they may appear to be in the eyes of members and friends of the institution...."[11]

Capen believed that academic freedom should be assured to students as well as to faculty members. He insisted that in a university pledged to academic freedom "students are free, in so far as the requirements of the several curricula permit, to inquire into any subject that interests them, to organize discussion groups or study clubs for the consideration of any subject, and to invite to address them any speaker they may choose; that censorship of student publications shall be based on precisely the same grounds and shall extend no further than that exercised by the United States postal authorities."[12]

We attempted to paraphrase in short statements the liberties which Capen asserted must be assured by any university which embraces the principle of academic freedom, and asked our group of National Merit Scholarship Corporation students, at the end of the first year in college, to check the ones with which they agreed. On some of the statements there was overwhelming

---

[11] Capen, S. P., *The Management of Universities*. Buffalo, Foster and Stewart Publishing Corporation, 1953, pp. 10, 25–26.
[12] *Ibid.*, p. 26.

T. R. McCONNELL

consensus. More than 90 per cent of the students agreed that educational institutions should assure "freedom to investigate any topic or question," "freedom from suppressive measures by special interest groups," and "freedom for students to study, investigate, and discuss any topic or subject that interests them." But only 71 per cent approved "freedom to publish the findings of all investigations; 65 per cent, "freedom to present any and all ideas in regular classes"; 75 per cent, "freedom to differ publicly with other faculty members"; 63 per cent, "freedom to differ publicly with administrators"; 62 per cent, "freedom to participate in any public controversy"; 61 per cent, "freedom for students' publications subject only to the censorship exercised by U.S. postal authorities."

We asked the same NMSC students to respond to these items at the end of the senior year, but possible changes in their attitudes have not yet been analyzed.

We have data for seniors at colleges A, B, C, and D comparable to those for NMSC freshmen. Without giving any of the data, it is perhaps sufficient to say that in general students in the four colleges fell into the same pattern of permissiveness and non-permissiveness as on the questions concerning civil liberties. The seniors in the three liberal arts colleges were also more liberal than the NMSC freshmen.

The interpretation of students' attitudes toward the liberties subsumed under academic freedom in our questionnaire will depend on one's expectations, and also on his own definition of academic freedom. If the expectations and definition are limited, it is possible, perhaps, to derive from students' responses some optimism concerning their future support of intellectual freedom in the university. But if academic freedom means to one what it did to Capen—admittedly his was an extreme position—he will find serious discrepancies between the ideal and the attitudes even of the NMSC freshmen. He will be still more concerned over the restraints which NMSC students in some institutions would seem to be willing to accept. He will be encouraged, on the other hand, by the responses of the seniors at colleges A, B,

T. R. McCONNELL

and C. Perhaps as seniors the NMSC students will come closer to the positions of the students in these three colleges.

Dr. McConnell reports four basic facts: 1) there are wide individual differences among students with respect to their attitudes on civil liberties and academic freedom; 2) students who are more tolerant, in the usual sense of the word, on these matters tend to choose certain schools over others; 3) seniors are generally more permissive than freshmen; and 4) there is significant change, from the freshman to the senior year, toward the tolerant position among students at some colleges, relatively small changes at others.

Findings 3 and 4 above are the ones that raise issues—and indirectly, at least, maybe some hackles. Education seems indeed to make a difference. Education at one college makes more of a difference than education at another.

Evidence, from Dr. McConnell and elsewhere, suggests strongly that college teachers do influence attitudes. Now comes the paralyzer: Does what I do in *my* classes make a difference? Am I influencing attitudes toward the more or less permissive? Should I be? If so, with what justification?

Conclusion

We have long been aware that colleges and universities are differentially selective in students' academic aptitude and previous scholastic achievement, although we have usually underestimated the magnitude of the differences among institutions. There is a growing amount of evidence that colleges and universities are also differentially selective or attractive in other important student characteristics. Recent studies have shown that the student bodies of particular institutions and groups of institutions may differ greatly in social and cultural background, educational and vocational goals, attitudes and values, and intellectual dispositions.[13]

[13] McConnell, T. R., "Differential Selectivity of American Higher Education." In K. E. Anderson, editor, *The Coming Crisis in the Selection of Students for College Entrance.* Washington, American Educational Research Association, 1960.

This paper has provided evidence that institutions are differentially selective in students' attitudes toward civil liberties and academic freedom. Although there were differences in attitudes toward these freedoms among students in Colleges A, B, and C, the most striking difference was between students in these three colleges and those in College D, a state college.

There may be a difference of opinion as to whether an educational institution should try to influence students' attitudes and beliefs in these realms. I confess I think it should, for to me, the education of the free man is impossible without academic freedom for both faculty and students, as a truly democratic society is impossible of attainment without the liberties presumably guaranteed in the Bill of Rights. As civil liberties are both ends and means in a free society, so intellectual freedom is both purpose and process in higher education. Without freedom of both teaching and learning, the liberation and discipline of the mind, which is to say education, is impossible.

The very idea that teachers are forming social attitudes as well as teaching subject matters stirs up, at least in some teachers, a conflicting fantod. But then the whole symposium centers around the notion that we are forming personalities as well as purveying knowledge. Not all teachers like this theme and this reality. Some perhaps dodge the issue. Others will want to face it openly and squarely and work out for themselves an intelligent and defensible stance with respect to their own influence on young personalities.

Commitment to intellectual and civil liberties is probably as much the product of campus life as it is the outcome of formal instruction. An atmosphere in which faculty members are fearful of external pressures or administrative coercion, or in which they are subservient to autocratic control is not conducive to intellectual independence on the part of either faculty or students. An institution which does not permit controversial figures to speak on campus—the University of California until recently was closed to political candidates or outside political speakers—or which censors its student

T. R. McCONNELL

newspaper is not likely to instill respect for free speech or a free press, unless, perhaps, its restraint becomes onerous enough to provoke rebellion.

A faculty which wishes to stimulate respect for civil liberties and intellectual independence will have a much more difficult task in some institutions than in others. The problem in Colleges A, B, and C, where students are strongly disposed toward these freedoms when they come, will be much less difficult than in College D, where a much larger proportion of the students come from limited social and cultural backgrounds. And if the NMSC students we have studied are at all typical of the student bodies of the institutions they attended, some of these colleges will find that they have many students who, when they arrive, are ready to accept and support intellectual and social constraints. A college which leads students to replace narrow attitudes with liberal values may make a greater contribution to American society than the one whose task is mainly to fortify the values of students who have already been emancipated.

Investigations at the Center for the Study of Higher Education indicate that the colleges which have been shown here to attract students with relatively tolerant attitudes toward intellectual and civil liberties also draw large numbers of students who are theoretically oriented, interested in ideas, flexible in their intellectual processes, complex in their perception of and response to the environment, and potentially creative.

While some institutions are fortunate to have students who are not threatened by ambiguity, who will accept responsibility for their own learning, who are critical, and who are capable of taking new intellectual directions, other institutions draw a correspondingly large share of students who are intellectually conventional, dependent, and rigid—characteristics associated with the authoritarian personality.

Studies by Dr. G. G. Stern and his associates at Syracuse University have shown that stereopaths can be changed, but that they can be disposed to less authoritarian and more flexible attitudes only by special methods of instruction.[14] This is but one example of the fact that the student's responses to classroom instruction, as well as to the other aspects of the college environment, will be in large part determined, not alone by his general mental ability, but also—and sometimes more significantly—by his social and cultural backgrounds, his attitudes and values, his interests and motivations, and other dominant attributes of his personality.

If the protection and promulgation of our basic liberties is in large part the responsibility of college men and women, we may well ask what attitudes toward them students bring to college and how these attitudes change during undergraduate years. Students' attitudes toward civil liberties and intellectual freedom are not matters of immediate importance alone to citizens in the larger society; they are necessary for the protection of the academy itself against the onslaughts of those who would curb the rights of scholars to investigate, to teach, and to exercise their privileges as citizens.

[14] Stern, G. G., "Congruence and Dissonance in the Ecology of College Students." *Student Medicine,* 8:304–339, April, 1960.

Chapter 3

IMPLICATIONS OF DIFFERENCES IN CAMPUS ATMOSPHERE
for evaluation and planning of college programs

The rationale for college self studies and for the evaluation of college programs is well established. It consists of three crucial questions: 1) what are the purposes of the program, 2) what resources and experiences are provided to help students achieve these purposes, and 3) how well do the students achieve them?

Under each of these large questions there are, of course, many smaller and more specific ones which must be asked, and much tested experience to draw upon in asking these questions. For example, purposes are most clearly understood as they are translated into specific behavior which exemplifies them. What, in observable attitude and action, thought and feeling, do the purposes mean? Unless one can answer this question, he cannot know what to look for in deciding how well the purposes have been attained. As to resources and experiences, what opportunities do students have to use the relevant resources and how widely are they used? What experiences are most widely shared and what are unique to special groups or individuals? What virtues do students attach to certain of these resources and experiences? Concerning results, what observations are systematically made, and how relevant are those observations to the purposes of the program? There are important questions, too, regarding the interaction between purposes, resources and experiences, and results. What were the students like at the beginning of the program? What are they like at the end of the program? What are they like 10 years later? What utilization of resources and what experiences are associated with the changes?

C. ROBERT PACE

43

What kinds of students change in what ways under what kinds of experience or conditions?

The increased interest of social scientists in colleges and college students as objects for research in their particular disciplines promises to enrich the meaning of these familiar evaluative questions. Harold Lasswell is reported to have said that the role of the social scientist is to complicate the job of the decision maker. The educator is a decision maker. Especially in recent years, social scientists have succeeded well in complicating the educator's job. Just at a time when educators were feeling comfortably familiar with the concepts of individual differences, and transfer of training, and aptitude and achievement tests, social scientists have introduced a host of new ones—role expectations and role behavior, membership groups and reference groups, congruity and dissonance, personality needs and environmental press, ego development and impulse expression, and many others. Some of these are well known within their particular disciplines, but others are relatively new even in that context and all of them are relatively new in the context of evaluation in higher education. One of these relatively new concepts, as applied to higher education, is the concept of environmental press, the explanation and meaning of which is the topic of this paper.

What are the experiences and conditions for student learning and living which the college provides? Whatever they may be, they define the environment, the college culture, the campus atmosphere. At a recent discussion, Dr. Benjamin Bloom[1] suggested that there were several questions in the minds of students and parents as they think about college. Can I get in? Will I survive? How will I have to learn? What will I learn and how will I be changed? Whom will I be with? What sort of life will I lead? As a college clarifies its purposes, and molds its environment to them, it provides answers to these questions. In so doing it creates its own special atmosphere and establishes its particular image. What sort of a place is Harvard, really, or Oberlin or Swarth-

[1] Conference on Consumer Research in Higher Education, September 26, 1960, New York City, sponsored by the Carnegie Corporation.

C. ROBERT PACE

more or Michigan or Stanford or Texas? Tentative answers to this "complicating" question are just beginning to emerge.

There is a long and distinguished history of research on the characteristics of college students, to which T. R. McConnell and Nevitt Sanford have given new enrichment; but there is no comparable history of research aimed at describing the characteristics of colleges.[2] To some extent, of course, the character of a college is determined by the character of the students it admits. Other information about a college however is much more commonly available. How large is it, is it coeducational or not, where is it located, when was it founded, what degrees does it offer, is it public or private, religious or non-secretarian, what does it cost? Having learned the answers to all these questions, one knows little that is important about a college. Suppose one asked the same kind of questions about a prospective college student. What is his height and weight, sex, residence, age, vocational goal, religious affiliation, and family income? Knowing all these things, one is still left in ignorance about what kind of a person the prospective student really is. The important knowledge concerns his aptitudes and interests, his motivations, and emotional and social maturity. In short, the crucial knowledge concerns his personality. So too, with the college, the crucial knowledge concerns its overall atmosphere or characteristics, the kinds of things that are rewarded, encouraged, emphasized, the style of life which is valued in the community and is most visibly expressed and felt.

Dr. Pace gives us a way of having an empirical look at the functional goals of our institutions. Such a look will often run counter to our theoretical and perhaps wishful, or at least unrealistic, picture of what our college is like.

Therefore, Dr. Pace may not find universal acceptance of the idea that a college or university can employ scientific procedures to learn about itself and then use the knowledge to handle its own affairs better.

[2] Pace, C. Robert and McFee, Anne. "The College Environment," Chap. III, pages 311–320 in *Review of Educational Research*, 30, 4, October, 1960.

The concept of environmental press was described in 1938 by the psychologist, Henry Murray.[3] Individuals were seen as having characteristic needs, and the strength and relationships of these needs was what characterized the personality. In corollary fashion, the environment was seen as having potentials for satisfying or frustrating these needs. The model for studying behavior was thus the interaction between personality needs and environmental press. In 1956, Stern, Stein, and Bloom[4] elaborated this need-press concept by applying it to assessment studies and showing that the prediction of performance was improved as one defined the psychological demands of the situation in which the performance was to occur. The psychological demands of the situation are the environmental press.

In 1957 Pace and Stern[5] constructed the first version of a test, called the College Characteristics Index, applying the concept of environmental press to the study of college atmospheres. The instrument was constructed as a parallel to the Activities Index,[6] which is an inventory of personality needs that had been previously constructed by Stern. Thus, a pattern of personality needs scales was paralleled by a corresponding pattern of environmental press scales. For example, a personality need for order would be suggested by liking such activities as: "keeping an accurate record of the money I spend," "arranging my clothes neatly before going to bed," and so forth. An environmental press for order would be suggested by such features of the college as: "professors usually take attendance in class," "in many classes students have an assigned seat," and so forth. Each instrument, the AI and the CCI, consists of 30

[3] Murray, Henry A., *Explorations in Personality.* New York: Oxford University Press, 1938.

[4] Stern, George G., Stein, Morris I., and Bloom, Benjamin S. *Methods in Personality Assessment.* Glenco, Ill.: The Free Press, 1956.

[5] Pace, C. Robert, and Stern, George G. *College Characteristics Index, form 457.* Syracuse, N. Y.: Syracuse University, Psychological Research Center, 1957.

[6] Stern, George G. *Activities Index, form 156.* Syracuse, N. Y.: Syracuse University, Psychological Research Center, 1956.

scales of 10 items, or a total of 300 items. In answering the CCI, students act as reporters, saying what they believe is generally true or not true of their college. The items refer to a wide range of topics—rules and regulations, facilities, student-faculty relationships, classroom methods, extra-curricular activities, etc. The argument is that all these characteristics and events and practices, added together, constitute an educational press upon the awareness of students. The aggregate awareness of students about their college environment constitutes a press in the sense of exerting a directive influence on their behavior. Preliminary results were reported by Pace and Stern[7] in 1958.

The emphasis which Dr. Pace places on the environmental factors in behavior will represent to many behavioral scientists an encouraging departure from the prevailing tendency to focus almost exclusively on factors within the skin of the single individual. Henry Murray's needs in the last 25 years of research and theory-building, have influenced thinking more than have Henry Murray's environmental presses. One can make the argument that social workers, parents, psychotherapists, teachers, counselors and personality theorists all would do better if they were able to think clearly about press as well as about needs.

Over the past four years, groups of students in approximately 100 different colleges have filled out the CCI.[8] In the Spring of 1959 a norm group of 32 colleges, representing a wide assortment of sizes and locations and shapes, was selected to develop standard scores for the scales. Much is now known about college environments from this testing activity and from various studies that have been made of the data. Some of the major results are described below.

Some things are true about all colleges. Students

[7] Pace, C. Robert, and Stern, George G. "An Approach to the Measurement of Psychological Characteristics of College Environments." *Journal of Educational Psychology*, 1958, 49, 269–277.

[8] Support for parts of this research program, much of it jointly conducted by Pace and Stern, has come from the College Entrance Examination Board, the Carnegie Corporation, the Social Science Research Council, and the Cooperative Research Program of the U. S. Office of Education.

everywhere agree that certain things are true about their college. By agree is meant at least 4 out of 5 students across the total norm group of 32 colleges, and at least 3 out of 4 in each sub-category of the norm group (private liberal arts, denominational liberal arts, universities, education, engineering, and business).

Thus, it is generally reported as TRUE everywhere that—

There are many opportunities for students to get together in extracurricular activities.

There is a lot of excitement and restlessness just before holidays.

Student papers and reports must be neat.

Classrooms are kept clean and tidy.

Most courses are very well organized and progress systematically from week to week.

Most of the professors are dedicated scholars in their fields.

Similarly, it is generally reported as FALSE everywhere that—

If a student wants help, he usually has to answer a lot of embarrassing questions.

Students don't argue with the professors; they just admit that they are wrong.

When students dislike a faculty member, they make it evident to him.

Students pay little attention to rules and regulations.

The student leaders here have lots of special privileges.

There are practically no student organizations actively involved in campus or community reforms.

Spontaneous student rallies and demonstrations occur frequently.

The campus and buildings always look a little unkempt.

"Alma mater" seems to be more important than "subject matter" at this school.

Students who work hard for high grades are likely to be regarded as odd.

In short, one might say that college campuses and

48

C. ROBERT PACE

classrooms are generally well manicured, the students are not especially belligerent or demonstrative but neither are they uninterested in reforms; faculty members are scholarly, and there is no stigma attached to hard work and honest inquiry.

Beyond these few common characteristics, however, colleges are vastly different from one another. By comparing the rank order of mean scores on the 30 scales one gets a general index of the degree of similarity between one environment and another. For the 32 institutions these rank order correlations ranged from +.93 to −.87.[9] Between some colleges the relative environmental pressures are nearly identical; between others the relative pressures are almost totally opposite. Between Swarthmore and Hamline, for example, there were 70 items characteristic of both schools, with characteristic being defined as agreement by 3 out of 4 students, or more. Sixteen items, however, were answered in exactly the opposite way at the two schools, meaning that more than 3 out of 4 students at one school said "yes" and more than 3 out of 4 students at the other school said "no." Here are some of these opposite characteristics:

Most courses require a lot of library work.

The professors really push the students' capacities to the limit.

Concerts and art exhibits always draw big crowds of students.

Students address faculty members as professor or doctor.

Professors usually take attendance in class.

There is a recognized group of student leaders.

Pep rallies, parades, dances, carnivals, or demonstrations occur very rarely.

Education here tends to make students more realistic and practical.

Moreover, the familiar structural classifications of schools—as liberal arts or professional, college or university, non-sectarian or denominational—are not very

[9] Pace, C. Robert. "Five College Environments," *College Board Review*, 1960, 41, 24–28.

good indicators of environmental press similarity. Between schools in any one of these structural categories, the rank order correlation of the press scales ranges from high to zero and sometimes negative.

Dr. Pace gives us evidence that college cultures do indeed vary widely. Perhaps one significant aspect of a college environment is the willingness of that college to expose itself to self-study.

The differences between college environments, across a wide assortment of schools, fall into several fairly clear patterns. There are certain kinds of pressures or characteristics which tend to go together in college environments generally. Five such clusters were recently described.[10] The first two are both strongly intellectual, with one more strongly oriented toward humanism, sentience, and reflectiveness, and the other more strongly oriented toward scientism, uncertainty, and competition. The third cluster emphasizes the practical and applied rather than the abstract or theoretical, and is heavily concerned with establishing status in relation to peers and accepting status in relation to authority. The fourth cluster exhibits a strong press toward group welfare, human relations, and social responsibility. And the fifth cluster suggests a rebellion against the well managed, group welfare oriented community.

These clusters form a pattern of interrelationships. The humanistic and scientific clusters are positively related, because of their common intellectual component, and both are negatively related to the practical, status-oriented cluster. The humanistic cluster, however, is unrelated to either the social welfare or the rebellion clusters. The scientific cluster, on the other hand, is negatively related to social welfare and positively related to rebellion. The practical, status-oriented cluster has a positive but low relationship to social welfare, and a somewhat higher positive relationship to rebellion.

[10] *Pace, Ibid.*

C. ROBERT PACE

What does the academic administrator mean when he speaks in favor of increased quality in his institution? Which of Dr. Pace's five primary clusters is the administrator wanting to make stronger? It may be that until he specifies the kind of high quality environment he's shooting for, he cannot succeed.

Distinctive patterns of college environment have predictable and demonstrable consequences. Two lines of evidence exist in support of this statement. The assumption underlying the use of the CCI as an indicator of the press of an institution is that if many students with high unanimity say that something is true about their school, this aggregate awareness constitutes a press on the students to behave in certain ways. Classifications of colleges stemming from the CCI can be compared with classifications made from other information. If these comparisons show the relationship one would expect if the assumptions underlying the CCI were true, then one can feel more confident about the probable validity of the assumptions. Several such predictions have been made.[11] For these predictions, schools have been classified into four types, based on CCI responses—humanistic, scientific, social welfare, and practical-status.

Nearly all of the predictions are supported by the obtained data. There are only two reversals of any significance. The social welfare schools were predicted to rank third in the proportion of liberal arts majors, and they turned out to have the highest proportion. The social welfare schools in the sample all happened to be women's colleges, a peculiarity which probably accounted for the result in this case, as well as for the same kind of reversal relative to the proportion of majors in applied fields. The second reversal in the predicted results is the higher than expected ranking of the practical-status schools on the two productivity indexes. It should be noted that all of these comparisons are based on a very small number of cases. There were only two to five colleges within any one grouping for which data were available to verify the predicted results. These tentative

[11] These predictions and analyses were made by Anne McFee, Stanford University, in the spring of 1960.

results, however, lend general support to the validity of the assumptions underlying the CCI.

TABLE 1

Predicted and Obtained Rank-Order Relationship Between Type of College Environment and Other Information About the College[1]

Type of School	SAT Verbal scores		SAT Math scores		Per Cent of Liberal Arts majors		Per Cent of majors in applied fields		Presence and number of fraternities		Productivity Index— Natural Sciences[1]		Productivity Index— Social Sciences and Humanities	
	P	O	P	O	P	O	P	O	P	O	P	O	P	O
Humanistic	1	1	2	2	1	2	4	3	3	2	2	3	1	1
Scientific	2	2	1	1	2	3	3	2	4	4	1	1	2	4
Social Welfare	3	3	4	4	3	1	2	4	2	3	3	4	3	3
Practical Status	4	4	3	3	4	4	1	1	1	1	4	2	4	2

P = Predicted.
O = Obtained.

[1] Note: For a description of the Productivity Indexes, see Thistlethwaite, D. L. College environments and the development of talent. *Science*, 1959, 130, 71–76.

One other prediction is of special interest. If CCI items measure aspects of the college important to the student, it is assumed that the pressure to adapt will cause appropriate personality changes in the students. Seniors will show traits different from those of freshmen, and these differences will appear in personality needs which correspond to the dominant press of the environment. This hypothesis is weakened somewhat by the fact that correlation analysis of the Stern Activities Index does not give rise to the same clusters of variables as the CCI correlation analysis. Nevertheless, there is sufficient similarity between the AI and CCI variables to warrant a tentative check on the hypothesis. The hypothesis is that personality differences between freshmen and seniors will be greatest in the areas where the college is perceived as exerting the greatest press. Data for checking this hypothesis were obtained from the recent Study

C. ROBERT PACE

of Cooperative Education.[12] The results are shown below:

TABLE 2
Personality Differences Between Freshmen and Seniors

	Liberal Arts Colleges		Engineering Schools		Business Schools	
Variables	P	O	P	O	P	O
Humanistic	1	1.5	2	2	5	1.5
Scientific	2	3	1	1	4	1.5
Rebellion	3	1.5	3	4	3	3
Social Welfare	4	4	4	3	2	4
Practical Status	5	5	5	5	1	5

The obtained ranks are close to the arrangement predicted for the liberal arts colleges and also for the engineering schools, but the hypothesis is not supported by the business school data.

It is a good bet that neither parents of college-bound students nor college students nor the many educational counselors, amateur and professional, are very keenly aware of the wide, subtle, and significant institutional differences Dr. Pace's methods have revealed. Should they be?

The best evidence that different environments have a differential influence on the behavior of students comes from studies made by Thistlethwaite[13] at the National Merit Scholarship Corporation. In 1959, he reported: "one type of college environment is associated with achievement in the natural sciences, while a different kind of environment is related to accomplishment in the arts, humanities, and social sciences. Productivity in the humanities is positively related to Humanism, Reflectiveness, Sentience, Harm-avoidance, and Understanding. It is negatively related to Pragmatism, Deference, and Abasement. Productivity in the natural sciences is positively related to Scientism, Aggression, and Impulsion,

[12] Wilson, James, and Lyons, Edward, *Work-Study College Programs.* New York: Harper & Brothers, 1961.

[13] Thistlethwaite, Donald L. "College press and student achievement." *Journal of Educational Psychology,* 1959, 50, 183–191. Also, "College press and changes in study plans of talented students." *Journal of Educational Psychology,* 1960, 51, 222–234.

and negatively related to Order, Deference, and Sentience." He went on to point out that there was some ambiguity in these results owing to the fact that most of the CCI scales contained items which referred to students as well as to faculty or other non-student aspects of the environment. He proceeded therefore to revise the scales into two categories, one referring only to the student press, and the other referring only to the faculty press. With these revised scales he found that "student cultures characterized by Humanism, Breadth of Interests, and Reflectiveness are associated with scholarly productivity (humanistic), whereas cultures characterized by Participation and Aggression are negatively related. . . Motivation to seek the Ph.D. in the natural sciences, on the other hand, seems to be stimulated by student cultures which are high in Scientism and Aggression and inhibited by those which stress Social Conformity."

Then, considering only the faculty press scales, he finds that "colleges outstandingly successful in encouraging undergraduates to get the doctorate in humanistic fields are characterized by excellent social science faculty and resources, a flexible, or somewhat unstructured curriculum, energy and controversiality of instruction, and informality and warmth of student-faculty contacts, . . ." Colleges high in natural science productivity are characterized, also, by informality and warmth of student-faculty contacts, but, beyond this, by relatively non-directive or non-predictable teaching methods, and the lack of close supervision.

In a study in 1960, he predicted that motivation to seek graduate education would be associated with certain characteristics of faculty and student press in the undergraduate college environment. He found that all his predictions about faculty press were confirmed, but that there was no evidence that student press influenced the aspirations of the National Merit students he studied. It seems quite clear from these studies that different college environments do have demonstrable consequences on student behavior, over and above the student culture which is part of the total college culture.

C. ROBERT PACE

Could a college or university, by taking thought, change the basic characteristics of its environment? Dr. Pace supplies evidence that much of the environment is formed by faculty, administration, and trustees. Suppose faculty, administration, and trustees agreed to change the college environment from a practical peer-status one to an intellectual, humanistic, sentient one? It might be accomplished in 20 years. But what if only the administration and trustees wanted the change while the faculty did not? This would be, to quote Dana Farnsworth, "as difficult as moving a graveyard."

To the question, "Do students make the college?" the answer is both yes and no. There are results from the AI and CCI, administered to students in 43 colleges, which show clearly that *students with strong needs in certain directions tend to be found at colleges which exert a strong press in those same directions.* The public image which a college has makes it especially attractive to students who sense that they would find such an environment congenial to them.

A correlation matrix was developed, based on the mean AI scores, and the mean CCI scores, for this group of 43 schools. This shows the extent to which students with certain kinds of needs are found in institutions with corresponding kinds of press.[14]

For three selected and most important scales in the humanistic press cluster—humanism, reflectiveness, and sentience—the median correlation with the three corresponding personality needs scales is .55. For the three most important scales in the science cluster—scientism, change, and negative order—the correlation with the corresponding three personality needs scales is .54. For the three most diagnostic scales in the practical-status cluster—practicality, dominance, and play—the correlation with the three corresponding personality needs scales is .23. For the four scales in the social welfare cluster, the correlation with the parallel personality scales is .60. And for the two scales in the rebellion cluster, the correlation with the parallel personality scales is .54. The median correlation between all 30 parallel need-press

[14] This matrix was prepared by George Stern, as part of an Office of Education sponsored research project, directed jointly by Pace and Stern.

scales is .35. For the special scales noted above, it appears that the similarity between student bodies and college environments is indicated by a correlation of about .55.

Translating this relationship into other statistical language, and projecting its meaning onto a broader plane, one might suggest that *about 30 per cent of the distinctive environment of a school is accounted for by the distinctive character of the students it admits. This leaves most of the potential impact of a college squarely up to the decisions of its faculty, administration, and trustees.* Environmental press is clearly more than the student culture alone.

Summary

Summarizing, and turning to implications, one can say that in the familiar rationale of evaluation studies, in which one considers purposes, programs, and progress, the meaning of "programs" has been extended by the concept of environmental press. It has been customary to look at the environment in various structural or functional parts—such as the general education curriculum, the student personnel services, the library resources with each being studied or evaluated in its own terms. It now seems possible and certainly fruitful to think about the environment as a whole. Many apparently disparate pieces of the environment fit together in a pattern of relationships, and these pieces cut across the familiar parts into which environments have usually been divided. Across the national scene the patterns of college culture illustrate the diversity of higher education. With variations in emphasis, the same patterns are revealed in the environments of individual colleges and illustrate the uniqueness of certain institutions. There are predictable and demonstrable consequences which follow from different major patterns of emphasis in college environments. These consequences cannot be fully explained by the selective distribution of students to environments which are already congruent with their needs. Nor can they be explained fully by the influence

C. ROBERT PACE

of student characteristics or student life within the total culture of the college.

Certainly the student who knows the various subcultures in his college should be better equipped to find his way into a productive pattern of college life.

The most important implication for evaluation studies lies in the new awareness of relationship between many different parts of the college environment. Whether a college class is taught by lectures or by discussions, whether the class size is large or small, whether the professor is permissive or strict, whether counseling is directive or non-directive, whether teaching machines or audio-visual aids are used liberally or not at all, whether general education courses are required or are selected from alternative offerings, all these, and many others, are relatively small phenomena in the total college culture. They are separately important, of course. But their real significance, and the clue to their influence, lies in the relationships between them. Do they add up to some dominant direction? Or is their possible influence dissipated through isolation and lack of reinforcement from the rest of the college environment? To the extent that a college environment is an unrelated assortment of policies and practices and events and features, its influence upon the student is probably small. To the extent that a college environment is a culture, in the anthropologists' sense of that word, its influence on the student is probably large.

One aspect of life that Dr. Pace does not deal with is the environmental press exerted from outside upon the academic culture itself. All academic cultures, especially those of public institutions, exist in a larger culture. Before we can think with greatest clarity about changing the college culture, we need not only to understand its present "personality," but we need to see clearly also the environmental press exerted upon it from outside—by alumni, by taxpayers, by the town in which it exists, by the national *zeitgeist*, and by the state legislature.

All things considered, however, there seems room for little doubt that Dr. Pace's kind of analysis can, in conjunction with the concern for the whole development of the whole individual, add significantly to the subtlety, the discrimination, the intelligence and probably the wisdom of our thinking, of our decision-making and our research in the areas of personality development in higher education.

Addendum

Granted the importance of college atmosphere, and the utility of the concept of environmental press as one way of expressing it, and the validity of results that have been obtained from the use of one particular measuring instrument, the CCI, there remain certain problems in some uses of the instrument which should be stated. There are ways of dealing with these problems which can be described, together with new analyses which may be made.

One problem was mentioned in Thistlethwaite's study, and that was the fact that items referring to students as well as to other aspects of the environment both occur in all of the CCI scales. An actual classification of items revealed that 45 per cent of them concerned student characteristics, extra-curricular programs, or informal student activities. Part of the environment of any college is of course created by the students, but the present instrument does not provide any systematic way of separating this influence from others. A second problem grows out of the fact that the larger and more complex an institution is, the more disagreement there is in the way its students answer the CCI items.[15] Closely related to this is the further fact that items referring to conditions or events which students are least likely to have encountered are often answered in quite different ways by different students.[16] Moreover, there is, as one would expect, more agreement about the dominant press of a college than about its less characteristic aspects.[17] The

[15] From a chapter by Pace, C. Robert. "The college characteristics index as a measure of the effective student environment" in a book, *The Study of College Peer Groups*, edited by Everett Wilson and Theodore Newcomb, 1961.

[16] From McFee, Anne, "The relation of students' needs to their perceptions of a college environment," *Journal of Educational Psychology*, 1961, 52, 25–29.

[17] Pace, *ibid.*, p. 17.

C. ROBERT PACE

fact that the CCI is designed to characterize the environment as a whole poses a third problem, especially in the larger and more complex institutions, because there undoubtedly exist important and influential subcultures in any complex college environment.

For people whose primary interest is in college evaluation rather than in the prediction of personal performance, an instrument which was more directly analytic of the environment might provide a useful supplement to the CCI. Such an instrument has been constructed and is now being used experimentally.

This instrument, called the College Characteristics Analysis[18] (CCA) enables students to report what, in their experience and opinion, is or is not true about the particular part of the university they know best—their own academic field or area, and the students they associate with most commonly and closely. Thus, the CCA provides a means of describing and comparing subcultures within the total environment.

There is an intentional bridge between the CCA and the CCI. Thirty-eight per cent of the items originally composed by George Stern and the writer for the CCI have been retained and used in the CCA. An additional 13 per cent were rewritten or revised in various ways.

Of the 210 items in the CCA, 57 are completely new, 40 are revised old items and 113 are unrevised old items. All items, however, were written, revised, or selected to fit a test blueprint which is different from the CCI.

The content of the items in the CCA is organized along two dimensions. The first dimension refers to the goals, objectives, or major emphases of the environment. Goals of higher education are grouped under four broad categories corresponding to four of the five clusters of environmental press variables which were described earlier: the first two are strongly intellectual, involving an interest in ideas as ideas and a primary emphasis on academic achievement, but with one more explicitly directed toward humanism and the other more explicitly directed toward scientism; the third goal encompasses

---

[18] Pace, C. Robert. The College Characteristics Analysis: Preliminary Comments. The author, 1960.

important practical and vocational objectives, and involves an interest in skills, and in external rewards and personal status; the fourth goal is concerned with those objectives which emphasize human relations, group welfare, citizenship, and social responsibility.

The second dimension along which the items are located refers to the major parts of the college or university community—the administrative community of the college or university as a whole, with its rules and procedures, the facilities and equipment provided, and various special features which transcend departmental or divisional boundaries; the academic community which refers to the faculty, curriculum, and instruction in the various major areas; and the student community which refers to student characteristics, extra-curricular programs, and informal student activities. In addition to the four major emphases described above, there are two shorter scales, referring only to the student community and concerned with rebelliousness and playfulness.

With this two-fold classification system, one can make a diagnostic evaluation of the college environment. For example, is the emphasis in the administrative community consistent with the emphasis in the academic community? Is the student community supportive of or at odds with the objectives of the academic community? Where does most of the support come for the major goals of the institution? Moreover, since the students' reports can be grouped according to major academic areas and according to major student associations, one can identify and evaluate the role of these finer subdivisions in relation to the objectives of the institution.

The insight which such a pattern of analysis might provide could greatly enlarge the benefit from college self-studies and evaluations. It is the business of educators to know what they want, and to learn, as best they can, at what points the environments they help to create are supportive of these purposes.

The press of the environment as a whole can be seen in relation to the needs of the personality as a whole, giving support to some needs and providing a counter thrust to others. The AI-CCI combination, with its need-press parallelism, facilitates the study of person-environment interaction.

The press of the environment can also be seen as a kind of operational definition of objectives or major emphases, with different parts of the total college community being supportive or not supportive of these major emphases. The CCA, with its diagnostic categories and its explicit concern for subcultures, facilitates a kind of internal analysis which may be particularly useful in program evaluation. The CCA is an experimental supplement to the CCI, hopefully enriching the total understanding which may be gained about the college environment.

Chapter 4

TEACHING MACHINES AND LEARNING THEORY

The reaction to the new teaching machine or "auto-instructional device" tends to fall at one extreme or the other: either to antagonism because this does violence to everything that we find precious in the relationship between the teacher and the learner, or to an enthusiastic acceptance of the machine as a solution to the teacher shortage and to the crisis in education generally. Obviously the appropriate attitude to be taken toward these devices is not to be *for* them or *against* them, but to see how they can best be used.

There has in the past been a tragic failure of learning psychologists to tailor and engineer their findings for practical use in the classroom. The teaching machines are in some sense an interesting breakthrough here. They are proposed by psychologists who believe that the machines incorporate principles of learning that have been established in the laboratory. Now we are prepared to find out whether they will deliver what is promised. They are likely to contribute also to general psychology, bearing on such problems as transfer of training, size of units, wholes versus parts, understanding versus rote learning, overlearning.

Some cautions are in order. Most of those who promote the teaching machines use a vocabulary of reinforcement, and speak of sequences of the subject-matter that are to be transmitted, as though we were still in the era of Ebbinghaus, Pavlov, and Thorndike. There are other teachings of the learning laboratory that have to do with anxiety, level of aspiration, achievement, power, and affiliation motives. They are among the most promising developments that we have in the present studies of learning, and they tend to get side-stepped when teaching machines are under discussion. Social learning, emulation, rivalry, identification with peers and with the teacher, are also part of learning. The fact that the teaching machine does not take care of all of these things is not to condemn it, but to keep it in its place.

A total educational program makes use of many resources: laboratories, libraries, museums, field trips, audio-visual aids, lectures, discussions, conferences. The teaching machine is not something to replace any one of these resources; it is, like the other items, something to be fitted into the total program.

If we wish to preserve what is precious in the teacher, we must leave the teacher unburdened enough to do these precious things. If the teacher can work beside the student in the laboratory, or can have time for some individual help on independent projects, or can help the student to invent or produce something original, then we will welcome anything that will free the teacher's time to do these things. It may be that the teaching machine, instead of displacing the teacher, will help the teacher to do the kind of job only a teacher can do. If the objection to the teaching machine is that it can only communicate something to the student, let us not forget that the teacher spends about 90 per cent of the classroom time in such communication, and often does not do it well.

It is a little shocking for a teacher to think of himself as an animated teaching machine, but maybe there is profit in the analogy. He is, like the machines, a dispenser of reinforcement and a purveyor of correct answers; also, whether he knows it or not, he is programmed. He probably is not as consistent as the machines in his meting out of reinforcement, not as trustworthy as a source of information and by no means as systematically programmed. How, then, can he compete with a machine? Obviously, he must conceive of his role in different terms. What terms?

The role and function of the teaching machines can be described in fairly precise and systematic terms. What about the role of the teacher? What is his function?

The teaching machine can let the student work at his own rate, but it cannot adjust itself to the student along any dimension other than the temporal one. The perceptive teacher can adjust, supposedly, to the unique personality of the learner.

ERNEST R. HILGARD

Some basic teaching principles hold true:

The use of some sort of acknowledgment of success, whether through reward, knowledge of results, or feedback is known to be efficacious.

Individual differences are known to be pervasive, and good teaching must respect them.

Understanding and problem-solving require some sense of self-initiated action on the part of the learner.

Because these are sound principles, we need to examine the advantages and disadvantages of the teaching machine in achieving them. Increasingly attention is being turned away from the "hardware" to the "programming." The programming of a course requires careful attention to the organization of knowledge, both logically and psychologically. In order to program, one has to know what he is doing; there can be no bluffing, and excuses for poor teaching won't work. The errors in programming will show up in the errors students make in trying to work through a program. This is one of the most refreshing features of programmed instruction: one cannot claim to be doing something he is not doing. Some programs are achieved with books, without the use of any machine at all (e.g., Blumenthal, 1960).

The teaching machine, as pointed out by Skinner, Professor of Psychology, Harvard University, is more nearly a substitute for a tutor than are such mass teaching aids as the motion picture. In common with the tutor it

1. respects individual differences in rate of learning,
2. gives knowledge of results as learning proceeds,
3. keeps the learner active,
4. lets the learner initiate his own learning by using "prompts" instead of rote memorization.

Each of these characteristics receives good support from learning theory. The old advice that we "learn by doing" is as good as it ever was. An active learner acquires more than a passive listener.

Why do students keep working away at teaching machines? They do —apparently for hours. Do we have here some evidence for a curiosity drive, a drive that we often underestimate? Does the fact that the student

**is actively manipulating something keep him going? Live teachers ought
to be able to compete successfully with the machines in keeping interest
and activity up. We probably do not. Why?**

In answering the question about whether or not teaching machines help students use their imagination, my own position is that they are very limited in this respect, and that imagination is better cultivated in other ways. However, a basic lesson in encouraging creativity may be learned from the machine. Teaching machines start where the student is and take steps he can do. We could possibly stimulate our own students to become more creative and imaginative in such areas as literature, art, music. Often we put before them models based on too high a standard and the discrepancy between what they can do and the model frightens them. Perhaps more people would learn to express themselves, with a sense of pride and satisfaction, through art, music, writing, and through other media if they were encouraged to try and actually to produce even in primitive ways. The high standard is thus attained, but more gradually.

To what extent may we utilize program or sequence logic on a broader scale to deal in more effective ways with the teaching of courses without machines? This question relates to the organization of knowledge. One issue concerns whether one needs to button something down cleanly and firmly, almost overlearn it, before moving ahead. Another alternative is that students move in overlapping units so that new materials and new knowledge are experienced before the earlier material is fully mastered. There is good evidence in the field of language teaching, for example, favoring reading discursive material ahead of the material one is ready to comprehend in detail. Reading ahead seems to help with the rhythm and the sound of language and aid in getting a broad sense of the meaning. If this is generally true, there may be some point at which with only partial knowledge one ought to move on and then return in some cyclical way to button up that which he is now motivated to understand. A good teacher uses all sorts of devices in learning situations. Perhaps a developing knowledge of program

ERNEST R. HILGARD

ming for teaching machines may help us to rethink our text books, teaching procedures, and lectures. This influence will certainly be an interesting by-product.

Some References

1. Blumenthal, J. C. *English 2600.* New York: Harcourt, Brace, 1960. (A "programmed" textbook on grammar and usage.)
2. Galanter, E. (Editor). *Automatic teaching: The state of the art.* New York: Wiley, 1959.
3. Lumsdaine, A. A., and Glaser, R. (Editors). *Teaching machines and programmed learning.* Washington, D.C.: National Educational Association, 1960.
4. Schramm, W. (Editor). *New teaching aids for the American classroom.* Stanford, California: Stanford University Press, 1960.
5. Skinner, B. F. The science of learning and the art of teaching. *Harvard Educational Review,* 1954, 24, 86–97.
6. Skinner, B. F. Teaching machines. *Science,* 1958, 128, 969–977.

Chapter 5

STUDENT PEER-GROUP INFLUENCE
and intellectual outcomes of college experience*

The Problem

Not long ago a group of social scientists met to consider a set of problems which might be summarized in the question, "How can we find out what happens to students in American colleges and universities, and why?" Being social scientists, we soon found ourselves "categorizing" the "sources of variance" in "institutional output." What this really meant was that a comparatively few kinds of things seem to be mainly responsible for the differences that one can observe among students—within a given college or among many—as they leave ivied walls and cloistered halls. Emerging students are different, we guessed, because they were different on first coming to college, because they met different kinds of faculty-administration influence and because they have done different kinds of things to each other while in college. Selection, tutelage, and peer influence, they may be labeled.

Having categorized the sources of differentiation, we then went on to rank them in terms of presumed importance. Somewhat to our own surprise, we found ourselves virtually unanimous. Selection, we thought (i.e., all things that students bring with them on arriving at college), more fully accounts for the final product than does either of the other sets of factors. Peer influences we rated second. Though most of us were college professors, we had no sense that we were, by assigning these rel-

* Adapted from a chapter in *The Study of College Peer Groups: Problems and Prospects for Research*, edited by T. M. Newcomb and E. K. Wilson. Social Science Research Council, forthcoming.

ative weights, necessarily denigrating our own roles as educators. It is possible that selection makes a difference not just because students on leaving are very much like the same students on entering college; perhaps also—or even instead—selection is important because some student characteristics, already present on entrance, make their possessors more likely to become different—in which case professors may provide the necessary mechanisms of change.

As to our second-rated set of factors, peer influence is not necessarily opposed to faculty influence; it is at least possible that the latter is mediated and reinforced by the former—in which case, again, the professor's role is essential even if not sufficient.

Whatever the facts of the matter, there is reason enough to conclude that on the contemporary American scene the effects of student peer groups are sufficiently important to justify the serious attention of social scientists. Everyday observation, theoretical expectation, and empirical investigation all point to their importance.

Dr. Newcomb's early statement that selection does more than teaching can to produce the kind of seniors we want brings humbling reality. Most of us as teachers cultivate the illusion that today's lecture or this week's discussion may lead students to everlasting insights and revolutionary steps toward maturity. Evidence indicates that we are much less influential than we think. How, then, can we keep our noses to the pedagogical grindstone? Can we gain satisfaction from the intellectual pleasure of exploring the world with our students? Do we have to reconcile ourselves to the mere enjoyment of our own expression of our own thespionic impulses? Do we take the stand that the changes we are bringing about remain significant but are too subtle for the behavioral scientists to capture in their crude net of measurement? Do we say to ourselves that if we are truly interested in helping increase the maturity of students, we should resign our college jobs and go back—or forward— to the primary grades, where we can work with greater effectiveness with less crystallized personalities? I'm not sure I want to go to class again until I can get answers to some of these questions.

Theory and Evidence

The theoretical grounds for assuming that student peer-group effects should be rather considerable are not

THEODORE M. NEWCOMB

particularly abstruse. In its general form the argument runs essentially as follows: People respond to a situation not necessarily as it really is but as they perceive it to be. And they perceive all but the simplest situations—especially human ones—not as they have been pre-ordained, by their physiological make-up, to perceive them but as they have learned to do so. The matter of learning to perceive—of acquiring habits of perceiving in one way things that might be perceived differently (and often are, especially by other people) is a very complex one indeed, but nearly all psychologists would agree that such habits are learned as a result of the successes and failures that follow from actions based on "right"and "wrong" ways of perceiving situations.

There are powerful reasons why groups have much to do with individuals' successes and failures, and thus with the kinds of perceptual habits that they acquire. This is true, first, because groups so often have it in their power to reward and to punish—as by applause or shame, or by the according or withholding of social status or of worldly goods.

One needs to know, dependably and in advance, what kinds of behavior will and will not be rewarded. Such standards come to have the psychological impact of ineluctability, and are sometimes referred to as "social reality." Successes and failures are matters of group life, second, because human beings want and need each other.

For the purposes of the present argument, the outcomes of these two bases of group power over its individual members are the same: individual members develop attitudes toward each other—most commonly favorable ones; and they develop consensual sets of expectations regarding each others' behavior and regarding important aspects of their common environment, by which their individual expectations of success and failure are guided. Such consensual expectations of each other's behavior are known as *norms*. Baldly put, groups have power over their members because the same processes of interaction that result in members' feeling favorably toward each other also result, simultaneously, in their adopting norms that enable them to aim at success rather than failure.

The final step of the argument, of course, is that student peer groups, as a special case of the general phenomenon, are subject to the general rules. A plausible case can in fact be made for the assumption that the general rules should apply *a fortiori* to student groups. College students (particularly in this country, perhaps) meet each other with a ready-made consensuality compounded of needs for independence from parents in a setting where independence is relatively possible, and of striving for adult status in a world that treats them half as children. These initial bases of consensus, together with the fact that students are inevitably thrown together in dining rooms, classes, and dormitories, inevitably result—and often rather quickly—in the joint processes according to which groups acquire power over their members.[1]

In sum, I believe that the theoretical reasons for expecting important peer-groups effects within American colleges are very convincing, and that the expectations have been well supported when they have been put to the proper tests. I shall later suggest certain conditions of peer-group influence that have emerged, or hypothetically would emerge, from such "proper tests."

A Framework for The Problem

It often happens, particularly in the world of human affairs, that the consequences of any event are more fully understood if viewed in the light of the circumstances of which that event itself is a consequence, than by viewing the event as "uncaused" (though for many purposes this procedure is unnecessary or even impossible). The study of peer groups is a case in point: peer-group formation is an outcome of antecedent events; the nature

---

[1] More substantial bases for the general position outlined above may be found in Asch (1952), Cartwright & Zander (1960), Festinger *et al.* (1950), Gardner & Thompson (1956), Hare *et al.* (1955), Newcomb (1950), Schachter (1959), Sherif & Sherif (1956), Tagiuri & Petrullo (1958), Thibaut & Kelley (1959).

THEODORE M. NEWCOMB

of members' experiences, and thus the effects of those experiences may be profoundly influenced by the circumstances attending the group's emergence. And so (in the language of contemporary social scientists) it is necessary to consider peer groups, alternately as dependent and as independent phenomena.

More specifically, the nature of student peer-group experience is sure to be influenced by the various factors having to do with student selection, and these in turn are influenced by and (in time) they also influence both the actual and the perceived nature of the college itself. In very direct ways, furthermore, various kinds of institutional arrangements—e.g., student living arrangements —influence peer-group formation.

Some Conditions of Peer-Group Formation

It is of course "natural" for people with common interests to associate with one another, and it is a truism that, in our own society at least, not only early but also late adolescents (including most college students) seem to have strong needs for acceptance by age and sex peers. The truism leaves unexplained, however, the entire matter of selection. Even in very small colleges, not every one associates with equal frequency or with equal intensity with all of his peers. There are wide differences among individuals; some are under- and some over-involved, in terms of local norms. Furthermore, there are many possible bases for peer-group formation, ranging from chance propinquity through more or less casual common interest to shared concerns of great moment.

The following discussion of conditions under which influential peer groups are likely to develop (like the subsequent discussion of their effects) is necessarily a general one. Colleges in this country vary enormously, in almost every conceivable respect; moreover, peer groups of the most diverse form arise within all but the tiniest colleges.

Associated with such variations in the nature of peer groups there are of course wide differences in individuals' motives in joining and remaining in them, differences in individual personality, and differences in degree and kind of impact. The rather general considerations noted below do not apply with equal force, or in constant ways, to all these kinds of groups, but in one way or another the generalizations may be nonetheless relevant.

In any case, there are three kinds of factors that may be considered of primary importance as independent—i.e., as contributing to the formation of particular peer groups.

Pre-college acquaintance. Particularly during early college experience, previous acquaintance—especially as established in secondary schools—may form the basis of college peer groups. One study of high school seniors' preferences among colleges (Coleman & Rossi, 1960) found that a small proportion of high school friends hoped to attend the same college. Neither this study nor any other known to me, however, provides much information as to the subsequent fate of pre-college friendships. It seems probable that many if not most of them are superseded by others developed in college with previously unknown persons. In the presumably rare cases where they do persist through a significant proportion of the college years, it seems more likely that they reinforce existing attitudes and values of the individuals involved than that they mediate new ones acquired through college experience.

Propinquity. One cannot very well develop peer-group relationships with persons whom one has never met. Neither does one develop them with all the persons whom one has met. But propinquity determines the probability of any two persons' meeting and, in particular, early propinquity in college—when most other individuals are relatively indistinguishable, since most of them are strangers—determines the probability of early meeting. This basic statement of statistical probabilities, together with a rather basic psychological consideration, has important consequences for peer-group formation. This principle, the consequences of which are in a certain sense conservative, must of course compete with other and sometimes overriding principles and therefore describe a probable rather than a required

THEODORE M. NEWCOMB

state of affairs. But the two kinds of probabilities, together, result in a considerably greater than chance frequency of persisting peer-group relationships that originated in "chance" encounters facilitated by propinquity, as in dormitory residence or classroom attendance.

In view of the fact that marriage rates—even within a single city—vary directly with residential propinquity of marriage partners (Cf. Bossard, 1932), we should scarcely expect that the formation of less intimate peer-group relationships would be immune to the same considerations, and the known facts support the expectation. Festinger *et al.* (1950),[2] for example, have shown that in a housing project for married students the closest interpersonal relationships (in a statistical sense) developed not merely on the part of those whose apartment entrance faced the same court, but also, in particular, among those who used the same stairways and other facilities. A more recent investigation (Newcomb, 1961) shows that, even within a small, two-floor house accommodating only 17 students, there were at first (but not following intimate acquaintance) significantly more close relationships among the eight men on one floor and among the nine men on the other than between men on different floors. Roommates, whose proximity to each other was greatest of all, were particularly prone to develop close relationships.[3]

The evidence concerning propinquity, and its attendant probability of interpersonal contact, has obvious implications for peer-group formation as related to the size of college populations. In small colleges, of course, where all students have frequent contacts with nearly all others, the student body as a whole is likely to have more important effects, as a peer group, than in larger insti-

[2] Festinger, L., Back, K., Schachter, S., Kelley, H. H., & Thibaut, J., 1950. *Theory and Experiment in Social Communication.* Ann Arbor: Institute for Social Research, University of Michigan.

[3] The finding concerning same-floor and different-floor relationships holds even when roommates, whose relationships were generally close, were excluded from consideration. . . . It should be added that all of these 17 men were total strangers to each other on entering the house, and they had nothing at all to do with the choice of their own roommates.

tutions. But this does not mean that the totality of peer-group influence is likely to be greater in small than in large colleges. Other things equal, the more intimate kinds of interpersonal relationships that characterize smaller rather than larger groups have relatively great impact upon group members; and subgroup formation is quite characteristic of very large populations as well as of smaller ones. At any rate, the essential significance of the factor of propinquity is somewhat as follows: For any individual there are many others, potentially, with whom he might form significant relationships. Those with whom he does in fact develop them are limited by opportunities for contact and reciprocal exploration, which in turn are influenced by physical propinquity. And, other things equal, he is most apt to maintain close relationships with those with whom he first develops them (as determined in part by propinquity). Thus the proper generalization concerning college size is not that peer-group influence is more effective, but that it is of more diverse nature in larger than in smaller colleges.

Insofar as we are interested in the study of formal peer groups (which are easier to identify than informal ones) it seems clear, from the available evidence, that they are likely to be found wherever local arrangements —of living, dining, studying, engaging in student activities—result in frequent associations among a given group of students. Not all individuals whose associations with each other are frequent will necessarily be subject— and certainly not in equal degrees—to the effects of the norms that inevitably develop under such conditions, but a large proportion of those who are influenced by such norms can probably be thus discovered.

Dr. Newcomb's results place great importance on the first contacts a student makes when he comes into the college environment.

A law of primacy seems to operate here. One somehow wants to think of ways in which the student's early contacts can be made highly diversified. Maybe we want to prevent love at first sight—or to get many more potential loves on the student's program. Maybe we should think in terms of a protracted John Paul Jones dance. Or maybe we remember the way the British, in World War II, allowed their air crews to choose themselves after extensive interpersonal contact.

THEODORE M. NEWCOMB

Similarity of attitudes and interests. Birds of a feather do flock together, and the kind of feathering that seems to be most essential for the human species is clearly marked by common interests. This truism both rests upon and illustrates some crucial principles concerning human interaction. People are most likely to interact— and thus, in terms of probabilities, to develop close relationships—when shared interest in some aspect of their common environment brings them together. An earlier principle that interaction tends to *create* consensual attitudes should not obscure the equally important one that interaction tends to *begin* on the basis of existing interests that are shared. The two principles, together, imply that interaction may lead to new (and often widening) kinds of shared interests. Also, of course, it may merely reinforce existing ones without leading to new ones.

Contiguity and common interests (or at least those assumed as common) together would seem to account for the beginning of most peer-group relationships. An initial basis may of course be provided by the common features of the shared environment, but the selective association that usually occurs within large groups, all of whose members have an environment in common, is likely to be based upon shared interests that are not inherent in the immediate situation—like preferred sports, hobbies, or tastes in music or sex partners. In my own study of the process of acquaintance on the part of small populations of college men, common interests in sports or college majors often served as a basis for early clique formation, but these did not necessarily persist; changes tended to occur with further opportunity to explore each others' interests. Closeness of interpersonal relationships after four months of acquaintance was in many cases determined more by sharing of general values (religious, perhaps, or aesthetic) than by more specific interests held in common.

Common interests include common problems, of course, insofar as the latter are not too private to be communicable. The problems of the late adolescent in our society may not be harder to bear than those of other ages, but they are commonly such as to invite college students to share them with each other. The struggle for independence is apt to be one of them, and such a problem is more shareable with peers than with parents or teachers. In college, moreover, most students for the first time find themselves cut off from intimacies with adults: they probably see little of their parents, and their teachers neither invite intimacies nor welcome them into faculty society. Such a combination of circumstances is hardly calculated to aid the student in his search for identity—precisely at the time when he is least certain about it. Small wonder, then, that students tend to be thrown upon each other: their common problems together with their relative isolation from others than each other make them ripe for peer-group formation.

To pursue the question of how common interests contribute to the formation of student peer groups, it is well to remember that the interests of groups, like those of individuals, may change. There is a well known principle in psychology according to which motives initially instrumental to the gratification of some other, overriding motive may take on a life of their own, independently of the goal to which it was at first subsidiary.[4] Means often become ends. An analogous principle may be applied to groups. A group already characterized by consensuality of interests and attitudes, and by interpersonal attitudes that are favorable, may persist as a group on the basis of the latter set of attitudes even though the former set has become dissipated. A group that has acquired considerable interpersonal solidarity may prove to be autonomous, in this sense, but it does not follow that a subsequent basis of consensuality can be dispensed with entirely. If the originally common interests have disappeared, they tend to be replaced by others, or if not, interpersonal solidarity is likely to decline, leaving nothing to hold the group together. The social-psychological fact seems to be that group continuity is fostered by high levels of consensuality of both of two

[4] Among various formulations of this principle, that of Professor G. W. Allport (1937) has perhaps been most influential; he uses the term "functional autonomy."

THEODORE M. NEWCOMB

kinds: favorable attitudes toward each other, and similar attitudes toward things of common importance—though most groups can tolerate less than a perfectly solid front.

In any case, the educator who despairs at the irrelevancies of student peer-group influences may take heart over the fact that yesterday's poisonous irrelevancy may, in the same group, become today's relevant meat. He may even anticipate that, as students reassort themselves, old groups giving way to new, some of the emerging groups will form around his favorite relevancies. He may, in fact, regard such possibilities as special challenges to his educational skills.

Some Conditions of Peer-Group Influences

Students' attitudes—rather than their general skills, or specific capacities, or basic personality characteristics— are most likely to be directly influenced by peer-group membership.

Attitudes, as social psychologists commonly use the term, refer to the ways in which an individual has learned to assess things with which he is more or less familiar. "Things" include any entity—cabbages or kings or concepts—that he recognizes and distinguishes from other entities. Assessment refers both to the qualities that he attributes to the thing in question and to his evaluation of it, in view of these qualities—evaluates, that is, in ways liking, fearing, approving, or their opposites. We generally think of attitudes as varying in intensity, or strength, in sign (favorable vs. unfavorable), and in generality (i.e., the inclusiveness of the entity to which they refer; one may have attitudes toward a specific man, toward men in general, or toward human beings in general). We often refer to highly generalized attitudes, especially toward non-concrete entities, as values.

Insofar as groups have power over their members, two processes tend to occur together, as group members continue to interact. Members become more favorably disposed to each other, and they come to adopt as their own certain group-shared attitudes, or norms, and to feel that those norms are right and proper. Both of these consequences (placing a measure of trust in others, and accepting their assessment of things) involve, in important ways, the yielding of power over oneself to others. But it is the second—which I have described as the sharing in group norms—that is of primary interest as an outcome of educational experience.

The import of these considerations seems to be as follows: Insofar as we are interested in what college experience does to students' attitudes we must, because of the nature of attitude formation and change, be interested in the groups to which students (wittingly or not) yield power over their own attitudes. Most attitudes—and particularly those in which educators are interested —are, as social psychologists like to say, anchored in group membership. This statement, let me hasten to add, in no way represents an advocacy of conformity, as opposed to personal independence and critical-mindedness. The latter represents a kind of value (highly prized by most social psychologists, incidentally) which, like most others, is nourished by group support, however narrowly selective. The assertion that, as a matter of empirical observation, values and other kinds of attitudes are nourished and even created via group membership carries no implication that any given instance of the general phenomenon is to be applauded or decried.

Insofar as the proposition is correct, however, it is heavy with implications for educators: How can we direct such kinds of influences in accordance with—rather than irrelevantly or in opposition to—our educational objectives? This question is really a double-headed one. It invites both scientific and "applied" replies—i.e., both statements of conditions under which the presumed effects are most likely to occur and prescriptions for creating those conditions. I shall touch only lightly on the latter.

At least four conditions that facilitate student peer groups' influence upon their members' attitudes appear to be well enough established to deserve mention. No one of them is an essential condition; perhaps any single one of them, under exactly the right circumstances,

THEODORE M. NEWCOMB

might prove effective in the absence of all of the others. Most commonly, however, several or all of these conditions exist together when marked effects have been noted.

Size of groups. Perhaps the most obvious of these conditions has to do with group size. Membership in very large populations is not likely, of itself, to bring about the strong interpersonal attitudes that are so important an ingredient in peer-group effects upon attitudes. Small groups, in which such interpersonal relationships can be established, often mediate the attitudes for which a larger population (like "the college") stands, but membership in the latter without the former's mediation would probably not be very effective. From the point of view of formal arrangements which result in group formation, however, relatively large groups have the advantage of making it possible for individuals to be selective in their more intimate associations. From this point of view, the formal group should not be so large that most of its members cannot recognize one another, nor yet so small as to discourage the formation within it of spontaneously formed, congenial subgroups. The combination of strong interpersonal attitudes engendered by the latter, and the strength of support provided by the more inclusive group of which the subgroup is a representative, is often an effective one.[5]

Homogeneity. A second condition involves relative homogeneity of group members. Homogeneity of age, sex, social class, or religious affiliation contributes to effective peer-group influence primarily because of the homogeneity of attitudes that tends to go along with such similarities. The more readily observable forms of similarity without their attitudinal counterparts will hardly suffice for the formation of effective groups. The fact that existing homogeneity of attitudes is so important to group solidarity has, of course, implications of conservatism: if group solidarity depends upon the simi-

[5] Witness, for example, the colleges within Cambridge and Oxford Universities, the Houses at Harvard and Yale, and several small colleges in which formal arrangements have resulted in groups of a few hundred that have proven capable of arousing effective group loyalties.

larity of members' attitudes, its continuing solidarity is likely to be threatened by lessened similarity in those attitudes. But the same fact also provides the possibility of exactly the reverse. As the late Professor Kurt Lewin used to say, apropos of the effectiveness of "group decision" under certain conditions, "it is sometimes easier to change the attitudes of an entire group than of a single individual"—simply because group support may be mobilized for change as well as against it. At any rate, if a group is not relatively homogeneous with regard to some existing attitudes of importance to its members, it will not have much power to change its members' attitudes.

Isolation. A third condition, relative isolation—communicative rather than physical—from groups having divergent group norms, is closely related to the second. Either the fact or the illusion of a membership homogenous in attitudes may serve to strengthen the conviction that those attitudes are "right." Many institutions of higher education, and many kinds of formal student groups within still more of them maintain policies of admission, which, together with their selective drawing power, result both in attitudinal homogeneity and communicative isolation. The effects of the combination are indubitably conservative, and also indubitably effective.

There is a particularly wry aspect of this condition of isolation from other groups in rendering peer groups effective. We faculty members who so often bemoan what we take to be the undesirable directions in which peer-group effects are expressed do a good deal to contribute to students' isolation from ourselves. And then we wonder why student norms are not more thoroughly permeated with our own.

Importance to individuals of attitudes that are group-supported. A final facilitating condition for peer-group effectiveness is also an obvious one: the importance to individual members of the group-supported attitudes. Other things equal, the greater the importance to them of the attitudes for which the group stands the greater the solidarity of the group, regardless of whether the sense of importance preceded or has been engendered by group membership. Again, the implications appear

THEODORE M. NEWCOMB

to be conservative, but again they are not necessarily so. It does not necessarily follow, from the fact that group members feel that something is very important, that existing attitudes (even consensual ones) toward it are immutable. It may follow, from the same fact, that its very importance requires accurate assessment of it, and group power may be mobilized toward recognizing new facts or widened perspectives from which changed attitudes follow. If so, the same group influence which previously resisted change now comes to support it.

In summary, groups become more effective influencers of their members under some sets of conditions than under others. The effective combinations of conditions are not infrequently present in contemporary American colleges, whether or not by design of their educational architects. Very often, too, they are not met—and perhaps fortunately so. The educators' objective is not necessarily that of maximizing peer-group influence, but rather that of understanding how, when, and why it occurs in order that its effects may be consonant with his purposes.

Peer-Group Influence and Educational Objectives

If, as seems to be the case, peer-groups are potent sources of change, then our task, as educators, may be stated as follows: How can we take advantage of students' potentialities for change, and of peer-groups' power to induce change, in such ways that change will most probably occur in the directions of our educational objectives?

One of the considerations that we need to bear in mind in trying to answer this question is the fact of the diverse motivations that students have in subjecting themselves to peer-group influence. Some students, for example, have strong tendencies toward conformity, while others seem to be compulsively deviant: both can find support from like-minded groups. Some need to be dependent upon authority, whereas independence is essential to others; while the latter may seem to be immune to peer-group influence, the fact seems to be that they need it as much as the others, but tend to find it in smaller and more selective circles. For some, membership in high-prestige groups is the crucial thing; positions of "leadership" or dominance, or perhaps just prominence, are required by still others. Some students become group members because of the interests or attitudes for which the latter stand, while others appear quite willing to adopt the norms of any group that becomes important to them for other reasons. Many of these and other motives are combined in the same person, as he finds different kinds of satisfactions in multiple and doubtless partially overlapping groups. The effects of peer-group membership will vary with such motives, and with the degree to which they find satisfaction through affiliation. But effects there will be, in any case, and whatever the motivations, or combinations thereof, there are comparatively few students in American colleges who are immune to peer-group influence.

For the most part such motives are perfectly normal ones. Students need the experience of mutual exploration; of learning to take different kinds of roles in teams, clubs, house groups; of finding themselves through social experiences without benefit of adults. These kinds of learning are legitimate objects of colleges, along with those of more intellectual and academic nature. For present purposes, however, there is a crucial distinction; the former objectives are reasonably well furthered, in most American colleges, by peer-group experiences; there are good reasons to doubt that this is true of academic-intellectual objectives.

Grounds for doubt on this score are not hard to find. As student bodies have become larger and less homogeneous in most American colleges, a kind of academic anonymity has arisen. Most students develop friendships with others whom they know as persons but not as students (in the literal sense). If peer groups of importance to their members include individuals who are sharing the excitement of academic-intellectual discovery, it is almost a matter of chance. Less and less probably, during recent decades, have individual students who know each other well, and who are important to each other outside

THEODORE M. NEWCOMB

the classroom, experienced shared excitement in the same classroom. With exceptions which, though not rare, are far too infrequent, the domain of peer-group influence overlaps but little with the intellectual domain.

College faculty members, by and large, are nowadays no less capable of offering intellectual excitement than they used to be. But for the most part they now operate in social systems where whatever excitement they offer tends not to be caught up, reinforced, and multiplied by virtue of being shared outside the classroom. Time was when colleges were typically small, their student bodies relatively homogeneous, and their general atmosphere community-like. Most of the changes of the past few decades have tended to deprive large numbers of colleges of these characteristics. The result has been that peer-group influences are as potent as ever, but increasingly divorced from intellectual concerns. These developments have not been premeditated, of course; they have been "natural" adaptations to new conditions, and perhaps they have occurred so gradually that the divorcement has been almost unnoticeable. But there is no need to assume that new conditions cannot be adapted to in ways that retain the desirable aspects of the *ancien regime*, as well as in ways that destroy them.

It is no accident that the more conspicuous exceptions to this general trend toward divorcement from intellectual concerns are colleges that remain small, relatively homogeneous, and community-like. My point is not that the divorcement can be halted only in small colleges, but rather that small colleges can, almost without taking thought, provide the essential conditions for mobilizing peer-group influence around intellectual concerns, whereas if larger colleges are to provide them, a good deal of thought will have to be taken. Students will in any case create their own peer groups, but the influence of the latter will not (even in small colleges) have much intellectual impact unless the conditions for sharing intellectual excitement are met.

One of the common student complaints, in larger colleges at least, is that "we never get a chance to meet the faculty." Most faculty members have some sense of guilt about this, and some of them go so far as to arrange an occasional tea for students. The assumption seems to be, on both sides, that there is some magic about "student-faculty contact." If magic there be, it is surely not intellectual magic. Let me cite one bit of evidence. An experiment was recently carried out at Antioch College, under the supervision of Professor E. K. Wilson (1961; Chapter 3). In eight different courses, including Humanities, Social Science, and Natural Science, different groups of students were subjected to modes of instruction involving two or three different frequencies of student-teacher contact. Some groups had "continuous surveillance of the teacher," others only "sporadic contact," and in still others students were "lone wolves studying—with the guidance of the syllabus—quite independently." Outcomes of these different procedures were evaluated in terms of various kinds of examinations, attitudinal responses, amount of "outside" reading, and in other ways. By none of these criteria were there any important differences, in any of the courses among the different procedures. Other experiments—though none so comprehensive—in other colleges have yielded similar results. There is no research evidence, as of now, to indicate that intellectual outcomes vary—other things equal—with frequency of student-teacher contact.

The probable reasons for such "negative" findings seem to be pretty clear. Outcomes of studying are determined by intellectual capacity, motivation, work habits, *and* by prevailing norms about how seriously studies are to be taken. At Antioch (as would have been the case in other colleges, in varying degrees), students assigned to the various experimental groups were more or less alike in subscribing to the local norms and presumably, also, the groups did not differ much in capacity and motivation. Teachers' influence, if it is to be effective, must be caught up in the norms of student groups, and the degree to which this occurs bears no necessary relationship to frequency of their direct contact with students. It can operate at a distance, mediated by some students so as to affect others. Indeed, if it cannot be made to operate in such manner the degree to which

THEODORE M. NEWCOMB

any but the smaller colleges can achieve their intellectual objectives seems to be very limited indeed.

Teachers' influence *can* operate at a distance—provided that colleges are willing to supply the necessary conditions. The major ones all stem from the elementary principle that individuals who spend a good deal of time together—particularly if they do so without a sense of constraint—jointly create norms, concerning their common interests, by which each of them is influenced. Like all general principles of social interaction, this is true in a statistical rather than in an absolute sense; there are bound to be individual exceptions. The applications of this principle that seem most likely to be effective are as follows:

First, there are facilitating effects of having a formal membership group that is both moderate in size and that is characterized by relative homogeneity of interests that are relevant to the desired outcomes. The assumption here is not only that small and influential peer groups are most likely to develop within larger, formal groups, but also that certain norms of the former can also be supported by those of the latter. The formal group should be large enough to provide a range of selectivity based upon individual preferences for companionship, but not so large that it will be improbable that most individuals will at least recognize each other. The implication here is that larger colleges should be composed of smaller units—300-400 being a reasonable idea.

Second, it is important to take advantage of the fact that students' living arrangements provide the major single source of daily contact. Peer-group influence is almost certain to be enhanced—for better or for worse—if there is a considerable overlap between membership in formal college units and in living units. As with the application of any principle, there is a danger here of conflicting with another principle—in this case that of providing opportunity for the development of new interests. Hence complete or compulsory overlap between these two kinds of membership units is probably inadvisable. In large and heterogeneous colleges or universities, however—where the problem of mobilizing group influence toward intellectual objectives is probably most serious—opportunities for the development of new interests are available in plenty.

Third, there should be overlap—both with formal college-unit and with living unit. In the typical large university it is hardly more than a chance occurrence if a set of students whose personal relationships are close find themselves simultaneously excited by the same lecture, the same book, or the same seminar, with resulting reverberations in their peer-group life, so that they reinforce and sustain one anothers' excitement. Such outcomes are predictably more likely if arrangements concerning college (or sub-college) membership, living-group membership, and classroom experience are so dove-tailed that groups of individuals who are important to one another come to share many interests, including intellectual ones.

Insofar as colleges are able to make curricular, residential, and other administrative arrangements that have such consequences, frequency of student-faculty contacts ceases to be a matter of concern. It is their *quality* that matters. Whether they be in the classroom or in the coffee-bar (preferably both), we need only ask whether contacts result in students' discovery that ideas are worth further exploration with each other. If so, teachers' influence is likely to be strengthened and multiplied; if not, the consequence is too often that it is multiplied only by zero.

Dr. Newcomb considers ways in which faculty members can have more effective social contact with students. There are two notions that arise on this point. First, one thinks about ways in which there can be *equal-status contact* between faculty and student. Somehow, faculty and students never do relate meaningfully as long as they are in role. Are there ways, better than softball games or dart throwing contests, in which faculty and students can relate on an equal status?

Secondly, faculty-student relationships are always difficult and strained as long as the faculty member is also a judge—as long as he grades the papers. The student is rarely able to divest the faculty member of those grim, black judicial robes. So, let's abolish examinations. Or less drastically, let's import outside examiners, so that teacher and

THEODORE M. NEWCOMB

student can become partners in the enterprise of meeting high standards of excellence.

In pointing to kinds of educational arrangements that resemble those typically provided by many small colleges, especially some decades ago, I am neither pleading for a single, standard model nor calling upon time to turn backward. My intended implications are just the reverse. Many small, community-like colleges, both of the past and of the present, have provided the basic conditions under which intellectual concerns have been caught up into the community life, but yesteryear's homogeneous communities can no longer provide today's pattern. Probably an outright majority of all students in American colleges and universities today are enrolled in institutions of more than 4,000 students. The educational advantages of the small, homogeneous community must nowadays be created and in diverse ways, in large heterogeneous institutions, and the required inventiveness is hardly beyond our capacities. I suspect that more effort has been expended in applying social-science findings to factory management and to the organization of mental hospitals than to the achievement of intellectual objectives in our colleges.

Student peer groups are here to stay, and so are colleges. I do not think that the one is about to become a cancerous growth within the body of the other; I prefer a different figure. I do think that, increasingly (in this country, at any rate) the social-psychological motors of student life are racing, disconnected from the wheels of intellectual development, and that the means of exploiting the power delivered by those motors are at our command.

The three views expressed by Drs. Sanford, Pace, and Newcomb are by no means dissonant, but they are also not yet consonant. Dr. Sanford emphasized the individual personality, seen from the inside out; Dr. Pace emphasized dimensions of the college environment; and Dr. Newcomb focuses on one significant way in which the environment has its way with the individual. Out of these three approaches, with, perhaps, some added elements, one can conceive of there being formulated

a complete and coherent theoretical picture of the individual in college. Such a development could add mightily to the significance of our research and to the coherence of our thinking about problems in the whole area. Also such a theory could help in the development of a systematic understanding of the young normal adult—an understanding that now really does not exist in spite of the frequency with which college sophomores serve as subjects in research.

References

Allport, G. A., 1937. *Personality: A Psychological Interpretation.* New York: Holt.

Asch, S. E., 1952. *Social Psychology.* New York: Prentice-Hall (Eds.).

Bossard, J. H. S., 1932. Residential Propinquity as a Factor in Marriage Selection. *American Journal of Sociology,* 38, 219–224.

Cartwright, D., & Zander, A., 1960. *Group Dynamics: Research and Theory.* Evanston, Ill.: Row, Peterson. (revised edition).

Coleman, J. S., & Rossi, P. "How High School Seniors Choose their Colleges." Study in progress, National Opinion Research Center, University of Chicago, 1960.

Commager, H. S., 1960. "Is Ivy Necessary?" *Saturday Review of Literature,* pp. 69 ff., Sept. 17.

Cooper, R. N., Green, R. H., and Humez, E. (Eds.), 1960. *Seminar on the Economics of Higher Education, Harvard University, 1958–59.* Cambridge: Harvard University Press.

Festinger, L., Back, K., Schachter, S., Kelley, H. H., & Thibaut, J., 1950. *Theory and Experiment in Social Communication.* Ann Arbor: Institute for Social Research, University of Michigan.

Gardner, E. F., & Thompson, G. G., 1956. *Social Relations and Morale in Small Groups.* New York: Appleton-Century-Crofts.

Hare, A. P., Borgatta, E. F., & Bales, R. F. (Eds.), 1955. *Small Groups: Studies in Social Interaction.* New York: Knopf.

Homans, G. C., 1950. *The Human Group.* New York: Harcourt, Brace.

Jacob, P. E., 1957. *Changing Values in College.* New York: Harcourt, Brace.

Merton, R. K., Reader, G., and Kendall, Patricia (Eds.), 1957. *The Student Physician: Introductory Studies in the*

THEODORE M. NEWCOMB

Sociology of Medical Education. Cambridge, Mass.: Harvard University Press.

Murphy, G., 1947. *Personality: A Biosocial Approach to Origins and Structure.* New York: Harper.

Newcomb, T. M., 1943. *Personality and Social Change.* New York: Dryden.

Newcomb, T. M., 1950. *Social Psychology.* New York: Dryden.

Newcomb, T. M., 1961. *The Acquaintance Process.* New York: Holt, Rinehart, & Winston.

Newcomb, T. M., and Wilson, E. K. (Eds.), 1961. *The Study of College Peer Groups: Problems and Prospects for Research.* New York: Social Science Research Council.

Sanford, R. N. (Ed.), 1956. Personality Development During the College Years. *Journal of Social Issues,* XII, No. 4.

Sanford, R. N., 1958. "The Professor Looks at the Student," *The Two Ends of the Log—Learning and Teaching in Today's College,* Cooper, Russell M., editor. Minneapolis: University of Minnesota Press.

Schachter, S., 1959. *The Psychology of Affiliation.* Stanford: Stanford University Press.

Sherif, M. & Carolyn W., 1956. *An Outline of Social Psychology.* New York: Harper.

Tagiuri, R., & Petrullo, L. (Eds.), 1958. *Person Perception and Interpersonal Behavior.* Stanford: University Press.

Thibaut, J. S., & Kelley, H. H., 1959. *The Social Psychology of Groups.* New York: Wiley.

Troller, A. E., (Ed.), 1958. *Long Range Planning for Education.* Washington: American Council on Education.

Chapter 6

WHO REALLY HELPS OUR STUDENTS?

Charles Frankel has observed that a student of European and American higher education will note that in comparison to European students American students "seem to be more closely supervised, more elaborately protected, more vigorously exercised and more solemnly prayed over."[1] Whether or not this tendency to increasing concern for the welfare of each student is serving a useful purpose in American education is a question that deserves our careful study.

College students have always had their troubles. More than a century ago Dr. Edward Jarvis of Boston deplored the effects of intense competition, rapid social mobility and expectations greater than could be realized. If students a century ago were confused about competition, social mobility, and rapid social change, those of today certainly must be more disturbed and hence even more entitled to intelligent help from their older colleagues. Many different kinds of special skills must be provided, many of them requiring long periods of preparation. Students thus have a wide variety of occupations or professions from which to choose, but any mistake that is made is likely to be very costly because of the penalties of starting anew in a fresh subject. The process of making a choice usually rules out many alternative lines of endeavour.

Who Are the Helpers?

If we are to answer fully the question as to who really helps our students, it would involve writing a history of

[1] Franckel, C., Ed., *Issues in University Education*. New York: Harper & Brothers, 1959, p. 123.

higher education. I shall concentrate largely on how the college or university itself can be used as an educational instrument, taking for granted the good results of excellent teaching in classrooms. It is my thesis that if the educational planning is good and if careful and continuous thought is given to relations between faculty members and students, fewer students will become emotionally disturbed and fewer will fail than if planning is devoted only to how and what material should be presented to students. If this is a reasonable assumption, many of the functions now relegated to psychotherapists, when they are available, could be performed by teachers and other counselors—which, of course, means more broadly based concepts of education than those most commonly accepted at present.

The most important of the influences which really help or hinder students are those which are mediated by the personal contact between students and other students and between students and members of the faculty and administration. Obviously, written material of college bulletins conveys some information and perhaps a little of the emotional climate of the institution, but these messages are taken for granted as attempts of the college to appear in the best possible light. Not until students sense something of the character, ability, and basic friendliness of their teachers do they begin noticeably to respond, either in approval of an atmosphere conducive to learning or disillusionment at being caught in a trap. The task of the faculty, and a neat trick it is, is to mold an environment which is not unbalanced in the direction of intellectual prowess yet one in which students sense that learning brings them more esteem and prestige than social and athletic activities. I think Mr. Hutchins overstated his case a bit when he indicated in 1936 that the universities should have nothing to do with character and body building, social graces and the tricks of the trades.[2] This I think of as the "brains on stilts" theory of education which seems to be a little thin. But anyway, we want an environment in which the standards are kept

[2] Hutchins, R. M., *The Higher Learning in America.* Chicago: University of Chicago Press, 1936, p. 77.

DANA L. FARNSWORTH

high with permissiveness (that's a fighting word—just throw it into one of your faculty meetings and see how many people get angry. The less they know about what the word means the more angry they will get, of course) as to how these standards shall be met, but with firm determination that they shall be achieved. The environment should be one in which the individual is respected, his personal situation considered, and the whole educational process should give satisfaction and a sense of meaning and purpose.

Since college administrators and teachers have begun to show an interest in the total effectiveness of students, not simply their capacity to acquire facts and restate them upon demand, a whole host of new questions has arisen, questions for which we have inadequate answers. You have heard many of them. What conditions in a student's earlier life predispose to strong personality and well integrated character development? Can we teach our present students how to rear their own children better than they were brought up? How can normal growth and development be better understood? What kinds of stress are helpful and which are harmful to optimum learning?

Obviously emotional conflict is good for those people whose character and personality structure is such that they can resolve conflicts as they go along. Equally clear, conflict appears harmful to those who are exceedingly vulnerable and who then suffer defeat after defeat and lose their confidence. What factors affect the students' vulnerability to stress? How is motivation for learning best encouraged? Is a marked contrast between high school and college conditions desirable or undesirable for the student? Among the students who become emotionally ill and withdraw from college, which ones are most likely to return to complete their work satisfactorily?

At Harvard we like to have students who leave for whatever reason stay out long enough to accomplish something worthwhile in the interval. In a small study made by former Dean Delmar Leighton a few years ago he found that of those who stay out less than a year and come back, about 35 per cent go on and get their degree. For those who stay out a year or longer, about 80 per cent go on to get their degree. Thus we are at the moment rather definitely of the opinion that when a person drops out of school or is given a leave of absence, he ought to stay out long enough to do something that gives him a sense of accomplishment before coming back. Otherwise, there is too much of a chance that he will repeat his original performance.

Is the prevailing attitude toward unusual behavior in a given institution likely to affect the prevalence of illness or of inappropriate behavior? One of the features of Harvard is the exceedingly great tolerance for any kind of behavior. A student must indeed be very unusual to be noticed in Harvard Square, and this is, we think, very good from the standpoint of most people. But for some students this is frustrating, because no matter what they do, they get little reaction. Some of them have even voiced the desire for a little less tolerance. Of course, part of our job consists in trying to help students develop intolerance of the right things. Many of our students are tolerant not only of things toward which they should show tolerance, but of situations which they should not tolerate. The development of *appropriate* intolerance and *appropriate* discrimination is, of course, the essence of good education.

These and other similar questions and problems are gradually developing into fascinating subjects for research in our colleges and universities. Opposition to such research is strong in many institutions. The opponents are not opposed to research per se, but they distrust tests and fear the effects of improper probing into essentially private affairs; many are not convinced of the validity of much social science research. This type of resistance is not new.

Fortunately, many research projects concerning students are now in progress in many of our colleges and universities. A recent conference sponsored by the Committtee on Personality Development in Youth of the Social Science Research Council at Andover, Massa-

DANA L. FARNSWORTH

chusetts brought together about 50 workers in this field.[3] A comprehensive program of research on medical students has begun to bring forth valuable publications.[4, 5]

The single most important influence in building a helpful environment to stimulate student responsibility and accomplishment is the attitude of the president. The idea that the institution is the lengthened shadow of a man is is certainly a valid one in terms of promoting those forces in a college or university which encourage mental health. From our point of view a good president is one who thinks of his students' welfare first, treats them with great fairness, and yet thinks of them individually and not as if they were all alike. One of the great qualities of the late president Karl T. Compton of MIT was that he treated students in terms of what they could become rather than what they were at the moment.

From President James R. Killian I learned another cardinal principle about relations between students and their colleges. One year I was serving as Acting Dean of Students at MIT and, as usual, problems arose calling for consultation with him. When I became concerned about the public relations effect of possible solutions to quandaries presented by students, he would say in effect, "Don't worry about MIT's reputation. It can take care of itself. What we should be concerned about is what is best for this particular student." Of course, a little reflection shows that in the long run such care is best for the institution's public relations.

I am in favor of the president who entrusts as much authority to students as they are able and willing to use in a responsible manner. It should be clearly understood

[3] Bidwell, C. E., *The American College and Student Personality: A Survey of Research Progress and Problems*. Report of a Conference on Research on College Influences on Personality. Andover, Massachusetts: Social Science Research Council, 1959.

[4] Gee, H. M., and Glaser, R. J., *The Ecology of the Medical Student*. Evanston, Illinois: Association of American Medical Colleges, 1958.

[5] Sanford, Nevitt, Ed., *Personality Development During the College Years*, Journal of Social Issues, Vol. XII, Nov. 1956.

that such authority is delegated and that it will ultimately be withdrawn if abused. If the president can have enough contact with student leaders to give them some idea of how decisions are made in a democratic organization, so much the better. I know of one president who meets at frequent intervals with about 15 representative students of his institution with whom he discusses all sorts of issues that are of importance to the institution's welfare. These sessions are "off the record;" no decisions are made, nor is reference made to the discussions at later official meetings. They serve to keep both administration and at least some responsible students aware of the crucial issues that confront them both.

A president may inhibit the development of students by inconsistency in making decisions, responding unwisely to pressures from parents and alumni, interfering with decisions made by his appointed representatives, being afraid of students, having too little contact with them and by exhibiting a lamentable lack of knowledge of student psychology.

A president who keeps himself informed about what is going on around his campus, watches the activities of the various departments with vested interests to protect and forward, keeps himself aloof from the lesser struggles, does not feel that he must be responsible for everything that goes on, and who makes decisions after the issues have been drawn clearly is in a position to influence students most favorably. The development of good morale, firm discipline, and high standards of intellectual accomplishment and behavior, all essential to good education, is infinitely easier with such a president than with one who is impulsive and arbitrary.

Director of Admissions

The director of admissions and his staff can be very helpful in creating the kind of environment in which education can flourish. Matching the abilities and needs of prospective students to the most appropriate colleges

DANA L. FARNSWORTH

should take precedence over more overtly partisan attitudes, but this is difficult if the college desires more students than it attracts. To entice a student to come to a college poorly suited to his abilities and purposes is as regrettable as some professors' trying to persuade students to come into their own fields regardless of their interests. Both of these practices are bad education. Doing a good job in one's own field of interest and showing enthusiasm for it is the ethical and desirable way of attracting others to it.

As I view his work, the director of admissions should be a continuous student of personality, growth, and development in order that he may avoid over-reliance on arbitrary guideposts and change his methods of procedure as his knowledge increases. A punitive or "keep those fellows out" attitude is not becoming to an admissions officer, nor should he admit students who seem certain to fail simply because of pressures exerted upon him. He should use tests as aids, not as exclusive yardsticks, and he could help in creating a more favorable climate for adequate consideration of emotional factors in education. He must be alert to indications of emotional health and should watch for these important warning signs in prospective students that all is not well emotionally:

(1) Consistent and persistent rebellion without regard to source or type of authority. Some rebellion in adolescence is practically normal in our culture; but when such a course is pursued blindly, it approaches the pathological. Some people almost make a career of it. In one form of this rebellion, the individual regresses to primitive, even anti-social, habits of sanitation—no baths, clothes unlaundered, unshaven if a boy, greasy, stringy hair if a girl. Another form consists of taking exception to all the customarily accepted rules for living together, along with continual questioning of the values by which an institution or society holds itself together. Some of these characteristics may be desirable, but as Ernest Jones has said, "A mere tendency to doubt and to ignore conventional opinions cannot in itself lead to originality in any significant sense; it may end only in social eccen-

tricity. It relates to true originality only when it is informed, i.e., only when the skepticism is founded on some objective reason and not on personal foible."[6]

(2) A long history of "acting out" feelings. Such persons are emotionally unstable, cannot profit from experience, tend to react on impulse heedless of consequences, and are usually at odds with one segment of society or another. They may be said to be suffering from character disorders, and their treatment is difficult and time-consuming. Their outlook is usually not encouraging.

(3) A clearcut history of mental illness with no treatment, or inadequate treatment, and aversion either to getting further help or facing their problems squarely.

(4) A consistent history of underachievement in comparison to test scores and other indices of intellectual capacity.

(5) Early and excessive use of alcohol. Such cases are fortunately rare, but their outlook for successful accomplishment is doubtful.

(6) Frequent changes of schools without similar moves by the family.

(7) Obvious parental friction resulting in any of the previous symptoms or any variety of other combinations

It should be emphasized that people with obvious signs of emotional conflict may at times do very well in college. If we exclude all who have potential emotional disorders, we would keep out practically all applicants. The ideal of admitting a class with no serious emotional conflicts is as impractical as the goal of admitting a class with no bottom quarter. It simply cannot be done as the armed services have pretty well demonstrated. The more practicable course is that of trying to avoid admitting those who would probably fail, and at the same time trying to help these applicants follow some course which for them will be constructive.

[6] Jones, E., *Life and Work of Sigmund Freud*, Vol. II. New York, Basic Books, 1955, p. 425.

DANA L. FARNSWORTH

Dr. Farnsworth mentioned that if we exclude students with emotional problems, we would exclude most of them. I wonder whether he was really serious.

Farnsworth: Any person who has lived in the Oliver Wendell Holmes sense or in the Schweitzer sense, has been deeply troubled over and over but has learned to resolve his difficulties. It is the very essence of maturity that we learn how to suffer, learn how to attain, how to cope with defeat without losing our morale in the process. And so, it is very difficult to think of a mature person who has not had serious emotional problems. This fact makes it most important that we not label students because if we label a person as schizophrenic, as manic-depressive, as psychotic, or as neurotic, this is decidedly unfair. All of us use mechanisms of defense from time to time which are inappropriate if used too often. The sick person is the one who keeps on regressing back to methods of defense that were appropriate in an earlier period but are not appropriate now; thus, there is both a qualitative and quantitative aspect involved.

Dean of Students

Another person who is in a peculiarly advantageous position to help students is the dean of students. A dean should not be maneuvered into a position in which he seems to be an antagonist of students. Instead, he should be their protagonist, a leader in representing their points of view to the rest of the institution, but at the same time a teacher who helps students develop attitudes that are consistent with what they ostensibly came to college to acquire—an education. He is seriously handicapped if he is constantly engaged in locating and punishing offenders against the social mores of the college.

Yet, the "web of morality" of the institution must be maintained, and it should be a part of student experience to know something, however slight, of how this is done. If the dean encourages and can work with a strong responsible student government, and the serious infractions of discipline are taken care of by a student-faculty committee, there is an opportunity to teach students much of what is necessary to preserve a decent community. As a police officer he has little possibility of influencing students. Students almost invariably respect deans who are, as they say, "honest" with them. I suppose they mean by this, fairness and frankness in communication without patronizing overtones.

As deans and their colleagues in student government (and in the faculty) study the conditions on their campuses that promote or delay maturity, they will inevitably delineate customs and conditions that require modification. As an example, the custom of requiring students to obtain excuses from a physician when they have missed classes, assignments, or examinations, has been found to be an exquisitely effective means of encouraging hypocrisy, exaggeration of the severity of illnesses, and sometimes clear dishonesty. Likewise, the promotion of intercollegiate athletics by making special payments, giving athletic schlarships, lowering scholastic standards for athletes, and encouraging athletes to take easy but worthless courses, encourages the kinds of standards which, if practiced in political life, lead either to exploitation of the public or to the offender's losing his position and reputation.

Parents

While thinking of those who really help students we should not forget parents. Their attitudes will reinforce or negate what the college attempts to do in the development of intellectual power, strong character, and continued desire for further intellectual development after leaving college. Study of children's needs will probably not change much those parents who have already sent their children to college.

Those who are new parents, or who will become parents in the next few years, (25 per cent of our students in college and graduate schools are already married) should know something of the basic psychological needs of children and how they may be provided. Every child needs love and affection, the feeling of being wanted, respect as a separate person, and room to move about and experiment without undue injury to himself. Since a child can imitate only what he sees or hears, he needs

DANA L. FARNSWORTH

proper standards of thought and behavior to emulate. As Erik Erikson so aptly says, "What we need is not a plan whereby relatively irresponsible adults can enforce morality in their children, but rather national insistence on a more *responsible* morality on the part of adults, paired with an *informed* attitude toward the development of moral values in children,"[7] A child needs stimulation alternating with periods of privacy and relaxation if his fantasy life, his romantic self, the poet in him, is to develop freely. A century ago Thoreau said that most people live lives of quiet desperation. Now they live lives of noisy desperation, with something of a mechanical nature always demanding attention.

But how can the schools and colleges teach these principles? Knowledge of these and similar principles is not enough, though I believe it is a desirable precursor of the kind of attitude and behavior so necessary in developing good family life. Whoever works out practical ways of effectively teaching our students the essential fundamentals of marriage and family living will really be helping them.

Teachers

In our discussion we have left out the people who should and do help students most—the teachers. They have done their job well, but they can do it better if those of us whose duty it is to support them can reinforce by a variety of indirect means what they try to do directly.

I have purposely left out of our discussion specialized counselors of various kinds, such as psychiatrists and psychologists. This is partly because of lack of time, but largely because of a special hope that we can gradually enlarge the scope of educational activities so as to include much of their work and make them unnecessary. We will never wholly succeed, but the more we equate teaching with counseling, the better. If only a small amount of time is available from such professionals, at

[7] Erikson, E. H., "Youth and the Life Cycle," *Children*, Vol. 7, No. 2, March-April, 1960, p. 49.

least half of it should be spent working *with* the faculty *about* student problems.

College teachers could probably be distributed along a continuum with respect to their attitudes toward serving as counselors. Dana Farnsworth says, "The more we equate teaching with counseling the better." It is probably dirty pool to take a sentence out of context and adumbrate it alone, but one can make a case that this sentence is an epitome of the burden of the paper and that it does raise quickly—and perhaps emotionally—some key dilemmas. The sentence very clearly implies that the whole person, not merely a disembodied cortex, goes to college. And it raises, directly or otherwise, some issues that can give a teacher considerable pause.

While I am personally inclined to be a mental health man, concerning myself with the personality development of my student, I have a sympathy for the pure teacher—the teacher who takes the stance that his job is the teaching of his subject matter. I have a feeling that the learning of a high skill or the mastery of a subject matter will sometimes do more than therapy can for mental health.

One of the best ways to learn about personality growth and development is to try to help students who are encountering psychological difficulties (including the academic) of any sort. A comparison of opinions and points of view by people of widely different backgrounds can be most helpful. The most valuable device for learning together (a faculty in-service training program) is the custom practiced in some institutions of holding a weekly luncheon meeting in some central place, attended by deans, tutors, chaplains, psychiatrists, psychologists, sociologists, directors of counseling services, house masters, or whoever may be responsible for or have an interest in students who are not living up to what is expected of them.

Dr. Farnsworth endorses periodic meetings of tutors, chaplains, deans, psychiatrists, and others concerned with students' personal welfare. This seems like a fine idea. But such meetings will be concerned 99 per cent of the time with students who are in personal and/or academic trouble. Why not similar meetings of similar people to talk about students who are doing well—but who might do better? Equal time for the trouble-free might achieve at least as much for the human enterprise.

DANA L. FARNSWORTH

The dean of the college or of students usually presides. The meetings are confidential. Any information previously obtained from students in confidence is not divulged without permission. The group has no authority, though the individuals have authority in other settings. Problems can be examined freely, the presence of persons with a variety of viewpoints being of enormous aid in this respect. Because of the presence of so many key individuals in the college, much time may be saved in analyzing and solving complex problems.

It helps greatly if the library acquires and conveniently arranges a collection of books on personality and interpersonal relations for the use of those faculty members and students who want to further their understanding of this field.

When we accept the view that the whole student comes to class, we somehow need to work out carefully our "theory" of what a whole student is like and about the proper—and unique— contribution the college can make to the development of more complete wholeness of personality. On the latter point, some faculty people and many students seem to underestimate the reality that the college or university is the only institution in the society devoted primarily to the *intellectual* development of the student. He can find social development, physical development, moral development and spiritual development in other settings. The unique and focal function of institutions of alleged higher learning is an intellectual function. While all forms of development should and can go along together, and while any distinction among the various forms of development is probably artificial, it seems somehow proper that the academic institutions emphasize above all else the use of the head at its best no matter what.

College should be a time both intense and enjoyable, aiding students in becoming ever more capable of attending to their own subsequent intellectual development. At the same time we should help them become aware of their responsibilities in the common tasks of enabling our civilization to survive. Sir Christopher Dawson says, "But our generation has been forced to realize how fragile and unsubstantial are the barriers that separate civilization from the forces of destruction. We have learnt that barbarism is not a picturesque myth or a half-forgotten memory of a long-passed stage of history, but an ugly underlying reality which may erupt with shattering force whenever the moral authority of a civilization loses its control."[8] Furthermore, "It would be a strange fatality if the great revolution by which western man has subdued nature's force for his purposes should end in the loss of his own spiritual freedom. But this might well happen if an increasing technical control of the state over the life and thought of its members should coincide with the qualitative decline in the standards of our culture."[9]

To my mind these statements suggest the most important problem to which we at this conference should be addressing ourselves.

Bibliography

Ackerman, N. W., *The Psychodynamics of Family Life*, New York: Basic Books, 1958.

Alexander, F., *Fundamentals of Psychoanalysis*, New York: W. W. Norton, 1948.

Allport, G. W., *Becoming: Basic Considerations for Psychology*, New Haven: Yale University Press, 1955.

Allport, G. W., *The Nature of Prejudice*, Cambridge: Addison Wesley, 1954.

Anderson, G. C., *Man's Right to Be Human*, New York: Morrow, 1959.

Angell, R. C., *Free Society and Moral Crisis*, Ann Arbor: University of Michigan Press, 1958.

Balser, B. H. (Ed.), *Psychotherapy of the Adolescent*, New York: International Universities Press, 1957.

Barclay, C., *Understanding the City Child*, New York: Watts, 1959.

[8] Dawson, C., *Religion and the Rise of Western Culture*. New York: Sheed and Ward, Inc., 1950, p. 24. Permission to include this quotation has been granted by The Society of Authors as the literary representative of Christopher Dawson.

[9] *Ibid.*, p. 14.

DANA L. FARNSWORTH

Burgess, E. W., and Fishbein, M., (Eds.), *Successful Marriage*, Revised Edition, Garden City, New York: Doubleday, 1955.

Davis, M., *Sex and the Adolescent*, New York: Dial Press, 1958.

Donham, W. B., *Education for Responsible Living*, Cambridge: Harvard University Press, 1944.

Eddy, E. D., Jr., *The College Influence on Student Character*, Washington: American Council on Education, 1959.

English, O. S., and Foster, C., *Fathers Are Parents Too*, New York: Putnam, 1951.

Erikson, E. H., *Childhood and Society*, New York: W. W. Norton, 1950.

Erikson, E. H., Selected Papers by, *Psychological Issues*, Vol. 1, No. 1, Monograph 1, New York: International Universities Press, 1959.

Erikson, E. H., *Young Man Luther*, New York: W. W. Norton, 1958.

Farnsworth, D. L., *Mental Health in College and University*, Cambridge: Harvard University Press, 1957.

Frank, L. K., and Frank, M., *Your Adolescent at Home and in School*, New York: Viking Press, 1956.

Fromm, E., *The Sane Society*, New York: Rinehart, 1955.

Funkenstein, D. H., (Ed.), *The Student and Mental Health: An International View*, New York: World Federation for Mental Health and International Association of Universities, 1959.

Gallagher, J. R. and Harris, H. I., *Emotional Problems of Adolescents*, New York: Oxford University Press, 1958.

Garrison, R., *The Adventure of Learning in College*, New York: Harper, 1959.

Goldesen, R. K., Rosenberg, M., Williams, R. M., Jr., and Suchman, E. G., *What College Students Think*, Princeton: D. Van Nostrand, 1960.

Harrison, G. R., *What Man May Be*, New York: W. Morrow, 1956.

Hein, F. V. and Farnsworth, D. L., *Living*, 3rd edition, Chicago: Scott, Foresman, 1959.

Jacob, P. E., *Changing Values in College*, New York: Harper, 1957.

Jahoda, M., *Current Concepts of Positive Mental Health*, New York: Basic Books, 1958.

Jersild, A. T., *The Psychology of Adolescence*, New York: Macmillan, 1957.

Josselyn, I., *The Happy Child*, New York: Random House, 1955.

Kluckholm, C., Murray, H. A., Schneider, D. M. (Editors) *Personality in Nature, Society and Culture*, 2nd Edition, New York: Knopf, 1953.

Lerrigo, M. O. and Southard, H., *Sex Facts and Attitudes, Parents Privilege, A Story About You, What's Happening to Me? Learning about Love*, The Dutton Series on Sex Education, Chicago: American Medical Association, 1955.

Levy, J. and Munroe, R., *The Happy Family*, New York: Knopf, 1938.

Lippman, H. S., *Treatment of the Child in Emotional Conflict*, New York: McGraw-Hill, 1956.

Livingstone, Sir Richard W., *Education and the Spirit of the Age*, Oxford, England: Clarendon Press, 1952.

Livingstone, Sir Richard W., *On Education*, Cambridge, England: University Press, 1954.

Lynd, H. M., *On Shame and the Search for Identity*, New York: Harcourt Brace, 1958.

McCarthy, R. G., (Editor) *Drinking and Intoxication*, Chicago: Free Press, 1959.

Mudd, E. and Krich, A., *Man and Wife*, New York: W. W. Norton, 1957.

Murphy, A., *Human Potentialities*, New York: Basic Books, 1958.

Murphy, L. B., and Raushenbush, E., *Achievement in the College Years*, New York: Harper, 1960.

Pearson, G. H. J., *Adolescence and the Conflict of Generations*, New York: W. W. Norton, 1958.

Riesman, D., Jacob, P. and Sanford, N., *Spotlight on the College Student*, Washington: American Council on Education, 1959.

Saul, L. J., *Emotional Maturity*, (second edition) Philadelphia: Lippincott, 1960.

Saul, L. J., *The Hostile Mind*, New York: Random House, 1956.

Seidman, J. M., Editor, *The Adolescent—A Book of Readings*, New York: Holt, Rinehart and Winston, 1960.

Stein, M., Vidich, A. J., and White, D. W., *Identity and Anxiety*, Chicago: Free Press, 1960.

Taylor, H., *On Education and Freedom*, New York: Abelard-Schuman, 1954.

Walter, E. A. (Editor) *Religion and the State University*, Ann Arbor: University of Michigan Press, 1958.

Weatherford, W. D., Jr., *Goals of Higher Education*, Cambridge: Harvard University Press, 1960.

Wedge, B. W., *Psychosocial Problems of College Men*, New Haven: Yale University Press, 1958.

White, R. W., *Lives in Progress*, New York: Dryden Press, 1952.

Whitehead, A. N., *The Aims of Education and Other Essays*, New York: Mentor, 1955.

Witmer, H. L. and Kotinsky, R. (Editors), *Personality in the Making*, New York: Harper, 1952.

Wylie, L., *Village in the Vaucluse*, Cambridge: Harvard University Press, 1957.

Chapter 7

CONFERENCE SUMMARY

A two-pronged question has been posed. Is not the ability and willingness to make value judgments the mark of an educated man, and does not the college have a responsibility to assist in enforcing the political, social, ethical, and moral values by which a society perpetuates itself? Let me address myself briefly to the first point. Certainly, education has to do with the ability and willingness to make value judgments. One of the limitations of recent scholarship and teaching in some instances in social sciences has been the avoidance of the question of values. One function of education is to confront the student with the problem of values in order that he may recognize that in making a decision, in choosing alternatives, he is in fact making a choice of values. Examination will lead to values that are increasingly significant and powerful in conduct.

In answering the question of whether or not the college or university has a responsibility to assist in enforcing the political, social, ethical, and moral values by which a society perpetuates itself, my own answer is, "No." It is not the business of education to enforce a set of values but, instead, to encourage the student to establish his own pattern of values and to revise this pattern as he continually examines his assumptions, his attitudes, and his own understandings. It is the continuous examination of our presuppositions and of our values that our society and education should enforce.

One of the threads running throughout this conference is that the outcomes of college education need to be redefined. There has been recurrent emphasis on the importance of the academic culture, but there has been a tendency to abandon the term "academic culture" and to talk about inducting the student into the intellectual life of the college or university. "Academic culture" seems to connote the conventional ways in which we express the student's progress through the curriculum. It also seems to suggest the conventional ways in which we ordinarily measure achievement, mainly by examinations that put a premium on a knowledge of well-established facts, principles, and methodology.

"Intellectual culture" is used to connote something more than a difference from the conventional academic requirements and marks. Such words as "imagination," "critical analysis," and "creative ability" and "invention" were used again and again, even in the talk on teaching machines which presumably are not yet adapted to the development of the higher critical and creative mental processes.

In its study of creative architects, the Institute for Personality Assessment and Research at Berkeley found that the most creative architects did not always get the highest marks or grades in their professional school years. They were more likely to be "B" students than "A" students. They were often rebellious; they were non-conformist, critical, not for the sake of rebellion, but for the sake of learning. In order to launch out in new directions they often had to repudiate or reevaluate critically what was offered them as sound architectural training.

I was impressed with the discussion of the importance of the faculty in connection with the more subtle aspects of intellectual development and learning. Many of us are threatened by the characteristics that are hallmarks of effective personal development and intellectual development of the students with whom we are concerned. If we are to make the most of students' potentialities, we will have to define desired outcomes in more subtle ways—in ways that allow for imagination, creative innovation, discrimination, sustaining intellectual interests, and intellectual independence.

Full Development

A second theme that appeared again and again is that education is more than intellectual development.

T. R. McCONNELL

Education is concerned with the full development of the person. Dr. Sanford has said that we cannot make any categorical separation of the intellect and the rest of the person. He stated that changes in what might be called intellect, that is, changes in knowledge and in modes of thought, would bring with them changes in the rest of the personality, just as changes in the rest of the personality leave the individual in a different state of receptivity to knowledge and ideas. I am not quite so sure the evidence is conclusive on the reciprocal influences of personality and intellect. Many individuals seem to insulate one area of personality from another. One can see many evidences of immaturity among the members of the academic community and in the community of scholars. Perhaps we should not assume that a highly intellectual person is always a person who is well-balanced in all of his characteristics.

Perhaps the diagrammatical model for the conference was the figure included in Dr. Newcomb's paper to represent the interdependent influences upon final student characteristics. The final outcome, he indicated, is a function of the interaction of the students' initial characteristics, the characteristics of the college, and the student culture.

Dr. Pace provided the means of determining the dominant culture or atmosphere of a college by aggregating students' perceptions of a large number of characteristics, events, and practices of the institution, which, taken together, constitute a pattern of presses on the behavior of students. Dr. Pace has demonstrated that there are dominant and distinctive college environments, but few institutions are monolithic. He pointed out that a large complex university may have a variety of sub-cultures and that a small college may not be entirely of a piece. An adequate characterization of a college, then, requires both a description of its dominant atmosphere and an identification of the important sub-cultures. Dr. Pace is now devising an instrument which will be adaptable for an exploration of these sub-cultures.

In one sense peer groups may be thought of as college subcultures. In reference to the individual student they may be considered a part of the environment, something contributing to the press of the institution on the student, or, as in Dr. Newcomb's model, may be included under student experience. In any case, peer groups are powerful determinants of individual behavior. In some colleges the fraternity system determines the schedule, states how much work students will do, and decides how students will expend their energy. Thus, many peer groups subvert the values which the faculty hold dear; a few peer groups, while not negative, may add little or nothing; and a few others may contribute to the intellectual and democratic values of higher education. The relevant question for education, then, is, in Dr. Newcomb's words, how can we direct such influences in accordance with, rather than irrelevantly or in opposition to, our educational objectives?

Disclaiming any desire to promote conformity by way of peer group organization, Dr. Newcomb is interested in devising and evaluating peer-group systems. Even though peer group pressures toward worthwhile goals can be capitalized upon, the problem of developing autonomy in the individual, whether in the intellectual or other behavioral domains, remains. One of the purposes of education is to strengthen the individual's autonomy, to help him arrive at the point where he is relatively, never absolutely, independent of group support. It is fair to say that we have as yet very little knowledge of the effectiveness of our educational effort. We need much more research of the kind reported by representatives of Texas colleges and of the kinds reported or proposed by the conference speakers.

Wide Research

Dr. Ralph W. Tyler made clear that the needed research should be done by scholars in a variety of fields —sociologists, psychologists, political scientists, anthropologists, educators, and others. These investigations are not only contributions to the solution of practical educational problems; frequently they are, as Dr. Tyler

T. R. McCONNELL

pointed out, contributions as well to the development of theory in the behavioral sciences. It is to be hoped that there will be more studies in Texas colleges of all factors in the Newcomb model, the input, that is, the characteristics of students at entrance; the output, that is, the attributes of students as they leave; their characteristics over time as they are alumni; and the processes by which we try to stimulate change in desirable directions.

I trust that we will not make the problems discussed unnecessarily complex, that we will not be afraid, as Dr. Hilgard suggested, to investigate less profound issues than those which the consultants have proposed. Anything which will help faculty members to deal with educational problems on the basis of evidence rather than on the basis of off-hand stereotypes will leaven faculty attitudes and promote reflection.

I believe fundamentally in the importance of establishing bureaus of institutional research. For colleges which have limited faculty and budgetary resources a bureau of institutional research does not need a large staff and an expensive budget. Rather, it needs limited central funds and staff supplemented by scholars from a variety of fields in the college or university. What I should like most to say following up Dr. Pace's emphasis on the importance of participation in self-studies is that the institutional research agency should not do research for the faculty, but with the faculty, not for the administration, but with the administration.

It is suggested that we need not be immobilized by the necessity for profound theoretical underpinnings of our research. Theoretical frameworks are useful; they are invaluable in that they help one to determine what problems are significant and provide useful bases for the interpretation of empirical findings. Nonetheless, theoretical constructs impose constraints too. Theoretical formation may blind us to facts which are important for us to see. The theory may be so domineering that it is possible for the researcher to write the report before he collects the data.

Dr. Hilgard perhaps would agree that the investigation of practical problems, if they are properly conceived and designed, may make a significant contribution to a developing theoretical structure. But I would not insist that only problems with large theoretical implications should be studied. A most significant way to change a college is to study its programs and to insure that members of the faculty participate in defining the problems, in conducting the investigations, and in reviewing their findings and the implications of the results.

During the conference Dr. Farnsworth has related what we ordinarily call mental health to the process of fruitful human development and of education itself. In so doing he has continually brought us back to the purpose of education as the full development of the person and to Dr. Sanford's admonition to evaluate all phases of college experience in terms of their contribution to the attainment of maturity.

Some Questions Submitted In Advance of the Symposium

How does the organizational structure of the college and also its self-concept affect the personality development of students?

What can we do as an institution to help produce a classroom climate that is warm, flexible, stimulating, and not paternalistic? At the same time, how can we maintain rigorous academic standards?

How can we assimilate the new faculty member into the campus culture more effectively?

PART II

HILGARD
LA GRONE
NARCISO

FARNSWORTH and MOORE

BOBBITT and FARNSWORTH

Chapter 8

STUDIES UNDERWAY IN TEXAS COLLEGES

All too frequently one must wait until several years after completion of a study before it is available to a wide audience. In Texas colleges a number of studies dealing with the problems of personality factors among both faculty and students as they influence college life have recently been initiated. Thus, it seemed appropriate to provide in the conference for a symposium dealing with research projects underway in Texas colleges.

Several months before the conference, Earl A. Koile visited a number of institutions in Texas, both to determine their interest in the conference and any current plans for systematic studies related to personality factors on the campus. Nine projects were uncovered. Because the symposium had to be scheduled in a session lasting no more than two and half hours, each participant was asked to bring a resumé, outline, or set of tables describing the significant aspects of his study. These abstracts were duplicated and given to all individuals present at the Wednesday afternoon session.

Each speaker was allowed only a few minutes for formal presentation, leaving 45 minutes at the end of the the afternoon for general discussion and comment. Obviously, only the chief points of these studies could be presented in the short period of one afternoon.

The nine studies were organized into four broad categories according to the primary emphasis of the research. Starting with a brief description of the project on mental health training and teacher education at The University of Texas, the only project dealing extensively with a longitudinal approach to the personality development of numbers of students, the program moved through three papers describing a total college study underway at Austin College and four papers concentrating primarily upon the attitudes, personality characteristics, and problems of adjustment of faculty members. Following the brief presentation of the nine studies, Ira Iscoe, Associate Professor of Psychology, The University of Texas, started the discussion period by offering general comments, tying together the independent studies.

The remainder of this chapter is devoted to abstracts of the nine studies as presented in the research symposium, followed in Chapter 9 by Robert F. Peck's paper dealing with the range of personality patterns on a college campus as they have emerged in his longitudinal studies of education students at The University of Texas. Considerable variety exists among these studies even though there is a common thread running through all of them. Some of the projects, such as the counseling research program at The University of Texas or the Austin College study, have been underway for several years and are nearing completion. Others, such as the brief report by James A. Young, Vice-President and Dean of Faculties of St. Mary's University, represent primarily a plan for undertaking a study. Each of the papers is introduced by short editorial comment intended to place the abstract in the broader context of the entire symposium. The abstracts themselves can only give the reader an introduction to the work in progress. It is hoped that each of the studies will appear as a separate publication by the principal investigators when the projects have been completed.

Personality Development

Robert F. Peck, Professor of Educational Psychology at The University of Texas, is reporting on a large scale action-research program dealing with the mental health training of future teachers in a college of education. Thousands of students have been evaluated in the course of this five-year study. In addition to Dr. Peck, the

WAYNE H. HOLTZMAN

project staff includes a number of other faculty members serving on the advisory committees to the study.

Among those taking an active part in the program are Glenn E. Barnett, Professor of Curriculum and Instruction and Associate Dean of the College of Education; Oliver H. Bown, Associate Professor of Educational Psychology; Ralph L. Duke, Associate Professor of Educational Psychology; Ben M. Harris, Assistant Professor of Educational Administration; Clyde I. Martin, Associate Professor of Curriculum and Instruction; Carson McGuire, Professor of Educational Psychology; and Donald Veldman, Social Science Research Associate III, Mental Health Teacher Training. Because this project is further along than most of the others and is particularly relevant to the theme of the conference, we have asked Dr. Peck to expand upon his abstract in a paper addressed specifically to the problem of describing the rich variety of personality patterns typical of college students. This more detailed report is given in Chapter 9 rather than in abstract form here.

General Student Development

Three of the studies deal with rather general aspects of the developing college student. The first paper, presented by H. Paul Kelley, outlines a series of projects undertaken as part of the counseling research program in the Testing and Counseling Center of The University of Texas. Dr. Kelley has chosen to list several dozen studies by a brief title and a sentence or two of description. The counseling research program is of considerable magnitude, involving several full-time research psychologists in the counseling field as well as a number of part-time staff members and graduate students. The four-year program of research was made possible by a grant from the Hogg Foundation to The University of Texas. As Coordinator of Measurement and Statistical Services, Dr. Kelley plays a major role in this research program. All of the studies are under the more general direction of Gordon V. Anderson, Director of the Center. Among the staff members most active in the program are G. Gerald Gonyea, Psychologist; Austin E. Grigg, formerly Assistant Professor of Psychology and Clinical Psychologist; N. Robert Altucher, Psychologist; Ira Iscoe, Associate Professor of Psychology; Kathryn K. Skinner, formerly Psychologist, The University of Texas; Frances F. Fuller, Psychologist; H. Paul Kelley, Assistant Professor of Educational Psychology and Co-ordinator of Measurement and Statistical Services; Earl A. Koile, Associate Professor of Educational Psychology and Co-ordinator of Counseling; and Ernest J. Doleys, Clinical Psychologist. The wide variety of studies underway in the counseling research program illustrates rather dramatically the key role played by a well trained research staff of a testing and counseling center when given adequate support.

The second study in this section is an unusual project at a small state college focusing upon the problems of motivation, academic attitude, and study habits of college freshmen. William F. Brown, Director, Testing and Guidance Center, SWTC, San Marcos, Texas, describes a significant experimental approach utilizing undergraduate upperclassmen as specially trained counselors for college freshmen. His results demonstrate how any small college with limited resources might embark upon a special program of student counseling centering primarily on motivation, attitudes, and study habits. Although this project has been given only modest support by a grant from the Hogg Foundation, it has already established itself as a successful program at Southwest Texas State College and has been introduced in one additional college in Texas.

The third study dealing with general student development is a brief report of student characteristics at Texas Southern University, a predominantly Negro institution in Houston. For the past several years Matthew N. Cooper, has been studying the aptitudes, interests, and personality characteristics of Negro students, particularly those who have not made a good academic adjustment to college. Some of the preliminary results of Dr. Cooper's work are reported by J. B. Jones, Associate

WAYNE H. HOLTZMAN

Dean of Students and Professor of Guidance and Special Education, Texas Southern University.

Counseling Research Program in a Large State University

H. PAUL KELLEY

The four-year program of research has involved many people and many projects, which can be described only briefly in this abstract:

A. Theory of Vocational Choice.
1. Sex Identity and Vocational Choice. (Altucher)
The hypothesis being tested is that persons with sex role uncertainty will be less clear as to their vocational interests than will persons who are more certain about their sex roles.
2. Response Preferences as Related to College Major and Sex. (Altucher)
It is expected that differences in preferences for abstract designs will be related both to the major subject area and to the sex of the university-student respondent.
3. Job Perceptions by High School and College, Business, and Technical Students. (Gonyea)
Job perceptions by students are being used to test Holland's hypothesis that job perceptions are most clearly differentiated within the interest area and ability level of the perceiver.
4. Dimensions of Job Perceptions: I. (Gonyea)
An analysis of the dimensions in terms of which university students perceive occupations yielded eight interpretable dimensions. In general, the usual interest groupings and conventional job classifications did not appear. Most of the dimensions could be interpreted as reflecting different needs among the perceiving individuals.
5. Dimensions of Job Perceptions: II. (Gonyea)
To extend the results of study A-4, Case II of Andrews' A-technique is being used to explore further the dimensions in terms of which university students perceive occupations.
6. Perceptions of Parents as Related to Vocational Goals. (Grigg)
An investigation is being made as to whether attitudes

towards parents are related to the kind of vocational choice made by college students, a view currently held by Roe.

B. Relationship of Background Experiences and Socialization Variables to College Performance and Experience.
   1. Educational-Vocational Development of High-Potential University Students. (Gonyea)
      The academic and vocational development of above-average university students is being studied in relation to selected personality and ability variables.
   2. Early History Correlates of Academic Performance. (Grigg)
      An investigation is being made of certain variables in the life history of a selected sample of university freshmen, and an examination is being made of the relationships of these life history variables to college grades, field of major subject, and leadership points acquired while in college.
   3. Perceptions of College Characteristics. (Iscoe)
      The perceptions of the characteristics of The University of Texas by freshmen, upper division students, and faculty members have been measured; the students' perceptions and incongruencies in perceptions will be related to their academic status and to subsequent academic outcomes.

C. The Role of a University Counseling Center.
   1. Survey of Faculty Perceptions of Students' Problems. (Grigg and Gonyea)
      Faculty perceptions were investigated in the areas of attitudes toward students with problems and kinds of problems observed among students.

D. Characteristics of Clients at a University Counseling Center.
   1. Personality Differences Between Clients with Vocational and Personal Problems. (Altucher)
      The hypothesis under investigation is that clients of the Testing and Counseling Center who have vocational problems will differ with respect to their manifest needs from clients who have personal problems.
   2. Deviant Responses in College Adjustment Clients. (Grigg)
      Berg's Deviation Hypothesis was supported by results which indicated that the deviant response scores of

H. PAUL KELLEY

freshmen who later became personal counseling or psychiatric treatment cases were significantly greater than the deviant response scores of a control group of non-clients. Freshmen who later became educational-vocational counseling clients did not differ significantly from the control group in their deviant response scores.

3. Characteristics of Counseling Clients at the U. T. Testing and Counseling Center: I. Relation to characteristics of the U.T. student body. (Kelley)
   In order to help view the activities of a university counseling center in the broader perspective of the total university setting, clients of the Testing and Counseling Center are being compared on a number of background and behavioral variables with the general population of students from which they came.

4. Characteristics of Counseling Clients at the U.T. Testing and Counseling Center: II. Background characteristics. (Kelley)
   To investigate more intensively the backgrounds of students who come to a university counseling center, a large number of demographic, experiential, and psychological factors are being examined.

5. Characteristics of Counseling Clients at the U.T. Testing and Counseling Center: III. Interview report data. (Kelley and Koile)
   To obtain a more detailed understanding of the behavior of the clients at the Center, data from each interview and each appointment are being recorded and summarized. Factors being studied include such variables as number of appointments in each contact series, case load by time and date, topic of interviews, outcome of interviews, and number of broken and unkept appointments.

6. Personality and Attitude Characteristics Associated with "Therapy Readiness." (Skinner)
   A formulation of the construct of "therapy readiness" within the framework of Roger's Self-Theory led to predictions that clients judged "therapy ready" (a) would be more anxious, less defensive, less comfortable, and less satisfied with their concepts of self than "not therapy ready" clients, but that the two groups would not differ on certain other personality variables, (b) would more frequently report attitudes re-

flecting realistic perceptions of counseling, and (c) would return for more counseling interviews than the "not therapy ready" client. All predictions were supported. (Doctoral dissertation.)

E. Criteria for Evaluating Outcome of Counseling.

1. Construct Validity of the Chicago Q-Sort: Frustration Tolerance. (Doleys)
   In validating the Chicago Q-sort against a criterion of frustration tolerance, results obtained, while inconclusive, tended to imply that the Q-sort does not measure validly that particular aspect of self-acceptance.

2. An Immediate Criterion of Vocational Counseling Success. (Gonyea)
   Former vocational counseling clients are being followed up after one year to determine relatively long-range effects of counseling on appropriateness of vocational choice, satisfaction of vocational objective, academic performance, and study skills; the relationship between these long-range outcomes and the immediate outcome of counseling will be examined.

3. Effects of Formal Training in Psychology Upon Performance on the Tolar-Reznikoff Insight Test. (Gonyea)
   It was concluded that scores on this test are inflated as a result of formal instruction in psychology. Unless it could be satisfactorily demonstrated that the test is measuring emotional rather than intellectual insight, this test does not appear useful as a method for assessing effectiveness of counseling.

4. A Scale for Self Description. (Grigg and Kelley)
   An instrument was developed, by the application of psychological scaling procedures, for the evaluation of self-descriptions in the areas of feelings, study and work habits, and social relations. The instrument was able to discriminate clients from non-clients; also scores on the scales for the client groups changed significantly following therapy, but no significant changes occurred after a five-week interval in a non-client control sample.

5. Holtzman Inkblot Technique in Relation to Counseling Outcome. (Kelley)
   Measures of counseling outcome are being investi-

gated for counseling clients to whom the Holtzman Inkblot Technique was administered.

F. Changes that Occur During the Counseling Process.
1. Changes in the Relationship Between Needs and Job Perceptions as a Result of Vocational Counseling. (Gonyea)
Under investigation are changes in the relationship between manifest needs and job perceptions as a result of vocational counseling.
2. Perceptions of Counseling as Related to Changes in Clients' Self Descriptions. (Grigg)
The perceptions by clients of their counselors and of their feelings during counseling are being examined in relation to the counseling outcomes as measured by the Self Description Test.

G. Client-Counselor Relationships.
1. Client-Counselor Interaction Study. (Gonyea)
Analysis of variance is being employed to test the significance of interaction between client and counselor needs, as measured by the Edwards Personal Preference Schedule, in relation to counseling outcome.
2. The "Ideal Therapeutic Relationship" and Counseling Outcome. (Gonyea)
When an attempt was made to relate counseling outcome to Fiedler's composite Q-sort of the Ideal Therapeutic Relationship, the results indicated little or no relationship. In general there seemed to be a slight tendency for the counselors judged most unlike the "Ideal" to produce the most favorable outcomes, when change on the Self Description Test is used as a criterion.
3. The "Ideal Therapeutic Relationship" and Client Comfort (Gonyea)
Examination is being made of the relationship between counseling outcome, degree of client comfort in counseling, and the extent to which the counseling relationship is judged to approximate Fiedler's "Ideal Therapeutic Relationship."
4. Influence of Sex of Counselor and Client on Client Expressions of Feeling During Counseling. (Fuller)
Preferences for female counselors were infrequent in all groups of clients. When sex and experience of the counselor, and sex, presenting problem, and counselor

preference of clients were controlled, female clients expressed more feeling than males in counseling interviews. Also, clients expressed more feeling in the presence of female than of male counselors, and male-female counselor-client dyads produced more feeling expression than when both counselor and client were males. Clients who stated no preference as to sex of counselor expressed more feeling and their increase in feeling expression from intake to first interview was greater than that of clients with preferences. (Doctoral dissertation)

H. Possibilities and Limitations of Group Counseling.

1. Pilot Study in Group Personal Counseling. (Gonyea and Altucher)
   Methods for establishing and maintaining personal counseling groups were explored, along with the behavior of student clients taking part in the groups. It was concluded that both voluntary and involuntary assignments into groups of clients seeking individual personal counseling were ineffective.

2. Pilot Study of Group Counseling for Self-Referred Students Who Are Academic Under-Achievers. (Fuller)
   Exploration is being made of procedures for working with students who refer themselves for participation in groups dealing with academic problems.

3. Pilot Study of Group Counseling for Self-Referred Students with Undetermined and Doubtful Majors (Fuller)
   Exploration is being made of procedures for working with students who refer themselves for participation in a group dealing with problems of vocational planning.

I. Prediction Studies.

1. Relationships between Information Given on an Information Form and Some Counseling Variables. (Altucher)
   Hypotheses are being tested concerning the use of responses to a pre-counseling questionnaire for the prediction of counseling behavior, specifically, type of termination, length of contact, and degree of resistance.

2. Selection of Dormitory Counselors. (Gonyea)

A test battery is being developed to aid in the selection of student counselors for women's residence halls.

Academic Adjustment Counseling Through Peer Group Interaction

WILLIAM F. BROWN

The number of young people entering college is expected to double within the next decade. As the college population increases, administrators will find it necessary to enlarge and revise current college counseling programs if they are to provide the necessary environment and services for the fullest development of each individual's potential. However, the prohibitive cost of maintaining an adequate guidance service utilizing traditional counseling techniques makes it mandatory that the range and complexity of the program be limited or that more economical procedures be developed for processing routine cases.

The objective of the research being reported was to develop and evaluate a counseling program employing peer group discussion procedures for transmitting test results, analyzing potential problem areas, and planning appropriate remedial actions. The experimental counseling program employed peer and group interaction dynamics and utilized scholastic ability, achievement, and attitude data to structure the guidance process. Specifically, the program incorporated the following unique characteristics: (1) utilization of the peer approach in that the counseling was accomplished by carefully selected and trained upperclassmen, (2) utilization of the group approach in that the counselor met with three or more students simultaneously, and (3) utilization of the motivation approach in that each student's study habits and attitudes were systematically surveyed.

The goal of the experimental counseling program was to help each student develop an effective study program. The following three-step counseling sequence was employed to achieve this goal: (1) report and interpret the results of ability, achievement, and attitude tests previously administered to all freshmen; (2) survey each student's study behavior and scholastic motivation and delineate potential problem areas; and (3) discuss organization and techniques for effective study and help plan appropriate corrective action for identified weaknesses.

Research undertaken during the 1959–1960 long session was designed to accomplish three objectives: (1) to evaluate the immediate and delayed effectiveness of peer group counseling for academic adjustment, (2) to assess the comparative effectiveness of male and female counselors with male and female students, and (3) to determine the optimum size and attitude composition of student groups receiving counseling.

Several statistical evaluations were made to facilitate research planning for the 1960–61 long session. Table I reports the results of this preliminary analysis of the program's immediate and delayed effectiveness for each sex. Data bearing upon the optimum size and attitude composition of student groups were not evaluated during this preliminary analysis.

Two criteria of immediate counseling effectiveness were employed in the research: (1) test-retest differential on the *Survey of Study Habits and Attitudes* (Form E57), and (2) post-counseling score on the *Effective Study Test* (Form E59). Table I reveals that three

TABLE 1

RESULTS FOR MATCHED CONTROL AND EXPERIMENTAL SAMPLES*
(Total N = 216 cases)

Criterion	Difference Between Counseled and Uncounseled *Female* Freshmen		Difference Between Counseled and Uncounseled *Male* Freshmen	
	Male Counselor	*Female* Counselor	*Male* Counselor	*Female* Counselor
1. Survey of Study Habits and Attitudes (Test-Retest Differential)	30.9**	23.0**	31.5**	11.5
2. Effective Study Test (Form E-59)	6.7**	6.2**	5.5**	5.6**
3. Point-Hour Grade Ratio	.58**	.46**	—.01	—.04
4. Quality Point Total	8.2**	7.5**	1.8	1.2

* Control (uncounseled) and experimental (counseled) subjects were individually matched on the following nine variables (1) scholastic aptitude (SCAT), (2) scholastic motivation (SSHA), (3) high school quarter rank, (4) high school size, (5) sex, (6) age, (7) course load, (8) employment status, and (9) place of residence.

** Counseled freshmen scored significantly higher than uncounseled freshmen (P < .01).

132   WILLIAM F. BROWN

of the four groups achieved significantly higher scores on all immediate criteria than did matched groups of freshmen who received no counseling. The fourth group (male students with female counselors) achieved significantly higher scores on the *Effective Study Test* only.

The two criteria employed to assess delayed counseling effectiveness were the one-semester point-hour ratio and the one-semester quality-point total. For both criteria, significant differences were found between counseled and uncounseled women, but not between counseled and uncounseled men. Although counseled women earned grades averaging almost one-half letter grade and 7.5 quality points higher than did uncounseled women, the grade averages of counseled and uncounseled men were nearly identical.

Further examination of Table I suggests that male counselors may be somewhat more effective than female counselors. Students advised by male counselors averaged slightly higher on almost all criteria than did those aided by female counselors. The only statistical significant difference, however, occurred for one of the immediate criteria of counseling effectiveness. The test-retest differential on the *Survey of Study Habits and Attitudes averages* 20 points higher for men counseled by men than for men counseled by women.

Another basis for evaluating the program's success might be obtained by analyzing the reception given it by the students themselves. Almost 85 per cent of the freshmen class requested counseling on their test results; nearly one-third of the counseled freshmen subsequently requested additional help with their study habits, vocational plans, or personal problems. Furthermore, the counseling responsiveness of men and women did not differ significantly.

The success of a program of this type is obviously dependent upon the selection and training of the upperclassmen serving as student counselors. The criteria for selection and training of counselors are outlined in Tables II and III, respectively. It should be noted that 20 of the 36 hours of counselor training employ the "buddy-system" training procedure.

TABLE 2

CRITERIA FOR SELECTION OF COUNSELORS

1. Top quarter of freshman class on academic ability measure.
2. Top quarter of freshman class on scholastic motivation measure.
3. Top quarter of freshman class in academic achievement.
4. Recommendation by dormitory head resident and house council.
5. Candidate for elementary or secondary teaching certificate.

TABLE 3

COUNSELOR TRAINING CYCLE

Activity	Training Hours Spring	Fall
1. Lecture: Testing and Guidance Activity Sequence	2	0
2. Demonstration: Counseling Process	2	2
3. Lecture: Effective Study Procedures	2	4
4. Lecture: Counseling Dynamics	2	2
*5. Laboratory: Counseling Materials Familiarization	2	2
*6. Practicum: Role-Playing Counseling Experience	2	2
*7. Practicum: Supervised Counseling Experience	0	4
*8. Practicum: Observation and Critique	0	4
*9. Practicum: Supervisor's Evaluation	0	4
	12	24

* Buddy-System Training.

Conclusions

The results of this preliminary analysis support one general and four specific conclusions.

1. The experimental counseling program has won a high degree of acceptance by the student body at Southwest Texas State College.

2. The program provided an effective means for communicating information about efficient study skills.

3. Although the program produced significant improvement in the academic achievement of women, the difference in mean grade-point averages of counseled and uncounseled men was insignificant.

4. Male counselors were slightly more effective than female counselors, at least when counseling members of the opposite sex.

A carefully directed program of academic adjustment counseling through peer group interaction is both a prac-

WILLIAM F. BROWN

tical and economical means for transmitting test results and analyzing study skills.

Some Personal-Social Factors Contributing to Academic Failure at Texas Southern University

J. B. JONES

This study was concerned with the determination of differences between college students who succeed academically and those who do not succeed. The search for significant differences was primarily in the area of social and personal adjustment.

Using the Army General Classification Test (First Civilian Edition), 51 good students were paired with 51 poor students on general scholastic aptitude. The good students all had grade-point averages of 1.0 or greater; the poor students had obtained averages of less than 1.0. Mean differences between the good and poor students were examined for statistical significance using scores on the following instruments: The Minnesota Multiphasic Personality Inventory; Guilford's Inventory of Factors STDCR; the Guilford-Martin Personnel Inventory; the Kuder Preference Record, Vocational Form G; the Group Membership Record; the American Council on Education Personality Report; and the "Who-Are-You" Technique.

A number of significant differences between the two groups of students were found. Since the good and poor students had been matched in scholastic aptitude, none of the differences could be attributed to general aptitude per se. As compared with the successful student, the poor student is significantly more likely to show the following personality characteristics:

1. Tends to be more careless, less self-critical, and to have less ability to comprehend the items or material presented to him.

2. Tends to be less self-analytic or meditative.

3. Tends to have interests more characteristic of the opposite sex (among the women only).

4. Is unlikely to be chosen by a classmate as a suitable partner for work on school projects.

5. Tends to give his teachers the impression he has less emotional balance.

6. Tends to use his name as the locus of his self-concept rather than such attributes as his achievements, aspirations, class membership, or family affiliation (on the W-A-Y Technique).

7. Aspires to a lower level of course grades in the future.

Total College Study

One of the studies can only be classified as a total college study since it involves periodic evaluation of students, interviews with faculty members, and complete reorganization of the curriculum for one large segment of students. The major curriculum study was made possible at Austin College by a grant from the Ford Foundation. An additional grant from the Hogg Foundation made it possible to construct a research design and carry out an evaluation program to determine the impact of the experimental curriculum as contrasted with the traditional curriculum already in being at Austin College. Initially the program of evaluation was worked out by E. Ashby Johnson, Professor of Philosophy and Theodore Nicksick, Associate Professor of Psychology of Austin College, with Lucile Allen and Wayne Holtzman serving as consultants. More recently J. Carter Parkes, Director, Testing and Counseling Center, took over the role of supervision at Austin College of the testing and evaluating program. The evaluation of students and changes in the attitudes, personality, and achievement level constituted one major aspect of the evaluation program. A second aspect consisted of a sociological analysis of the faculty and staff organization based upon individual interviews conducted by Dr. Allen with faculty members. Dr. Parkes is reporting only on the program dealing with student characteristics.

Impact of an Experimental Curriculum Upon Students at Austin College

J. CARTER PARKES

Basic Integrated Studies Program
    Background—The Basic Integrated Studies (BIS) pro-

WAYNE H. HOLTZMAN

gram was undertaken by Austin College after several years of self study and departmental efforts to draw up better programs of instruction. Concerns of more than local nature were in our minds in undertaking this program. For one thing, we had the feeling that the often expressed opinion that the small Christian liberal arts college is on the defensive to justify its existence is well grounded and that it is imperative for such schools to take the initiative in the affairs of higher education. Furthermore, we worked under the conviction that more economical use must be made both of faculty and student time if we are to cope with the financial problems of higher education. Perhaps the most vital consideration was that of coping with the steadily increasing pressure for both broader and more intensive studies to be brought into the restricted time of the college years. We believe that we have reached the limit in dealing with this problem by simply adding new courses to the traditional curriculum. Therefore, it is important for us to determine what is really essential and the ways in which this important subject matter can be presented within a circumscribed period of time.

Preparation—The period of faculty preparation for inaugurating the BIS program was extremely brief. It is possible to debate endlessly regarding the merits of various types of curriculum design, and some form of action was deemed preferable to indefinitely prolonged discussion regarding equally plausible approaches. Through correspondence and visits we gained some familiarity with a dozen college and university programs across the United States. This information was invaluable in designing the BIS program. The Fund for the Advancement of Education approved our request for a grant in June, 1958. Fourteen members of the faculty were involved during the summer of 1958 in planning the first year of operation.

Objectives—Several rather specific objectives were outlined for the BIS program:

1. That part of the college curriculum regarded by the faculty as essential for every student should form the core of the program. It was not anticipated that the experi-

mental program would be the exact equivalent of any particular combination of existing courses.

2. This material should be presented in a manner that would enable the student to have a more thorough grasp of the inter-relatedness of knowledge and of the social and personal implications of the various academic disciplines.
3. The student should be given an increased sense of responsibility for his own academic enterprise.
4. The overlapping of subject matter which takes place in strictly departmental offerings should be minimized.
5. The student should be prepared for a large measure of independent work during his junior and senior years.

Level of the BIS Program—The BIS program was pitched at a level of difficulty appropriate for the top two-thirds of the entering class in anticipation of rising admission standards over the next five years. We presumed more rigorous selection of students and somewhat stronger preparation from the high schools than would be the case for the entire freshman class in 1958. It is still an open question whether this experimental program offers most promise for general college use or for use with only the more gifted student.

Evaluation of Curriculum Experiment at Austin College—The description and evaluation of the basic integrated studies program and its impact upon the faculty and students at Austin College consist of two major parts: (a) a sociological analysis of the program's impact upon the faculty, students, and entire social system of the college as revealed by a series of personal interviews and observations of faculty and staff members; and (b) the assessment of changes within individual students as measured by psychological tests and personal interviews.

The second part of the evaluation program has focused primarily upon changes in the students as measured by psychological tests of social attitudes, personality characteristics, social adjustment, and educational achievement. Under the direct supervision of Wayne Holtzman, with the close collaboration of Theodore Nicksick and, more recently, J. Carter Parkes, Director of the Testing and Counseling Center at Austin College, the objective phase of the evaluation has involved repeated testing of individual students in the freshman classes entering Austin College in September 1958 and September 1959. Some testing has also been completed for the freshman class entering Austin College in September 1960, in order to provide a means of measuring any change in the population of freshman students across the three-year period.

The major focus of the evaluation has been geared to the group entering Austin College in 1958, when it was possible to set up rigorous experimental and control groups, each consisting of approximately 32 students. The experimental group was comprised of all students following the BIS program. The control group consisted of students matched with the BIS group for motivation, aptitude, sex, and other relevant background characteristics in order to provide a basis for evaluating change due to the experimental program. In the summer prior to arriving on campus, all of the control cases had expressed the same desire to participate in the new BIS program as did the students who were actually admitted. Initial differences between the two groups were truly random at the start of the experiment.

Of the original 66 students in the experimental and control groups, 45 were still enrolled 18 months later when most of the retest measures were obtained. About 40 students from the original groups have enrolled for the 1960–61 academic year. Some attrition was unavoidable due to students who failed or transferred out of school for other reasons. The number of students who left the program was approximately the same in both the experimental and control groups. Either in the spring or early fall of 1960, the following instruments were re-administered to students from the BIS and control groups: (a) the USES General Aptitude Battery; (b) the Iowa Test of Educational Development, Sections 5, 6, and 7; (c) Brown's Student Biographical Inventory; (d) the Survey of Study Habits and Attitudes; (e) the Opinion Questionnaire containing five social attitude scales; and (f) the Holtzman Inkblot Technique. Together with initial scores on these same tests, these data have been punched on IBM cards and were analyzed during the month of October, 1960, to determine the extent to which there is any difference between the experimental and control groups.

In addition to the above measures that were obtained in the fall and winter of 1958–59 and again in the spring and fall of 1960, first year grade-point-averages, sociometric nominations, and attitudes expressed in the College Characteristic Index are available on most of the students in the 1958 freshman class.

For the entering freshman class of 1959, only group tests were obtained. Twenty-six students—10 women and 16 men—comprised the group who matriculated in the BIS program. No control group was set up at the beginning of the fall term for the 1959 freshmen, since it was unfeasible to obtain rigorous, random placement of students in the same manner as was done for the 1958 group. Instead a quasi-control group will be constructed in a *post hoc* manner by matching students from the 1959 freshman class at large with the BIS students on the following variables: (a) verbal and quantitative scores on the CEEB Scholastic Aptitude Test; (b) size of hometown; (c) sex of student; (d) major field of study; and (e) type of dormitory residence. Initial scores on several of the test variables may also be taken into account to obtain close matching of the BIS and control groups.

Measures available on the entire freshman class of 1959 consist of the following: (a) the CEEB Scholastic Aptitude Test; (b) the Survey of Study Habits and Attitudes; (c) the Student Biographical Inventory; and (d) the Opinion Questionnaire. It is contemplated that in the spring of 1961, the entire 1959 freshman class will be retested on these same variables (with the possible exception of the CEEB Scholastic Aptitude Test) to determine the extent to which the students in the BIS and matched control groups differ from each other. In addition a standard achievement test, such as the Iowa Test of Educational Development, may be given to the BIS and control groups, depending upon the outcome of the current analysis on the 1958 groups.

General descriptive analyses have been made for the

J. CARTER PARKES

entire freshman class of 1958. Intercorrelations among 27 variables have been computed, as well as mean and standard deviations, separately for men and women. This descriptive analysis has revealed some interesting student characteristics that can be compared in a general way with student populations at other colleges. A similar analysis will be undertaken for the smaller number of variables collected on the 1959 and 1960 freshman classes. A study of any significant trends across the three freshman classes will reveal any changing characteristics of the student population during this critical period of reorganization at Austin College.

The Faculty

The last four studies presented by the research panel deal mainly with the characteristics of faculty members rather than students. The first paper by Lucile Allen concerns primarily the problem of translation from graduate student to faculty member in several Texas colleges. The study is just getting under way and Dr. Allen reports only the major objectives of the project, the research methods, and several preliminary observations from her initial interviews. It is interesting to note that in this kind of research, special care must be taken to plan the study with the full collaboration of key representatives of both the faculty and the college administration. Since only a small number of individuals are interviewed and observed, the anonymity of the participating faculty members is difficult to preserve unless only rather general findings are reported.

The second paper by Reece McGee presents a descriptive study of regular junior faculty members in two large state universities. Dr. McGee's report is part of a series of studies that he has been undertaking for a number of years on the sociological aspects of academic life. This particular study is presented in a little more detail than most of the abstracts because of the complex nature of the accompanying tables and the general interest of college personnel in Dr. McGee's results.

The third speaker in the series dealing with faculty studies was James A. Young, vice-president of St. Mary's

University in San Antonio. He reported briefly on plans that are just getting underway for a major self-study among his college faculty. Since the proposed study has hardly moved beyond the initial stages, no abstract is presented here.

The last paper in the symposium was presented by Richard Evans and deals with an empirical study of the values and attitudes of faculty members toward the use of television in the classroom. Dr. Evans' study is particularly timely because of the great surge of interest in utilizing television for college instruction.

A Study of Role Conflicts and Congruences Encountered by the New Faculty Member as He Enters the Culture of a College or University Community

LUCILE ALLEN

In collaboration with staff members of the Hogg Foundation, a study has been planned which will investigate the role of the new faculty member on several college campuses. Since the project is just getting underway, only general plans can be reported at this time. Among some of the issues and questions to which this study is addressed are the following:

A new faculty member conducts a high percentage of classes for beginning students as well as for upperclassmen. When he enters the classroom, how does he perceive his role? Is this perception consistent with the bases for promotion and with the norms of acceptance by his colleagues? Are his personal goals related to research achievement or to a concentration upon classroom teaching or both? Or upon other activities and objectives?

What are the organizational arrangements and the channels of communication which early acquaint him with the purposes of the university or college, with the specific expectations of the administration for him, and with acceptance into the academic group by his colleagues? Are the official provisions for his induction as a member of the college community and its value system supported by the value systems of other informal groups in the college community with whom he comes in contact at this early stage in his academic career?

What is the movement during his first year in his perception of his role and the value systems to which he responds? Are his original purposes strengthened? Has he shifted to a new set of objectives? Is he confused? Or, does he see himself playing several roles with conflict or with consistency?

Any project dealing directly with the interpersonal relations and self-perceptions of faculty members must include a number of precautions to avoid disturbing either the individuals or the social system being studied. On each of the two campuses to be studied during the 1960–61 academic year, a small faculty advisory committee has been established consisting of at least one top administrator and behavioral scientist familiar with social organization. It is hoped that the advisory committees may also include a representative of the Board of Trustees.

Research Procedures

The main method for obtaining information is the open-ended, structured interview conducted at least twice with each new faculty member—once immediately after the faculty member arrived on campus early in the fall of 1960, and again in the spring of 1961. Particular note was to be made of any discernable shifts in roles, value systems, or conflicts that arose during the first few months of teaching on the new campus. All of the interviewing was done by Lucile Allen.

Prior to carrying out the main study in two Texas colleges, a pilot study was conducted at a west coast university. The interview outline and a related questionnaire grew out of this preliminary effort. A shorter questionnaire was planned for use with departmental chairmen, division heads, deans, provosts, and presidents at a later date but before the end of the academic year.

Preliminary Results

Thirty initial interviews of new faculty members have been completed and were to be used in the spring as a check against the second interview with the same faculty members. While no conclusions can be drawn from these limited data, several interesting notes might be mentioned. These illustrations are taken from notes collected at the west coast university as well as the two Texas institutions.

1. Several of the faculty who had been on a campus a week or more, but who had not met any classes, had already concluded that the aims and goals of the university were somewhat different from what they had interpreted them to be before their arrival.
2. The large majority of the faculty had little idea as yet as to how promotions are determined and what criteria are used.
3. A point that came out in the interviews was that six of the thirty faculty members had parents born outside this country. This foreign background seemed to affect their understanding of the quality of the student body and the campus mores.

A systematic analysis of the interview data will be made at the end of the academic year. Specific findings will be reported separately to each college president and to his advisory committee, with care taken to preserve the anonymity of the individual faculty members. If the findings prove of sufficient general interest, a report of the research will be published.

The exact purpose, procedure, and personnel of the study on a certain campus rests with the authorities of that college and with its advisory committee. The Foundation will publish no inclusive report nor any comparison of various colleges unless requested by the participating colleges.

Some Occupational Concomitants of Academic Degrees
REECE McGEE

The Problem

A neglected area of empirical study is the occupational consequence for the individual professor of his possession of the Bachelor's, Master's, or Doctor's degree. Equally lacking are data to support what "everybody knows" about the consequences for the individual of having a degree from this or that university or institutional source. It is the purpose of this paper to offer some data.

The literature on higher education, both sociological and educational, is replete with discussions of the degrees themselves, their "real" or "actual" meanings and their intended ones, calls for reform in degree-programs and hiring practices,[1] and with statistics about the nature of the employment of degree holders. Several sociologists have studied what could be called "elements of the academic personnel process," sometimes with attention to certain aspects of degree-holding such as "inbreeding."[2]

It is overwhelmingly agreed by all commentators, (and, indeed, "everybody knows") that, as Jacques Barzun puts it, "The Ph.D. Degree has become the union card of the American college teacher . . . A young man on the educational market without a Ph.D. must en-

[1] *c.f.* Winfield D. Armentrout, "Is College Teaching a Profession?" *School and Society,* Vol. 73, pp. 373–374, June 16, 1951; Harold R. W. Benjamin, "Ph.D.'s Preferred," *Journal of Higher Education,* Vol. 19, pp. 189–193, 218, April, 1948; William W. Brickman, "The M.A. and the Ph.D.," *School and Society,* Vol. 66, pp. 169–174, August 20, 1947; Irwin A. Buell, "The Master's Degree," *Bulletin of the American Association of University Professors,* 30:3, Autumn 1944; Stuart C. Dodd, "A Ph.D. Defined in Three Tenses," *Journal of Educational Sociology,* 30:9, May, 1957; Ellsworth Faris, "Too Many Ph.D's?", *American Journal of Sociology,* Vol. 39, 1933–36; John D. Garwood, "Attention College Seniors," *American Mercury,* Vol. 79, pp. 66–68, December, 1954; E. H. Sturtevant, "Selection and Retention of Faculty Members," *Bulletin of the American Association of University Professors,* 25:4, October, 1939.

[2] *c.f.,* Theodore Caplow and Reece McGee, *"The Academic Marketplace,* (New York: Basic Books, Inc., 1958); F. Stuart Chapin, *Contemporary American Institutions,* (New York: Harper and Brothers, 1935), pp. 152–154; A. B. Hollingshead, "In-group Membership and Academic Selection," *American Sociological Review,* 3:6, December, 1938, pp. 826–833, and "Climbing the Academic Ladder," *American Sociological Review,* 5:39, June, 1940, pp. 384–394; Paul Felix Lazarsfeld and Wagner Thielens, *The Academic Mind,* (Glencoe, Ill.: The Free Press, 1958); C. Wright Mills, *The Sociological Imagination,* (New York: Oxford University Press, 1959); P. A. Sorokin and C. A. Anderson, "Metabolism of Different Strata of Social Institutions and Institutional Continuity," *Instituto Poligrafico dello Stato,* Vol. 9, Rome, 1931, (seen only in summary by this author); Logan Wilson, *The Academic Man,* (New York: Oxford University Press, 1942.)

deavor to look as if he were working for one, because even junior colleges and state teachers' colleges will take nothing less in a member of their staff."[3]

The data presented herewith generally confirm what "everybody knows," but suggest that the necessity for the possession of the Ph.D. as a prerequisite for academic employment is vastly overrated. (Indeed, for a small but significant minority of professors no degree at all is necessary.) They also suggest that where the professor's degree is *from* may be just as important as what it is.

The Data

Data were drawn from the faculty personnel records maintained by the presidents' offices of two large state universities. Records for all fulltime regular junior faculty members (rank of assistant professor or below) at both institutions were examined and certain items coded and recorded on edge-punched cards. The institutional records of 675 individuals are represented. Since both universities are among the ten largest academic institutions in the country, both are state-supported and draw students from wide hinterlands, and both operate in the faculty labor market of the major universities of the country, it is not unreasonable to conclude that their faculties are probably comparable in many respects.

Information about the occupational backgrounds and experiences of faculty members was cross-tabulated to ascertain the effects upon individuals of their possession of the various degrees and the institutional sources of those degrees. All relationships so ordered were tested by Chi Square. The accompanying tables report the findings of this analysis. In order to assess in some measure the social location of any judgments about the worth of the degrees or their sources which might be empirically expressed in differential occupational experience or treatment of the faculty members considered, each table is divided into three general categories: Those experiences ("Job Factors") which are exclusively under the

[3] *Teacher in America*, Little, Brown—Atlantic Monthly Press.

REECE McGEE

control and the direction of the university, those which are partially so-controlled, and those over which the university has little or no control.[4] Relationships shown in the tables are expressed as percentages for ease of comparisons.

The Findings

Table 1 shows the relationship between highest academic degree possessed by junior faculty members and certain aspects of their jobs. Considering the variables in Category I, those factors totally controlled by the university, it is overwhelmingly apparent that the doctoral degree is closely related to attainment of the rank of assistant professor and frequently contributes to initial appointment in that rank. It is interesting to note, however, in view of the very common belief that the Ph.D. is a prerequisite for college teaching, that 136 individuals have only the bachelor's degree and an additional 285 have only the master's. (Not represented in the table are the 13 men from the two universities who have no academic degrees at all.) Men with B.A.'s only are almost certain to receive their first university appointment as an instructor or similar low rank rather than as an assistant professor, and their chances of becoming assistant professors without further degrees appear to be only slightly better. Men with M.A.'s are as likely to become assistant professors as to remain instructors, but are less likely to be appointed in that capacity originally. About half of those with the doctorate were originally appointed as assistant professors and almost three-quarters of them now hold that rank.

From these findings it would seem as if the common belief that the Ph.D. is a *prerequisite for* college teaching is actually a mistaken interpretation of the fact that, in most disciplines, men with Ph.D.'s *do* college teaching.

---

[4] Professional productivity and the possession of research grants are considered "partially controlled by the University" in that productivity is in some part a function of opportunity and support which may only be provided by the University, and that in both institutions under consideration, the consent of the University is necessary for a faculty member to accept a research grant. Both control research funds which may be disbursed at their discretion as well.

TABLE 1

Highest Academic Degree Among the Junior Faculties of Two
State Universities by Various Job Factors
in per cent

Job Factors	Highest Academic Degree			Chi Square	P-Value	Contingency Coefficient
	Bachelor's	Master's	Doctor's			
Category I: Totally Controlled by University:						
Present Rank						
Instr. & Other	81	54	29	98.3	<.001	.36
Asst. Prof.	19	46	71			
Total	100	100	100			
N	136	285	254			
Rank, 1st Appointment						
Instr. & Other	92	70	51			
Asst. Prof.	8	30	49	78.9	<.001	.33
Total	100	100	100			
N	132	284	251			
Years Served in Jr. Rank						
1–6	82	64	76			
7 and over	18	36	24	16.7	<.001	.16
Total	100	100	100			
N	135	286	253			
Annual Class Load*						
1–6	55	54	73			
7 and over	45	46	27	14.7	<.001	.18
Total	100	100	100			
N	78	189	150			
Category II: Partially Controlled by University:						
Productivity#						
Productive	18	47	69			
Unproductive	82	53	31	92.6	<.001	.35
Total	100	100	100			
N	135	286	254			
Possession of Research Grants						
Grants	4	7	20			
No Grants	96	93	80	30.9	<.001	.21
Total	100	100	100			
N	135	286	254			

TABLE 1—(Continued)

Highest Academic Degree Among the Junior Faculties of Two
State Universities by Various Job Factors
in per cent

Job Factors	Highest Academic Degree			Chi Square	P-Value	Contingency Coefficient
	Bachelor's	Master's	Doctor's			
Category III: Uncontrolled by University: Memberships in Learned Societies						
Memberships	56	71	83	34.1	<.001	.22
No Memberships	44	29	17			
Total	100	100	100			
N	135	286	254			
Offices in Learned Societies						
Offices	9	18	18			
No Offices	91	82	82	6.8	< .05	.09
Total	100	100	100			
N	135	286	254			
Listings in National Reference Works						
Listings	1	7	18			
No Listings	99	93	82	34.6	<.001	.23
Total	100	100	100			
N	135	286	254			

* Expressed on *Semester* basis, excluding summer.
# Defined as any publication or presentation directed to a professional audience, and including individual pieces of creativity in the graphic arts as well as literary, musical, and dramatic works.

Clearly so also do a number of men without the Ph.D. Since these data are from two *major* universities, it is reasonable to assume that as a matter of fact *most* college teaching is done by men without Ph.D.'s, for that degree is generally to be found in greatest proportions among the faculties of the major universities.

The association between degrees and time served in junior rank is less clear than the foregoing relationships. The majority of all three categories of individuals are in their first six years of university service. The small proportion of men with B.A.'s who have served longer than six years may indicate either attrition or the attainment of more advanced degrees, while the 24 per cent of Ph.D.'s in that group might be expected to be a residue of men deemed unpromotable. The data do not permit us to examine these hypotheses. The contingency co-efficient of the association is low.

It is plain that men with the doctoral degree generally teach less than men with the B.A. or M.A. only. The similarity in proportions of the latter with annual class loads of seven or more (45 per cent and 46 per cent respectively) suggests that in this respect they are treated alike, perhaps as "work horses" in their departments. Note, however, that the contingency coefficient of the association between degree and teaching load is relatively low.

With regard to Category II, those variables only partially controlled by the university, there is again a high positive association between professional productivity and the possession of advanced degrees. In view of similar though lower, associations between possession of advanced degrees and teaching load and research grants, this result may be a function of the training and motivations for productivity learned in the process of acquiring the doctoral degree as well as of opportunity to produce. (That 18 per cent of men with only the bachelor's degree fall into the "productive" category may be an indication of the ubiquity of the belief that it is necessary to "publish or perish.")

With regard to the possession of research grants, the table may demonstrate that such grants are not usually for junior faculty members since, at best not over 20 per cent of the subjects have or have had them. In the absence of similar figures for senior staff, this finding is inconclusive. It is apparent, however, that for those junior faculty members who do get them, there is a correlation between attainment of the doctorate and the chance of getting a grant.

For the variables of Category III, which are uncontrolled by the university, positive associations between the possession of advanced degrees and opportunities for professional accomplishment similar to those already seen may be viewed, indicating that whatever the factors of motivation and decision may be which determine the events, they are similarly associated with the attainment of advanced degrees on the part of the individual. In other words, Category III demonstrates that not all of the distinctions existing between the groups of men with different degrees are the consequences of university decision or action.

Table 2 depicts associations between the source of highest academic degree (whatever that degree may be in the case of the individual) and the job factors of Table 1. Since both universities studied are definitely "major" institutions, the institutional sources of degrees listed are "inbred," indicating that the individual has his highest degree from the university where he is employed, "other major" indicating its source at another outstanding school, or "minor" which is a residual category. In Category I, barring only "present rank" (where 41 per cent of men with inbred degrees as against 38 per cent of those with degrees from minor institutions are assistant professors) it is apparent that the junior faculty member is most advantaged by having a degree from a major university other than the one by which he is employed and is most disadvantaged by employment in an institution of which he is the inbred product.

In Category II the dominance of the major university degree is again asserted over those inbred or those from minor institutions in the matter of professional productivity and possession of research grants. The chi square and contingency coefficients of the latter associations are substantial, possession of grants being found in proportions twice as great among individuals with major university degrees as among the inbred or the products of lesser schools.

In Category III only one of the three variables checked distinguishes individuals by the source of their degrees: There is a low (although highly significant) positive association between lack of inbreeding and membership in learned societies. Men may not be distinguished with statistical significance on the basis of

TABLE 2

Institutional Source of Highest Academic Degree Among the Junior
Faculties of Two State Universities, by Various Job Factors
in per cent

Job Factors	Inbred	Minor U.	Other Major U.*	Chi Square	P-Value	Contingency Coefficient
Category I: Totally Controlled by University:						
Present Rank						
Instr. & Other	59	62	35			
Asst. Prof.	41	38	65	9.93	< .01	.12
Total	100	100	100			
N	241	173	261			
Rank, First Appointment						
Instr. & Other	94	78	61			
Asst. Prof.	6	22	39	79.79	<.001	.33
Total	100	100	100			
N	235	171	259			
Years Served in Jr. Rank						
1–6	57	80	81			
7 and over	43	20	19	43.4	<.001	.25
Total	100	100	100			
N	236	173	265			
Annual Class Load#						
1–6	49	62	71			
7 and over	51	38	29	16.7	<.001	.20
Total	100	100	100			
N	153	95	170			
Category II: Partially Controlled by University:						
Productivity†						
Productive	44	44	59			
Unproductive	56	56	41	14.3	<.001	.14
Total	100	100	100			
N	237	173	265			
Possession of Research Grants						
Grants	8	8	16			
No Grants	92	92	84	68.19	<.001	.33
Total	100	100	100			
N	237	173	265			

REECE McGEE

TABLE 2—(Continued)

Institutional Source of Highest Academic Degree Among the Junior
Faculties of Two State Universities, by Various Job Factors
in per cent

Job Factors	Institutional Source of Highest Degree			Chi Square	P-Value	Contingency Coefficient
	Inbred	Minor U.	Other Major U.°			
Category III: Uncontrolled by University: Memberships in Learned Societies						
Memberships	65	72	80			
No Memberships	35	28	20	15.8	<.001	.15
Total	100	100	100			
N	237	173	265			
Offices in Learned Societies						
Offices	19	13	16			
No Offices	81	87	84	3.39	<.20	.07
Total	100	100	100			
N	237	173	265			
Listings in National Reference Works						
Listings	8	7	12			
No Listings	92	93	88	4.61	<.10	.08
Total	100	100	100			
N	237	173	265			

° Defined as including any institution which had granted over one thousand non-medical doctorates by 1956 and including foreign universities in that category.

Expressed on *semester* basis, excluding summer.

† Defined as any publication or presentation directed to a professional audience, and including individual pieces of creativity in the graphic arts as well as literary, musical, and dramatic works.

office in learned societies or listings in national reference works, although the differences in the latter are in the direction we might expect from the evidence above.

Table 3 represents the cross-tabulations of Table 2, this time for men with doctoral degrees only. One of the weaknesses of the former confrontation having been that "highest degree" might mean any of the three here considered, it had seemed possible that some of the relationships exposed (e.g., those appearing to disfavor

REECE McGEE

the inbred) were the consequence of the presence of graduate students in the junior faculty. These being eliminated by the selection for study only of men with doctoral degrees, we may now suppose that any relationships discovered will be more purely the consequences of the dependent variables considered, or of other factors associated with them.

In Category I it may be observed that the inbred and those with doctoral degrees from other major universities share similar proportions (79 and 71 per cent respectively) of individuals in the rank of assistant professor, while only 58 per cent of men from minor institutions hold that rank. The association is significant only at the 10 per cent level; but when we examine the following two "job factors" it becomes clearer: 7 per cent of the inbred were originally appointed at that rank (as against 53 per cent of other major university products) but 64 per cent of the inbred have been members of the junior faculty for seven years or more while only 13 per cent and 10 per cent of men from minor and major universities, respectively, have remained in junior status that long. Class loads are so similar between the three groups that the differences may be equally the result of chance or discrimination.

In Category II differences in productivity among faculty members with the doctorate are negligible (supporting our earlier observation that the association between productivity and advanced degree may be the result of training). With regard to the matter of research grants, it appears to be more advantageous to have a degree from some other major university than to be inbred or to have originated in a minor school. (Note, however, that the contingency coefficiency of this association is relatively low.) In Category III it appears that men with doctoral degrees from minor or other major universities are more likely than the inbred to be members of learned societies but do not differ from them significantly (and, indeed, only little numerically), on other variables.

TABLE 3

Institutional Source of Doctor's Degree Among the Junior Faculties of Two State
Universities by Various Job Factors
in per cent

Job Factors	Institutional Source of Doctor's Degree			Chi Square	P-Value	Contingency Coefficient
	Inbred	Minor U.	Other Major U.[*]			
Category I: Totally Controlled by University						
Present Rank						
Instr. and Other	21	42	29			
Asst. Prof.	79	58	71	5.4	<.10	.14
Total	100	100	100			
N	61	45	148			
Rank, First Appointment						
Instr. & Other	93	58	47			
Asst. Prof.	7	42	53	39.54	<.001	.36
Total	100	100	100			
N	61	45	148			
Years Served in Jr. Rank						
1–6	36	87	90			
7 and over	64	13	10	72.51	<.001	.47
Total	100	100	100			
N	61	45	148			
Annual Class Load#						
1–6	80	91	84			
7 and over	20	9	16	2.33	<.50	.10
Total	100	100	100			
N	61	45	148			
Category II: Partially Controlled by University						
Productivity†						
Productive	72	71	68			
Unproductive	28	29	32	.41	<.90	.04
Total	100	100	100			
N	61	45	148			
Possession of Research Grants						
Grants	10	13	26			
No grants	90	87	74	8.77	<.02	.18
Total	100	100	100			
N	61	45	148			

TABLE 3—(Continued)

Institutional Source of Doctor's Degree Among the Junior Faculties of Two State
Universities by Various Job Factors
in per cent

Job Factors	Institutional Source of Doctor's Degree			Chi Square	P-Value	Contingency Coefficient
	Inbred	Minor U.	Other Major U.°			
Category III: Uncontrolled by University						
Memberships in Learned Societies						
Memberships	67	89	89			
No Memberships	33	11	11	17.60	<.001	.26
Total	100	100	100			
N	61	45	148			
Offices in Learned Socieities						
Offices	21	13	18			
No Offices	79	87	82	.62	<.80	.05
Total	100	100	100			
N	61	45	168			
Listings in National Reference Works						
Listings	20	11	19			
No Listings	80	89	81	1.75	<.50	.08
Total	100	100	100			
N	61	45	168			

° Defined as including any institution which had granted over 1,000 non-medical doctorates by 1956 and including foreign universities in that category.

Expresses on *semester* basis, excluding summer.

† Defined as any publication or presentation directed to a professional audience, and including individual pieces of creativity in the graphic arts as well as literary, musical, and dramatic works.

In summary, it appears that what "everybody knows" about the nature of academic employment is more or less true in a vague and general way; this is probably to be expected in a profession devoted to the creation and communication of ideas and facts. In certain areas where it is not true, (i.e., the necessity for the Ph.D. as a prerequisite for a university appointment), the disparity between the popular knowledge and the actual fact may be the result of recent fluctuations in supply and demand in the academic labor market with which the popular knowledge has not yet caught up, of the general nature of such knowledge, and of simple ignorance of facts. Perhaps this present mapping of such facts may help to dispel that ignorance.

Values and Attitudes of University Professors— Some General and Specific Findings

RICHARD I. EVANS

Apathy and outright hostility on the part of university faculties have seriously jeopardized the growth of television in teaching. However, when professors are given the opportunity to spend a period of time thoroughly experimenting with the medium as a device for improving instruction rather than as a device for teaching larger numbers of students, they may shift toward more favorable attitudes in regard to television instruction. This fact was evident in research currently in progress at a large, urban southwestern university.

Under terms of a Title VII research grant from the U. S. Office of Education, the writer and his research staff are attempting to look objectively at the value systems of professors and the social psychology of attitude change. In particular, we are interested in developing ways of overcoming unwarranted resistance to change in teaching behavior, using resistance to television instruction as an example. Theoretically, the present investigation becomes a field study of the dynamics of attitude change.

Several points of resistance to television instruction are apparent in the findings. For example, most professors have seldom, or never, lectured before colleagues or administrators. Therefore, television instruction is threatening to some, since it would force them to expose their teaching product outside of the classroom.

A psychological instrument, an adaptation of the Osgood semantic differential, was administered to the faculty and yielded expressions of attitudes toward an array of concepts including respondents' attitudes toward the use of television as a function of their own philosophy of education, personality organization, and general background. Ninety per cent of the entire faculty responded. Sixty faculty members most resistant to television instruction and 60 most favorable to television instruction were selected, on the basis of the attitude toward television concept responses, for follow-up depth interviews. Almost all agreed to the interviews. Comparisons between professors positive or negative in their attitudes toward television will be made on the basis of the variables measured in the present study, in order to allow an analysis in depth of this form of resistance to change.

Among the preliminary findings is an indication of the self-image of the professor. Eighty-five per cent of those responding tended to regard themselves as "good" teachers. On continuum scales they regarded themselves as rough, honest, active, fair, strong, fast, pleasant, hard, and valuable. This self-image is interestingly at odds with the student image of most professors.

One question in the interviews, employing a quasi-role-playing technique, concerns the possibility of hiring Charles Van Doren as a university instructor. A majority, acting hypothetically as a university president, would not have hired Van Doren, with the principal response category indicating that they considered his television performances and subsequent testimony "immoral" and at odds with the general ethical code of the professor. Those favoring hiring Van Doren felt, as revealed in the principal response category, that a professor should not be responsible to a university for activity off the campus which did not affect his teaching ability.

Though replies in depth interviews to a group of projective questions tended to indicate that professors, on the whole, have a more equalitarian rather than authoritarian social outlook, upon closer examination, it was discovered that many professors had developed a facade of overt responses which tended to conceal authoritarianism.

With respect to the attempt to change attitudes toward instructional television, two large university departments which previously had been unwilling to participate in television instruction were induced to take

RICHARD I. EVANS

part for one semester in an intensive program for the improvement of teaching by first encouraging them to make extensive use of television and film facilities at the university.

Because of its immediate playback and erasure characteristics, the video tape recorder appeared to be an ideal instrument to be used in this experiment. A maximum opportunity was provided the two departments to explore the improvement of teaching possibilities inherent in the video tape recorder. Staffs of the involved departments prepared several lectures for video tape presentation to general, large-enrollment classes. In addition, each professor privately viewed some of the tapes which he had made, which were not shown to the staff as a whole. Individual and departmental impressions of the project were prepared.

Following the "experimental" semester, the faculty was retested. This experimental situation offered an opportunity to test the hypothesis that such faculty ego-involvement and "cognitive field saturation" with television instruction would be a device to change faculty attitudes. On the basis of preliminary results, the hypothesis was supported—attitudes toward television instruction became more favorable. Behavioral changes are also being noted; some members of the two departments are beginning to employ some television in their instruction.

In addition, responses of the faculty members who utilized the video tape recorder in the present study indicate great promise for it as a device for self-improvement in teaching, a possibly significant educational use of this device aside from its present use in commercial television.

Chapter 9

STUDENT MENTAL HEALTH

the range of personality patterns in a college population

Until the last decade or two, most attention and sophisticated study had been directed to the educative process at pre-college levels. In recent years, however, there has been a growing interest in and study of the personalities, motives, and values of college students, as represented by the other members of this conference, and by numerous other researchers.

The task is more difficult than it might seem at first glance, for many of the most important aspects of personality are inherently value-laden. No one can talk about behavior that has a social impact without making his hearers think, either explicitly or implicitly, about the relative "desirability," or "likability," or "moral goodness" of that behavior. Similarly, when the "inner" psychology of a person is being discussed, sooner or later questions of "happiness," "maturity," or mental health are raised; and these, too, are value judgments. As Smith has pointed out, it is neither possible nor desirable for behavioral scientists to withdraw from the scene when these inescapable value judgments enter.[1] Nonetheless, as scientists we properly worry whether our assessments of people are objective, honest descriptions or whether they are heavily biased by idiosyncracies of personal perception or by culture-bound formulae which may or may not do justice to the facts and the objective consequences of behavior.

This paper describes a current study which, as one of its objectives, is trying to identify and describe the many different kinds of personality patterns to be found

[1] Smith, M. Brewster, "Mental Health" Reconsidered: A Special Case of the Problem of Values in Psychology. *American Psychologist*, 16:6, 209–306, June, 1961.

ROBERT F. PECK

161

among college students. What is more, whether wisely or not, it is trying to meet the problem of defining mental health in terms of positive, effective ways of meeting life, and assessing the degree to which one or another person achieves such effectiveness.

The major purposes of this present report are three-fold:

1. To describe the wide range of mental health to be found in a college population;
2. To illustrate the very different kinds of personality and behavior patterns to be found even at the same level of mental health; and
3. To discuss some implications of the natures and needs of students for their teaching and guidance during college.

The University of Texas Program: "Mental Health in Teacher Education"

Overview

This five-year study is supported by a grant to the College of Education by the Training Branch of the National Institute of Mental Health. Its overall objective is to produce mentally healthy teachers who have good understanding of people, and the ability to teach their subject matter in such a way that they promote *both* efficient learning and good mental health in their pupils

In order to attempt this, we are revising some of the content and some of the teaching methods in certain sections of all the required courses in the teacher preparation program. Provision is also made for considerably more individual counseling than is ordinarily offered to undergraduates. This is closely linked with their course work.

Needless to say, all such procedures are experimental. To test their effects, a multifaceted program of observation and measurement is underway. Pre-post measures of attitude and personality, amounting to some 10–1 hours of testing, are given at the sophomore and senior level, to the "experimental" students and to a comparable "control" sample. Up to now, data have been gath

ROBERT F. PEC

ered on about 2,000 students, of whom about 400 started their sophomore education course as "experimental" students, randomly selected from the total sophomore group.

These data consist of the following instruments: California Psychological Inventory, Mental Health Opinion Scale, Bown Self-Report Inventory, School Situations Analyzer, T.A.T. (group administered, as are all instruments), Peck Biographical Information Form and the Peck Sentence Completion (both in its conventional form, and in a one-word-answer form which we plan to subject to a new kind of computer analysis—psychological rather than statistical). Several other instruments have also been used, once, so that about 500 students have responded to Cattell's 16PF, a revised form of Ryans' Teacher Characteristics Schedule, Heil's Manifold Interest Inventory, the Brown-Holtzman Survey of Study Habits and Attitudes, and Pace's College Characteristics Index.[2] (From the last-named we will derive the students' picture of the University.)

These data are in the process of varied analyses. Distribution statistics are, of course, obtained on all. The several questionnaires have all been factor-analyzed, to identify the basic dimensions they actually measure. The California Psychological Inventory, for example, appears to measure not the 18 scales currently listed in the manual, but only four factorially distinct dimensions.[3] All quantified scores and ratings have been, or are being, intercorrelated. Correlations are planned with the following kinds of data, also.

A staff of observer-recorders is making detailed logs of events in the college classrooms. From these, evidence will be drawn to describe the group process, and also to give behavior anecdotes for selected students.

A sociometric instrument has been developed, and has

[2] Pace, C. Robert, and Stern, George G., "An Approach to the Measurement of Psychological Characteristics of College Environments," *Journal of Educational Psychology*, 49:269–277, October, 1958.

[3] Mitchell, James V. and Pierce-Jones, J., A Factor Analysis of Gough's "California Psychological Inventory," *Journal of Consulting Psychology*, 24:453–456, 1960.

been given to all sophomore, junior, and senior students in the past year. It attempts to gather peer judgments on personality factors (matching those in the rating and questionnaire instruments) and on teaching-related behaviors.

All experimental students, and some controls, are observed twice by a recorder, during their semester of practice teaching. At the end of that semester, the recorders interview each student's supervising professor and cooperating teacher, to obtain a picture of the student's behavior during practice teaching.

Individual "exit" interviews have been held with all experimental students who have finished their senior year, in order to accumulate depth information regarding the impact of the college years. Interviews are also being held with a sample of "controls."

Appraisal of all students in practice teaching, by their pupils, is underway. About 300 practice teachers have been described by about 9000 pupils, thus far, using a descriptive questionnaire which yields factor scores on three dimensions of teaching behavior.

The research plan further calls for intensive on-the-job study of a sample of those students who do go into teaching after they graduate. (This is a small proportion of the original "starters.") Completion-of-college or drop-out statistics, as well as the quality of college performance corrected for aptitude differences, are being correlated with all other data.

First, appropriate synthesis of all these data will ultimately provide adequate validation of various methods for predicting individual behavior, personal adjustment, and teaching performance, we hope. Secondly, it will permit description and analysis of the nature and course of the personality development and attitude changes of all the many kinds of people we lump together as "college students." It is planned to gather comparable data, on a more modest scale, from students in other parts of the University; our present students are chiefly arts and sciences, or education majors. Thirdly, some advances in the basic science of assessment may emerge. Program CAP (Computer Analysis of Personality), now in the

ROBERT F. PECK

planning stage, potentially offers a break-through toward turning the present art of individual assessment into an explicitly defined set of scientific rules and procedures.

The Individual Case Studies

Individual, longitudinal case studies are being made of both experimental and control students. One object is to permit more precise assessment of the impact of college experience on the students. This is a more appropriate method for studying changes in mental health than mass measurement of groups of students. For example, a move toward greater spontaneity might be generally accepted as an improvement in mental health for a student who started out as an excessively shy, self-restricting person; whereas the same change, on the same dimension, might be generally regarded as a regression in mental health for another student who started college as a rather unthinking, unorganized person, given to all-too-free expression of the moment's impulse.

Another purpose is also being pursued: a basic study of the kinds of personalities, and their distribution, in a cross-section of "normal" college students. A great many studies have been made with one or another questionnaire instrument, measuring a score or so of characteristics, at most. Relatively few students have gone to the depth of Murray and few of these have undertaken to study a total college population, even by selective sampling.[4] A great deal remains to be learned about the proportions of different personality types, and different mental health levels, in college populations.

Nine representative students are described below, to illustrate the extremes and the middle of the mental health distribution. The data on which their portraits are based were obtained in the following way. About two years ago, the group they represent were all enrolled in the introductory sophomore course in educational psychology. There were approximately 500 of these students, most majoring in arts and sciences, some

[4] Murray, Henry A., and others, *Explorations in Personality*, New York, Oxford University Press, 1938.

in education. They all responded to a ten-hour testing program which included what we call the "projective battery": the biographical information form, the sentence completion, the School Situations Analyzer, and selected Thematic Apperception Technique pictures. (See the Addendum to this chapter, for details.)

A random sample of 103 students was drawn from this population. Twenty males were included. (The illustrative cases described below are limited to girls simply to avoid the complication of introducing sex-differences in personality, in addition to the other differences among these nine students.) The projective battery of each student was independently analyzed by four judges: Carson McGuire, Robert Peck, Donald Veldman and James Horger. Each judge rated the student on 69 variables of personality, character, and anticipated behavior in later teaching situations. The four judges then discussed the case and prepared a single set of consensus ratings on the 69 scales. Using the correlations of their earlier, independent ratings in the Spearman-Brown formula, the reliability of the consensus ratings may be estimated to exceed .85.

From the 69 scales, 50 were then selected which dealt primarily with traits of personality and character.[5] These 50 scales were correlated and factor-analyzed. A Varimax rotation completed the "boiling down" of 32 of the variables into four distinct personality factors. (The remaining 18 variables cannot be simply explained by these four factors, but represent some additional dimensions of personality.) The composition of the four factors is shown in the Addendum, Table 1.[*]

Individual factor scores were then computed for the 103 students, using the Lackland Multiple Regression Program to derive beta weights. These weights (see Table 1) were multiplied by the student's original ratings, to derive a factor score for each subject, on each factor.

[5] Peck, Robert F., Havighurst, Robert J., et al., *The Psychology of Character Development*, New York, John Wiley, 1960.

[*] Details of this analysis will be given in a forthcoming article by Donald Veldman and Robert Peck. Veldman carried through all statistical analyses on the IBM 650 computer.

ROBERT F. PECK

Thus, four different dimensions of personality were identified:

I. Conscience-ruled stability *vs.* unprincipled impulsiveness
II. Creatively intelligent autonomy *vs.* dull, unthinking dependence
III. Loving affection *vs.* cold hostility
IV. Relaxed, outgoing optimism *vs.* anxious, self-preoccupied pessimism

Another of the original 69 ratings was a summary evaluation of "overall mental health." The four personality factors correlated .40, .54, .27 and .63 with this mental health rating. It is of interest that mental health, at least as seen by these researchers, is not simply defineable by any one of the four factors, but by a combination of all four factors, with considerable variance left over, for some other variables to explain.

The students' scores on these four factors were correlated with their scores on several of the self-report questionnaires. The results, shown in Table 2, 3 and 4 of the Addendum, are a considerable number of correlations in the .25 to .50 range, significant in both a statistical and a psychological sense. Since "public" self-appraisals, as on questionnaires, are by nature less than perfectly valid, a relationship of about this order with the judge-assigned factor scores might be anticipated if the judges' ratings are themselves valid.

Much more direct and objective validation of the personality ratings was desired, of course. For the group as a whole, and for the additional hundred or two students still to be rated, comparisons are to be made with all the other kinds of behavioral data being gathered: observations of college classroom behavior; instructors' interviews and appraisals; peer sociometric descriptions; counseling interviews; descriptions and appraisals of practice teaching behavior by supervising professors, cooperating teachers and pupils; observation records of practice teaching behavior; and exit interviews with the students.

The nine students whose portraits are about to be sketched (with identities disguised), have been thoroughly studied, using all available data from their sophomore through their senior years. The descriptions are organized in the way they were first tentatively prepared from analysis of the projective battery, along with the ratings they were given; but the vignettes are a synthesis of all the facts that could be discovered about them, from all the sources listed above, cross-checked and cross-confirmed to a convincing degree. Needless to say, it is not possible to get the necessary information about all students. Imperfect criterion data remain one of the most stubborn and critical obstacles to the validation of assessments and predictions, from whatever data one starts. These nine girls have been selected because their personalities and behavior patterns are known beyond reasonable doubt.

These brief sketches do not by any means include all the features of any one student's makeup, as need hardly be said. They are merely an effort to convey an overall picture of each girl, touching on a few outstanding characteristics that uniquely mark her behavior pattern. They do not systematically cover the same dimensions of personality in all the cases. On the contrary, their purpose is partly to depict a few of the very different kinds of people to be found in college, and partly to suggest, if only in an impressionistic way, the large number of personal characteristics which no one has yet managed to gather into a comprehensive system for describing and explaining all the different kinds of people in the great melange, the "normal range."

The one common set of measures included in all sketches are the scores on the four rating factors. If anything, this illustrates further what a small segment of personality any small number of dimensions encompasses. Moreover, even in the limited realm of personality characteristics related to mental health or academic performance, which were selected for initial study, some 18 characteristics did not fall within the four-factor system. Since there are unquestionably a large number of

ROBERT F. PECK

personality characteristics which have nothing necessarily to do with mental health, and which consequently were not included for measurement, it is evident that the number of dimensions necessary to describe the personalities of these students is of a large order.

It might be noted that individual descriptions like these, with purely personal information edited out, have been found extremely useful in the teacher education program, when conveyed verbally by a skilled counselor to the student's practice teaching supervisor. Judiciously communicated and judiciously weighed, such insights into the student have made it possible to place students more intelligently, and to guide them with much more precise attention to both strong points and places where they need constructive help. This, at least, is the report of the practice teaching supervisors who have availed themselves of this information.

Personality Sketches of Some Representative Students

Three cases are described below at each of three levels of mental health: low, middle, and high. The object is two-fold: to illustrate, and at least briefly describe, the extremely wide differences in adjustive capacities which occur within what we commonly regard as the "normal" population of college students; and, secondly, to illustrate the great diversity of personality patterns that occur at the same general level of adjustment.

Low Mental Health

The Amateur Call Girl

"Faye" grew up in a coldly hostile, working class home. She frankly is convinced that both her mother and her father "hate her," and she reciprocates this feeling in kind. Bright and observant, she has learned to admire "smart operators." "Work is for suckers," expresses her own view. Yet she recognizes that it is necessary to keep up a socially acceptable front and she has managed to do this, if in an undistinguished way, throughout

ROBERT F. PECK   169

high school and college. She has worked full-time for periods of several months to earn money that her parents would not give her for college expenses.

A pretty girl, she has plenty of male admirers. Her extremely unhappy experience with her father has made her intensely bitter and hostile to men; yet at the same time, she has a very deep craving for male attention and response. Since, in addition, she has a decidedly sensuous capacity to enjoy physical pleasures, it is not surprising that she has a fairly lengthy history of sexual affairs. (She did not quite announce this in so many words, but she has made it plain by repeated, barely veiled references.)

On the other hand, she has quite a stern conscience. She feels intense disgust for herself, frequently, for her feelings of hostility toward her family and others around her, as well as for her sexual promiscuity. The guilt about her hostility is decidely the more emphatic.

Just about the only reason she can see for sticking it out through college is to get a mark of respected status which she only vaguely perceives but powerfully wants. The only goal in life that she is able to define for herself is to do modeling. Apart from that, as she frankly and unhappily states, she has no clear idea what she wants out of life or where she is going.

She has a rather strong streak of perverse anti-conventionalism. She has enough good sense not to indulge this entirely too far, but she does let it slip out often enough to shock and alienate a good many people of her age. She does not want to live a disorderly life or to bring misfortune or punishment on herself. The trouble is that she has passionate hungers which she can't stand to have frustrated for long. She gets intensely angry when she must refrain from indulging her impulses directly. Yet, being a highly complex person, with a vision of what a good life could be, she does exert a good deal of self-discipline much of the time. The problem is that she generally does this after she has gone astray and has learned the penalty of a wayward course "the hard way." She seems likely to settle down realistically into being a responsible worker; but her private life seems all too

ROBERT F. PECK

likely to continue to be an unhappy mess for many years to come.

Her rating on overall mental health was six, next to the bottom of the scale. Her factor scores described her as quite extreme in the direction of unprincipled impulsiveness, and also as coldly hostile. She is not a dependent girl, however, and her better than average imagination and intelligence help to keep her from being more than slightly below average on factor II, intelligent autonomy. On factor IV, though, she was definitely toward the anxious, self-preoccupied pessimism end of the scale.

The Lost One

"Sally" is a tragic example of the lost, lonely child who is struggling to hang on to reality, without anyone's realizing that she is anything other than a "nice, average young girl." She is so unobtrusive, and her lapses from reality-contact are so quiet and undramatic, that almost no one had noticed anything very much amiss in her behavior or adjustment until she happened to be included among the students who were to be intensively studied. She has just about average intelligence for the college population and got through a large urban high school with passing grades, sufficient to admit her to college. By her sophomore year, however, she was failing in her college work. She was not succeeding in much of anything else, either. She lived in a room by herself and belonged to no campus organizations. The latter is an unusual pattern for most girls at the University.

She has always striven hard to live up to the expectations of her parents and friends. These have frequently puzzled and confused her, and left her very unclear about what she should do. Consciously, she pictured herself as being sufficiently liked by other people around her, but it is almost as if she were surrounded by a glass shell. She could see others, and they could see her, but there was almost no real communication of personal feeling or responsiveness, except at a superficial level. She had learned, unfortunately, to avoid and evade efforts to draw her out and get her to express her true feelings and thoughts. She subtly retreated behind a facade of bland clichés and the conventional responses that she knew were expected.

Behind this bland exterior, and at a rather deeply repressed level, there was "confusion, fury, and violence" as she unwittingly revealed in one of the projective situations, in her own words. Technically speaking, she was judged to be in a state of ambulatory schizophrenia, probably moving toward a catatonic psychotic breakdown, with rather strong paranoid undertones.

Her overall mental health rating was at the lowest point on the scale. Her factor scores put her at the average level for affection and kindness of behavior, although this was undoubtedly more by a crude, primitive kind of projective, wistful longing-for-response, than by a mature ability to give love. In a similarly ambiguous way, she received an average score on stability versus impulsiveness, but this was made up of extreme and opposite ratings on the several components of this factor. She was outwardly extremely restrained, but inwardly intensely reactive and unstable in her moods. She had a punitive, though poorly integrated conscience, but her judgment and self-control were so erratic that she already showed signs of pathological lying and near-psychotic irresponsibility in her behavior. Needless to say, she had a very extreme score for anxious, self-preoccupied pessimism.

None of this analysis was communicated to anyone, for a firm commitment had been made at the outset to keep all such information confidential. However, an instructor in another part of the University noted her disorganized thinking and referred her to the Dean of Students and to the Health Center. As far as could be learned, she was diagnosed as extremely disturbed, and counseled to withdraw from college for rest and treatment. She would soon have been suspended for academic failure, in any case. She left the University and has not been heard from since.

ROBERT F. PECK

"Carolyn," unlike either "Faye" or "Sally," generally knows exactly what she wants and moves forcefully and immediately to take it. She is proud of her good looks. She says that people think of her as a "fun-loving, irresponsible party girl." She is quite right, according to her peers' estimate. When she is thwarted, however, she has a viciously ugly side that she has no compunction about exposing. In short, she bears all the hallmarks of the "spoiled brat." She comes from a highly visible, socially ambitious family. Both her mother and father are very active in the highest status cliques in her home town.

Some clues to the family dynamics which might explain her present nature are more than hinted in one of her TAT stories. She describes the death of a girl's parents as they are coming to the hospital. They are going to see their daughter and her husband who have just been horribly injured in an auto accident. At the end of the test she remarked that she liked that picture because "This is the way people are most of the time. News is always surprising to the parents or adults. It reminds me of my parents."

There were so many other evidences of acting-out tendencies, and of just barely unconscious impulses of a violent intensity, that the research staff were moved to suggest the girl be observed rather carefully for signs of forceful antisocial behavior, in the future.

Not all of her acquaintances are "wise" to her. She is an attractive girl and she can be extremely charming whenever she puts her mind to it. She earned election as "most popular girl" in her high school, and was active socially. She had a decidedly above average academic record. Now that she is in college, she is a member of a high status sorority, but is on academic probation.

Most girls can't afford to let it be obvious, but a number of them dislike and distrust her—and rightly so. She is a destructive manipulator when she is challenged or crossed. There was more than one example of her swift and devastating moves to revenge herself when she thought she had been crossed. She demands a great deal of personal attention from whomever she is with. At the same time, she strongly resists any effort to "dominate" her. (There seems little risk that anyone will ever succeed in actually controlling her, let alone dominating her.) When her temper is not getting the best of her (in ordinary social circumstances, she can firmly control her overt behavior), she is an extremely poised, self-confident, and forceful person. She thinks in a highly conventional mode, with conservative, not to say reactionary, values. She does not understand anyone who is different from herself in his specific views or value system. Basically she is a willful, egocentric young woman, with a highly stimulating, forceful personality, who seems likely to impose herself on a great many people throughout life, with little concern or regard for the consequences to them. Since she is violently hostile and vindictive on only slight provocation, her influence is destructive, in human terms, all too often.

She was rated next to the bottom in overall mental health, a little below average on intelligent autonomy and outgoing optimism, below average on capacity for loving affection, and decidedly on the side of unprincipled impulsiveness.

Average Mental Health

The Nice Young Thing

"Sue" is a very likable girl who said more than she probably realized when she said, "What I want to do most is to lead a good Christian life and live up to everything that is expected of me." She does, indeed, conduct herself in a friendly, decently disciplined manner. She trusts authority figures completely, almost fatalistically accepting their directions. Basically she is an extremely passive person. As long as she can earn the pleasures of personal approval by doing what others ask, she is happy. When this does not work, she is almost utterly helpless

She was an average student in high school and active socially. She seems to be in college only because her father wants her to be. She has an unsatisfactory academic average and feels at times that she is "a complete failure to my parents." She suffers a great deal from her poor performances, repeatedly referring to her feelings of inferiority, wounded self-respect, and even a rather sincere conviction of worthlessness, at moments. At the same time, she cannot accept the fact that she might have no more than modest intelligence, in view of the evidence of her grades. As a matter of fact, there is a good deal of evidence that she by no means has inadequate intelligence for college work. There is some evidence that she has considerable unconscious resentment toward her father which might unwittingly influence her study habits and performance. Her real ambition is to "quit school and travel abroad."

To balance the picture, it should be said that in the relatively simple, domestic areas of life she does responsibly and reasonably well anything that she is carefully taught to do. As a member of social organizations she is a dependable attender, if never by any stretch of the imagination a leader. She would never do anything unkind or dishonest. Her character profile showed her to be overwhelmingly of the conforming type; but in that pattern she is quite stable and dependable in trying sincerely to do what the respectable people around her want and approve.

She fell exactly at the middle of the population on overall mental health. Her factor scores showed her to be distinctly above average on conscience-ruled stability, above average on affection, just about average on outgoing optimism and decidedly below average on autonomy, toward the unthinkingly dependent end of that continuum.

The Well Equipped Operator

"Peggy" started out in life as an indulged child. She was voted the "friendliest girl" in her high school and says that she was "always having a good time with no worries about school." She made an excellent academic record in a sizable urban community. Now that she is in college she is earning barely above average grades, has joined a sorority and is active on a number of committees. She rather frankly resents her parents' complaints about her lack of effort in school.

She loves the limelight, and devotes most of her effort toward achieving high social visibility and personal recognition. She has adequate intelligence and can be shrewdly observant, but she tends to be quite lazy in her thinking and prone to biased, subjective judgments. She is complacently self-satisfied, and rather self-indulgent. She might not exhibit her present level of adjustment if she were a long distance from home, or could not turn to her parents at frequent intervals. As it is, she says home is the place where "I release my tensions." This seems very likely indeed.

While she is presently hesitant to accept the responsibility of marriage and motherhood, this seems primarily to come from a reluctance to give up the fun of being a child "free of responsibility." She very much likes to be appreciated by men and seems most likely to "accept" a husband, ultimately, in order to fulfill her wishes for comfort and status. Her narcissism and selfishness are marked enough to suggest that she will expect more indulgence and more praise and appreciation than her efforts and contribution to a family would warrant. Nonetheless, she would probably do her "job" in a reasonably responsible way in the routine of homemaking.

She can be catty, lazy, and act "superior" when things don't please her. On the other hand, if people are nice to her and don't press her very hard, she can be pleasant and cheerful in return. She is never one to fight for an idea or a principle. As she says, "it's not worth it." She would rather go along and be a "good sport." Primarily expedient in her character type, she has the intelligence and surface attractiveness to be a rather successful operator in casual social interaction.

She fell at the middle of the range in overall mental health. Her factor scores showed her to be decidedly above average in relaxed, outgoing optimism, and slightly above average for stability of behavior. She was rated slightly toward the unthinkingly dependent end of factor II and rather decidedly toward the hostile end of factor III.

"Mary Ann" is the second child of lower middle class parents. She had an above average grade record in high school and was active in several school-affiliated organizations, although she held no offices or positions of leadership. In college she has maintained a C average and has no membership in social or campus organizations. As a sophomore she became engaged to a boy two years older than herself, and married him a year and a half later. She continued in college, planning to teach while he completes advanced professional training.

"Mary Ann" is a somewhat shy and insecure person, generally restrained; but she is a quietly stable and sensible girl who places considerable personal value on being useful and helpful to others. She is not really very happy, partly because she is so restrained that she does not have too many effective ways of initiating action to achieve the effects she very much wants to accomplish. She is responsible and sensible in sizing up practical matters and in handling them, although she is not a very enterprising person. She is not one to figure out new ways to get a job done, on her own. Nonetheless, she readily follows the lead set by some responsible person. She does not impress herself very forcefully on anyone, but people her own age, as well as supervisors, find her quietly cooperative and friendly.

She has some mildly warm feelings for children. This, coupled with her desire to be helpfully useful to others, has attracted her toward teaching. She works conscientiously to do the job in a well organized, businesslike manner. She has a strong tendency to go by the rules at all costs, and her somewhat underdeveloped capacity for self-assertiveness, even when she believes in what she is doing, moderately reduces her effectiveness as a teacher below what it might otherwise be.

The one place in her life pattern which is less than satisfactory is not in her outward behavior, but in her inward feelings about life and herself. She feels quietly disappointed in a low-key way, and there is a distinct possibility that unless she is reassured by genuinely interested, personal attention from people she likes and respects, she could easily become progressively disillusioned with life in the years ahead.

Overall, she fell at the middle of the student population in mental health. Her factor scores showed her far above average in conscience-ruled stability; just average on loving affection; slightly below average, toward unthinking dependence; and toward the end of anxious self-preoccupied pessimism. The dominant element in her character structure was judged to be the irrational conscientious component.

High Mental Health

The All-Around Go-Getter

"Hope" is the second oldest of six children in a family where both parents are college graduates, both have been active in politics, and both have been "fighting Liberals." In addition to maintaining a high academic record in high school, Hope was active in extracurricular affairs. She was elected president of her class in a large urban high school, was active in various kinds of public speaking, and in general was regarded as a "natural leader." She has continued this pattern in college, maintaining a high grade average, serving as one of the publication editors on campus, and as chairman of several committees. At the same time, she has worked part-time on campus during the week and assisted in church on weekends.

She is an extremely intelligent, observant young lady whose most striking characteristic, perhaps, is her precocious maturity in her interests and in her way of thinking. Equally impressive is her vigorous, action-oriented striving for creative self-realization. A sturdily independent individual, she is actively and deliberately working to make the utmost use of all her various potentialities, intellectual, social, and esthetic.

This extremely busy pattern of life brings her considerable personal satisfaction. It is so demanding that on occasion she does get slightly weary and slightly cynical about it, but this mood rarely lasts long. She

ROBERT F. PEC

tends to do her major communicating and sharing with other people through the medium of ideas and words. She is just a little remote and restrained in her emotional relations with others. This does not at all reduce her deeply felt and firmly adhered-to sense of responsibility, both in work roles and in her interpersonal relationships.

She is genuinely creative in her use of her imagination. She is still youthfully vulnerable in this spot. If her ideas are rejected, she goes almost into a state of shock and mental immobility for a short time. She has not yet learned to divorce her ideas from her self, and from her personal pride. She is honest and unafraid, nonetheless, and almost defiantly asserts her views, whatever she may think their reception will be. She is not necessarily completely wise in her behavior, and there is enough evidence of underlying anxiety about emotional security to keep her from reaching the top of the scale in mental health. She was actually rated just one step from the top of the scale. Her factor scores put her at the absolute top on creative, intelligent autonomy; just average on loving affection; but above average on conscience-ruled stability, and a little above average on outgoing optimism.

The Happy Homemaker—Plus

"Cynthia" has always "had everything": a loving family, keen intelligence, unusual beauty, an invincibly happy disposition, and a rich capacity to enjoy the diverse pleasures of life. Her childhood, by her own account, was "golden." In high school she enjoyed an active social life while unobtrusively making very high grades. She was chosen for minor offices in several student groups but neither sought nor was put into positions of top leadership.

During her freshman year in college she married a young man who was headed for graduate work in a specialized field of business management. She has carried a full academic load and made an A average. She has also dived into homemaking with exceptional zest and personal pleasure. During her second year of marriage, to be sure, she faced up to the fact that she had married early, partly in order to maintain an unbroken pattern of comfortable family-based security. She now experienced some doubts about the wisdom of her choice; but, having made it, she resolutely decided to turn all her opportunities to good account and firmly suppress any further misgivings.

In a less solidly developed personality, her somewhat Pollyanna-like insistence on looking at nothing but the good side of things might lead to trouble. This would require, however, the presence of rather strong fears or resentments which, accumulated under repression, might eventually break through her composure. In her case, this condition just does not seem to arise, nor does she give it much chance to occur. While her "idealistic" system for making life turn out happily would be far from foolproof for most people, for her it works. There are several reasons for this.

In the first place, her very happy, secure upbringing has given her a deep faith in life, a genuine expectation that it is going to be good, and thus a readiness to recognize and capitalize on whatever good things come along. Moreover, with very little experience of harm in her life, she has unusually few persisting fears or angers from past frustrations. If this were all, she might be naively vulnerable to harm. She also has, however, a keenly practical, open-eyed awareness of what is going on, and a firm, powerful will to achieve control over every situation in which she finds herself. She is not much interested in power for its own sake; but she has no intention of letting events or people thwart her determination to lead a life which is at once happy, respected, and useful. She has a good deal of insight into other people, and is fundamentally honest with herself on major issues.

There is some mild element of expediency in this, at times. Indeed, on one or two occasions people have thought her a "phony," "shallow," or too good to be true. In her classes, her social life and her teaching, however, most people have demonstrated enthusiastic respect and liking for her. One observer noted, "During the hour the class's attention was excellent, and the pupils were

ROBERT F. PECK

eagerly responsive. She was friendly, relaxed and very poised. She seemed to *charm them into learning.*"

During her practice teaching she taught one unit in such a way that she led the pupils from a well planned study of scientific facts to a session of creative writing. At this point the children were inspired to vivid, downright poetic imagery that brought one of those rare moments of spontaneous joy to the classroom, shared freely and delightedly by all.

"Cynthia" plans to teach for three or four years until her husband has finished graduate school and has made a start on his career. Thereafter, she plans to rear a family and "be a good, helpful wife to my husband." In the process, she will undoubtedly continue to indulge her rare capacity to luxuriate in the odors and sounds and sensuous pleasures like "the smell of fresh coffee in a pine kitchen—children tumbling in the yard—a spicy-hot pumpkin pie bubbling in the oven."

Her original ratings put her at the top of the mental health scale. Her personality factor-scores put her at the top on creative autonomy, loving affection, and outgoing optimism. She was rated considerably above average, too, on conscience-ruled stability. Her character structure was judged to be predominantly rational-altruistic.

The Future Queen Mother

"Eleanor" is a remarkably mature young woman for her years. She is so complexly differentiated in her personality that no one view of her tells anything like the whole story. On the one hand she strikes many people as quiet. Yet, underneath her cool self-possession, she is a woman of vivid emotion and powerful vitality. Those who know her well are struck with her quick-wittedness. She is never without a fast "comeback" to a jest, or to life. At the same time, she is very serious-minded about making an unqualified success of her career, her marriage and, indeed, anything she undertakes. She simply does not allow herself to fail; and if she should, she would manage to succeed at something that was closely related.

She is a *thinking* person, to a degree that few people

are. She is willing to face all facts and come to terms with them, and then go on to explore life further. Yet she is far from being a coldly intellectual person. She shows a vivid, vital joy in living, and a real interest in other people.

She is deeply in love with the fellow student whom she married in her senior year. She has arranged all her plans around this marriage. It seems no accident that she shares in common with her husband similar basic values, abilities, and interests. For his part, he appears likely to earn success in his own field, of the kind she finds so necessary to her self-respect.

She has had her share of human difficulties. She comes from a family which is highly respected in the community, but which has suffered more than one severe misfortune due to illness. Her father is a successful man, both in his career and in the community. She has a deep admiration for him. At the same time, at an unconscious level she betrays an element of hurt cynicism where men are concerned, possibly because he left her alone so much since her adolescence began. No doubt stimulated by her admiration for her father, she also shows a latent drive for power that could overwhelm people if it got out of control. One other potential problem is her quick temper, which she rarely shows now, but which she is well aware of possessing. All this being said, one of her chief characteristics is the firm, effective way in which she deals with these problems. For the most part, she simply controls them; in part by sheer strength of character, and in part by her remarkably level-headed, constructive style of acting, leavened by her sense of humor. Such tensions as remain, she expresses through occasional flights of dramatic fantasy which are themselves enjoyable, temporary excursions from the mundane world.

Eleanor shows unusual wisdom for her years, and unusual powers of constructive self-discipline. One can almost foresee her growing into the role of the dowager queen in later life, ruling by sheer strength of character and by unflinching, penetrating honesty. She will not

182   **ROBERT F. PECK**

always be happy, but she will never shirk her responsibilities.

She was ranked at the top of the population on overall mental health. Her personality ratings put her at the head on creatively intelligent autonomy. She was judged far above average, also, for outgoing optimism. Her capacity for loving affection was judged above average, but not outstanding. Her demonstration of conscience-ruled stability was scored above average, also. In character, she was considered an outstanding example of the rational-altruistic person, with a moderate leavening of expediency but almost no ungoverned impulsiveness or irrational conformity.

The Distribution of Personality Types in the Student Body

Faye, Sally, and Carolyn are not typical college students, fortunately. On the other hand, neither are Eleanor, Hope, or Cynthia. In the present study the raters were instructed to assume a normal distribution of all characteristics, in the total population to be rated. In the first 103 cases this kind of distribution has been rather closely approximated. This means that only five or six students out of the sample of 103, whether male or female, are as seriously disturbed or seriously disturbing as the three girls at the lowest end of the mental health scale. By the same token, no more than half a dozen students out of this sample are as well developed and promising as the three girls described at the top end of the scale. The great majority of students fall somewhere in between these extremes, with the average represented by Sue, Peggy, and Mary Ann.

Characteristics of the Low Group

The students with the poorest mental health, represented here by Faye, Sally, and Carolyn, show the following characteristics in common. (In the total sample this group also includes some men.)

1. Many intense, primitively self-centered desires.

2. Strongly conflicting feelings about major aspects of life. The specific nature of the emotions vary from person to person. For example, Faye seems to feel guilt

in conflict with her hunger for affection, whereas Sally feels fear in conflict with her longing for human support. Carolyn appears to suffer chiefly from the conflict between her desire for active response from people, and frustration and anger when they don't give her as much as she wants. In any case, the presence of strong, repeated conflict characterizes this group.

3. Relatively poor forethought and self-discipline. In one way or another, these young people show a short-sighted grasping for satisfaction, or for an imagined "safety" as in the case of Sally, which only leads to losses in the long run.

4. Destructive interpersonal behavior. Whether obviously or subtly, openly or covertly, students such as these flee from, antagonize, or alienate many of the people of their own age. Where evidence on their earlier lives is available, it appears that they learn to act this way in the context of unhappy, mutually frustrating familial relationships.[6]

Characteristics of the Average Group

Sue, Peggy, and Mary Ann represent the average or "typical" student. As in an earlier pilot study,[7] the present data indicate that the majority of college students who fall around and below the mean have the following characteristics in common:

1. They are dependent social conformists. Their life experiences have unavoidably left them with little practiced skill at thinking for themselves, and not much impressive self-assurance or faith to motivate them to try.

2. They get along half-ineptly, on a rather thin diet of human happiness and healthy pride. Although these college students are presumably a highly select subgroup in the American population, a majority of them fall a long way short of the idealized picture, widely held, of the "normal" person as a happy, vigorously pur-

[6] Peck, Robert F., *Measuring the Mental Health of Normal Adults*, Genetic Psychology Monographs, 1959, 60:197–255.
[7] Peck, Robert F., *Personality Patterns of Prospective Teachers. Journal of Experimental Education*, 29:2, pp. 169–175, December, 1960 (b).

ROBERT F. PECK

poseful, clear-thinking person. Their lives little resemble the radiant, joyful existence of the "typical college student" portrayed in our mass media. While the more maladjusted of them can be described in conventional clinical terms of neurosis or even psychosis, most of this half of the college population seem less to suffer from distorted development of their personalities, than from insufficient training and example. The available evidence suggests that the Sues and the Mary Anns of the college world show their relative lack of well-developed skills for living because they have grown up with parents who, with the best will in the world, are able to do little better themselves. Alternatively, an expedient conformist such as Peggy seems to come from parents who themselves know no more than to seek the shallow appearances of human worth and happiness, for want of any deeper understanding or greater skill.

3. Most of them show a pervasive anxiety, of a tolerable but uncomfortable kind. A great deal of this anxiety seems not to stem from guilt over specific transgressions, or fears of desertion by family, as happens in the case of neurotic disorders. Much of the anxiety seems rather to stem from a quite accurate perception on their part that their lives lack shape and purpose. Most of them would have a hard time putting it into words, and they often try hard to hide this painful sense of meaninglessness from themselves, but it becomes evident when they seriously contemplate where they are going in life, and what they hope to find. Rollo May has well described this kind of anxiety.[8]

The existentialists, and a good many other intellectuals in recent years, have attributed such pervasive anxiety to the overshadowing threats of the H-bomb, fear of communist domination of the western world—or vice versa, the uncertainties aroused by the rapidity of technological change, and other society-wide or world-wide phenomena.

Actual study of these students suggests that this sophisticated explanation is almost irrelevant. Very few of

[8] May, Rollo, *The Meaning of Anxiety*, New York, The Ronald Press, 1950.

these young people show any deep personal awareness of international conflicts, any realistic fear of atomic war, or any great anxiety about conflicts at the national or state level. They actually show little deep concern about these issues, which are far removed from their everyday lives. On the contrary, their mental horizons are close and narrow, bounded largely by their families and by the relatively few people with whom they interact meaningfully on the college campus.

If they worry about their inability to shape their lives meaningfully, they usually have good cause in their immediate, personal lives. Their anxiety is essentially a realistic one. They do, in fact, lack the purpose or the skill to set and pursue worthwhile goals.

4. They have the desire and the courage to keep going. Whatever the defects of human support or training they have experienced, whatever their deficiencies of skill or will to shape their own lives meaningfully, these young people do achieve occasional visions of what a fully realized life could be. They wish deeply that there were more success and happiness in their lives than they find, but they do not give up on that account. They find some pleasures, some causes for just pride. Perhaps, above all, they have a hope that the future will somehow be better. However wishful this may be, however ill-buttressed by effective efforts of their own, this hope gives them a downright stubborn persistence in going ahead.

Characteristics of the High Group

The students at the high end of the mental health scale show many differences among themselves in personality and life style, but they also share certain features in common:

1. They are strongly motivated to build self-realizing lives. They seem to be happiest and most successful precisely when they are most vigorously living out one or another of their diverse human capacities.

2. They have diversified personalities, well developed on many sides. Their personal relationships are as deeply important to them as is their intellectual grasp of life.

ROBERT F. PECK

They are effectively active in social affairs of one kind or another; at the same time, they show a good deal of self-insight and take time to become well acquainted with their own inner thoughts, feelings, and needs. They savor the physical pleasures of life with unashamed enjoyment, and yet they are basically disciplined in their behavior, rarely giving vent to a selfish impulse in an unthinking way. Thus, they have developed over a long period of years their physical responsiveness to life, their intellectual inquiry into its meaning, their emotional relationships with other people, and their exploration of their own spirits. Evidence in this study, as elsewhere, suggests that this kind of differentiated development of the many different potentialities of which every human being is capable, is essential for the attainment of full happiness and mental health.

By way of contrast, the apparently "simple" people among the student population turned out upon closer examination to be far from simple in their inherent structure of capacities and needs. If their surface "simplicity" masked repressed needs and unused capacities, as it usually did, they showed many signs of unhappy frustration, often without being able to identify its source. Following the ideas of Carl Jung[9] and Gardner Murphy,[10] the lesson could be drawn from the average and below average student that unused human capacities press for use, for expression and fulfillment; disuse of these capacities leads to active internal stress, discontent or depression.

3. They experience powerful emotions gladly, and find life deeper and richer for it. In part, this is probably because most of their feelings are of a happy or positive kind; but even intense negative feelings, when they occur, do not teach them distrust of the emotional side of life.

4. They think clearly and farsightedly. In this regard, it may be no accident that the healthiest students tend

[9] Jung, Carl, *The Integration of the Personality*, London, Kegan Paul, Trench, Trubner, 1940.
[10] Murphy, Gardner, *Human Potentialities*, New York, Basic Books, 1958.

to have superior intelligence, in most cases. It is true that there are some extremely bright students who are maladjusted, but there seem to be few really fully developed, mature students who do not have intelligence in the upper range of the college population. In short, good intellectual endowment does appear to help considerably in learning to manage life effectively.

In any case, whatever the general level of their intelligence, these healthy students show a richness of imagination and a free, actively applied creativity that rarely occurs among the less well adjusted students. They show this creativity in the various ways the term is commonly understood: unusually effective expression in speech or in writing, imaginative ideas for entertainment or social activities, and the like.

5. They are integrated people. Complex and differentiated though they are, they feel, think, and act in a self-disciplining way that unites thought, feeling, and purpose. Even the healthiest of them may show what would be called a neurotic complex if it were the dominant element in the personality. Eleanor, for instance, could rather accurately be said to have a mild Oedipal conflict that is unresolved. The important thing is that each student's overall personality is so firmly and healthily organized that a good deal of stress can be tolerated at times, or even recurrently in one limited aspect of life, without seriously impairing effective living.

6. They are genuinely ethical in their motives and in their behavior. It is not nearly as much of an effort or a strain for them to treat other people thoughtfully and decently, as it often is for the less adjusted people. One reason is that they have much more unconflicted feelings of liking for people, in general. When other people feel good, they feel good, quite simply and directly. Their character tends to be predominantly of a rational altruistic kind, by reasoned intent and by personal choice.

7. They like other people, and others seek their company. They are effective in their human relationships, in a mutually satisfying way. They may or may not be highly active in a variety of social groups; the important

ROBERT F. PECK

thing is the high quality of their relationships in the groups to which they do belong.

8. These young people, too, have problems. Their lives have in no case been without disappointments or frustrations. Thus, they illustrate that good mental health is not "adjustment" in some sense of static contentment, requiring no effort. On the contrary, good "mental health" is simply a way of talking about a vigorous, continual process of coping effectively with each day's new problems. Hope, Cynthia, and Eleanor demonstrate, too, that good adjustment is an inner quality, not to be measured merely by income, social background, or membership in a high-status sorority. In contrast, less well adjusted Carolyn and Peggy are also highly visible members of much sought-after organizations; but it does not do much to make them deeply happy, nor are they really warmly trusted or deeply liked by the other girls. The motives for social action make a great difference, it appears.

Some Implications of the Study

If all students came to college with an eager thirst for knowledge, a quick grasp of ideas, and firm self-discipline for the voyage of intellectual discovery—*if* this were true, or even nearly true, our traditional ways of managing the efforts of college students would be reasonably workable. Our objective would be attainable: To turn out graduates who for the rest of their lives are vigorous, open-minded seekers of truth, and broadly informed judges of the good and the beautiful in all aspects of life.

The facts seem to be otherwise, however. We have postulated a model of the college student which describes no more than a quarter to a third, perhaps, of our students. The rest are greatly different from this hypothetical model, in their natures and in their needs.

No doubt it is humanly inevitable that our basic model of "the typical college student" has for generations led us to adopt the easiest and the cheapest strategies of teaching and of student guidance.[11] It has not worked.[12, 13] Judging from much evidence, it seems safe to say that there is a great qualitative difference between the extremes of the college population, greater even with regard to mental health than in intellectual ability. To gather 30 students at random into one class, as we commonly do, and treat them as if they were somehow uniform units who would respond similarly to some standard treatment, is clearly to misconceive the nature of the situation. The values, the motivations, even the ability to think in an organized fashion will vary tremendously in such a group.[14] It is undoubtedly cheaper to process students by the thousands, but it simply does not do the job we wish it would do. Much more discriminating attention to the individual characteristics of students is needed if we are to come anywhere near the objectives for which society looks to our colleges.

The present grouping of students into three levels is much too crude to do justice to all the individual differences which distinguish the people within any one group. At least, though, this may be a small improvement on the single, standardized model of "the college student" which has been so long and so widely assumed in practice. A brief review of some salient characteristics of each group may suggest some reasonably specific principles that should inform our choice of teaching strategies in dealing with this particular kind of student.

The Low Mental Health Group

Since the habits of thought of these students are commonly disorganized and ill-directed, and since they never would get much help from their families, only two alternatives seem possible. Either we give them,

[11] Williams, George, *Some of My Best Friends are Professors*, New York, Abelard-Schuman, 1958.

[12] Jacob, Philip E., *Changing Values in College*, New York, Harper, 1957, 174 pp.

[13] Riesman, David, *Constraint and Variety in American Education*, New York, Doubleday Anchor Books, 1958, 174 pp.

[14] Heist, Paul, "Diversity in College Student Characteristics," *Journal of Educational Sociology*, 33:279–291, February, 1960.

ROBERT F. PECK

in school, the intensive support and guidance that is lacking at home, or the service professions should establish criteria which would exclude from their staffs persons who have traits of destructiveness and irresponsibility, such as these prospective leaders show.

With young people in these straits, the very nature of their situation requires that the adult who aspires to help them work out a healthier, more productive way of life must provide not only a great deal of detailed guidance, but must also fulfill the security-giving functions which the parents failed to fulfill. The work of Bettelheim, Redl and others with severely disturbed children offers a close analogy.

The Average Group

This middle-majority of students ask overly simple questions of life and expect overly simple formulae by way of answers. Their relatively stereotyped habits of thinking appear to be due to inadequate parental training. With the best will in the world, they cannot quickly and easily alter this state of affairs. They memorize, they do not question. They take notes and they write, but they do not necessarily understand, nor do they long remember. This is the outcome, that is, as long as these young people encounter the world of ideas primarily through the impersonal medium of large lecture classes, with instructors whose natural interests incline them to communicate with students in a largely impersonal manner. It is a basic fact about these students that before they can learn to care about a new set of ideas, they have to feel a personal interest toward, *and from,* the person who is trying to communicate the ideas. Put negatively, this characteristic reaction can be termed dependent conformity, or subjective, personalistic thinking. Viewed positively, if they are approached on an individual level, with genuine interest in their personal thoughts, feelings, and concerns, such an interest awakens a strong response in them. At the beginning, it is largely an emotional response, a hunger for personal attention; but with patience and clear purpose, students like this can slowly be led to assume modest but increasing amounts of independent thought and work.

It is no use trying to force the pace with these young people. To give them wide freedom of choice at first, without detailed guidance, usually is to paralyze them with anxious indecision, or drive them into defensive irritation with the instructor. What would look like a wonderful freedom to mature students looks like frightening chaos to these average students, at first. They need to be led toward more autonomous habits of thought by small degrees, with plenty of personal encouragement, if they are ever to achieve much growth in this direction.

The High Group

If it were not for the concurrently high opinions of their friends and agemates, and the testimony of psychological evidence quite removed from academic operations, the designation of these students as extremely healthy might be suspect, for the majority of them are a college professor's dream from a purely intellectual standpoint. By comparison with their agemates, in almost every aspect of their lives, these students show firmly entrenched habits of vigorous initiative, clear thinking, objectivity, and foresight. Almost all of them find at least some part of their college studies deeply meaningful and attractive. They are strongly motivated to learn, for in addition to their practical awareness of the utility value of knowledge, they find a keen pleasure in the very process of achieving understanding.

For students such as these, the ideal college program differs markedly from the programs proposed for the other two groups of students. For these people, the following conditions seem desirable: 1. A rich library and an array of informed, stimulating professors, to supply a wide variety and depth of ideas. 2. A loose rein, with wide opportunities to follow their own natural curiosities and interests. 3. Just enough guidance to teach them how to move efficiently and quickly on the track of whatever information they seek. 4. Active, personal support from at least a few inspiring teachers, to show them further

ROBERT F. PECK

horizons than they yet have seen. 5. Challenge, and more challenge, to the utmost limit of their capacities.[15]

If these conditions can be provided, these healthy young people can be expected to make steady progress of exactly the kind we have always posed as our objectives for a broadly liberal college education. While this is scarcely a new suggestion, it may bear noting that these conditions are by no means typical in all college classes. Indeed, observation of a wide range of classes suggests that this is more the exception than the rule. (Williams, 1958)[16] As in the case of the other two groups, although in a different way, our traditional methods of teaching and guiding students may need to be considerably changed.

The Moral of It All

The very idea of any program which requires such arduous and expensive changes in college operation can readily be attacked on grounds of impracticality. The validity of such an argument rests, of course, on the values our society holds. If, as a society, we are content to have college-going largely a social ritual, with smaller and smaller proportions of the ever-increasing mass of students finding deep intellectual challenge and inspiration, then a program such as this is indeed impractical. If, however, we value the lifelong effectiveness of our children as much as American business values the efficiency of its employees, then something like this kind of program becomes practical in the deepest sense. Many aspects of this program are already being carried out in business corporations. Individual assessment, selective placement, carefully individualized developmental guidance, selection of supervisors and trainers, study of effective ways of conducting human groups—all these are already being used by many American corporations.

[15] McConnell, Thomas R., *The Rediscovery of the Gifted Student,* Berkeley, California, The Center for the Study of Higher Education, 1959.

[16] *Op. cit.*

Only such a program in colleges will actually achieve the results we want.

In the end, the issue comes down to a few simple questions. Are we willing to pay the bill? Are we willing to evaluate, select, and place faculty members with the best assessment procedures now available? Are we willing to evaluate and guide students selectively?

Much of the cost of a study like the present one goes into basic research on the proper design and use of procedures. While it is too early yet to make specific proposals with assurance, it does look as though some of the assessment methods and some of the teaching procedures could be applied to advantage in many colleges. They could not be done without any extra cost at all, but a reasonable economy seems quite possible.

College teachers themselves could be chosen with increased discrimination. A great deal of highly skilled, highly expensive effort has been poured into ways of identifying and developing astronauts, jet pilots, business executives, physicists, and salesmen. Perhaps it is time to muster the findings from behavioral science into the service of our own profession. It may be time to marshall our skills to recruit, select, and train some of the very best young people to be found, for careers in college teaching.

References

Heist, Paul, Diversity in College Student Characteristics, *Journal of Educational Sociology* 33:279–291, February 1960. (a)

Jacob, Philip E., *Changing Values in College*, New York, Harper, 1957, 174 pp.

Jung, Carl, *The Integration of the Personality*, London, Kegan Paul, Trench, Trubner, 1940.

May, Rollo, *The Meaning of Anxiety*, New York, The Ronald Press, 1950.

McConnell, Thomas R., *The Rediscovery of the Gifted Student*, Berkeley, California, The Center for the Study of Higher Education, 1959.

Mitchell, James V. and Pierce-Jones, J., A factor analysis of Gough's California Psychological Inventory, *Journal of*

Consulting Psychology, 24:453–456, 1960.

Murphy, Gardner, *Human Potentialities*, New York, Basic Books, 1958.

Murray, Henry A., and others, *Explorations in Personality*, New York, Oxford University Press, 1938, 761 pp.

Newcomb, Theodore M., *Personality and Social Change: Attitude Formation in a Student Community*, New York, Dryden Press, 1943, 225 pp.

Pace, C. Robert, and Stern, George G., An Approach to the Measurement of Psychological Characteristics of College Environments, *Journal of Educational Psychology* 49: 269–277, October, 1958.

Peck, Robert F., *Measuring the Mental Health of Normal Adults*, Genetic Psychology Monographs, 1959, 60:197–255.

Peck, Robert F., Personality Patterns of Prospective Teachers, *Journal of Experimental Education*, 29:2, pp. 169–175, December, 1960.

Peck, Robert F., with Havighurst, R. J., and Cooper, R., Lilienthal, J., and More, D., *The Psychology of Character Development*, New York, John Wiley & Sons, 1960.

Riesman, David, *Constraint and Variety in American Education*, New York, Doubleday Anchor Books, 1958, 174 pp.

Smith, M. Brewster, "Mental Health" Reconsidered: A Special Case of the Problem of Values in Psychology, *American Psychologist*, 16:6, 209–306, June, 1961.

Williams, George, *Some of My Best Friends are Professors*, New York, Abelard-Schuman, 1958.

Addendum

The Projective Battery

A. Thematic Apperception Technique

Eight pictures are used: Murray's 1, 2, 6GF, 8GF, 12F, 19; and Alexander's A-3 and A-5. These are administered in class, using slides.

B. Biographical Information Form (Peck)

A four-page questionnaire, this elicits life history information. It also asks about interests, attitudes, and about major experiences, and plans for the future. This form has been specially adapted for use with prospective teachers.

C. School Situations Analyzer

This instrument, constructed chiefly by Bown, with some

assistance by Barnett, Veldman, and Peck, presents a series of verbal pictures of normal crises that are frequently encountered by teachers. Each situation is followed by a series of open-ended questions or statements to be completed.

D. Peck Sentence Completion

    1. Form 2-D

This is a 90-item form adapted from earlier versions specifically for this study of teaching-relevant attitudes and behavior. The responses can be of any length.

TABLE 1

*Scale Content, Factor Loadings, and Optimum Weights for Scales
Selected to Estimate Four Rating Factors*

Scale	Content	Loading	Beta-Wt.
Factor I	*Conscience-ruled Stability vs. Unprincipled Impulsiveness*		(.94)
8	restrained, calculated judgment vs. impulsive, snap judgment	.820	.158
18	controlled, restrained emotionality vs. loose, impulsive emotionality	.845	.283
20	seldom shows anger vs. often angry, attacking	.737	.117
24	stable mood, little fluctuation vs. labile, changeable mood	.755	.122
31	respectful to authority vs. defiant, rebellious	.693	.030
52	non-amoral character vs. amoral character	.837	.215
53	non-expedient character vs. expedient character	.691	.098
55	irrational-conscientious character vs. non-irrational-conscientious character	.532	.142
Factor II	*Creatively Intelligent Autonomy vs. Dull, Unthinking Dependence*		(.97)
1	full reality, awareness vs. constricted, undifferentiated perception	.857	.144
3	high thought capacity vs. low thought capacity	.864	.212
6	rich, complex fantasy life vs. dull, unimaginative	.738	.066
7	creatively productive vs. little creative expression	.857	.156

ROBERT F. PECK

TABLE 1 (Continued)

*Scale Content, Factor Loadings, and Optimum Weights for Scales
Selected to Estimate Four Rating Factors*

Scale	Content	Loading	Beta-Wt.
11	intense reactivity vs. mild or shallow emotional reactivity	.610	.224
29	dominant, ascendant, competitive vs. submissive, following, yielding	.761	.000
37	insightful regarding others vs. unskilled in analyzing motives	.750	.055
38	socially shrewd and knowledgeable vs. socially naive and unthinking	.684	—.026
39	self-directing, independent vs. dependent, little initiative	.840	.163
42	self-insightful vs. little self-insight	.722	.020
45	persistent, tenacious vs. quitting, gives up easily	.736	.045
54	non-conforming character vs. conforming character	.680	.097
56	rational-altruistic character vs. non-rational-altruistic character	.645	.062
Factor III	*Loving vs. Coldly Hostile*		(.81)
21	affectionate, kind vs. undemonstrative of affection	.752	.470
68	strong identification with children vs. little identification with children	.736	.421
Factor IV	*Relaxed, Outgoing Optimism vs. Anxious, Self-preoccupied Pessimism*		(.91)
14	relaxed, comfortable emotionality vs. anxious, many specific fears	.814	.223
16	elation, hopefulness vs. depression, hopelessness	.798	.310
19	composed, relaxed vs. fearful, tense	.785	.268
22	proud, self-satisfied vs. ashamed, self-critical	.719	.274
23	optimistic, cheerful vs. pessimistic, sour	.711	—.086
25	basic trust vs. distrust of people and life	.719	.000
26	socially adaptable vs. socially unadaptable	.621	—.269
27	socially outgoing vs. isolated, withdrawn	.697	.278
32	positive regard for family vs. negative attitude toward family	.664	.051

TABLE 2

Correlations of Rating-Factors with Survey of Study Habits and Attitudes,
Bown Self-Report Inventory, Mental Health Opinion Scale

Test	Scale	Factor Scores I	II	III	IV
SSHA	Scholastic Motivation	318†	285†	—035	182
SSHA	Study Habits	429†	179	099	142
SSHA	Educational Philosophy	166	120	—153	005
SSHA	Teacher Valuation	218°	096	072	—018
SSHA	Achievement Drive	434†	167	—017	139
SSHA	Procrastination Orientation	329†	181	—155	116
SSHA	Self-confidence	171	433†	—091	256†
SRI-1	Self	185	214°	096	373†
SRI-1	Others	187	029	378†	297†
SRI-1	Children	162	—034	191	056
SRI-1	Authority	390†	023	315†	329†
SRI-1	Work	274†	042	110	172
SRI-1	Reality	252†	152	060	254†
SRI-1	Total	349†	102	285†	359†
MHOS	Total (Part 1 + Part 2)	115	514†	069	007

N = 87 subjects, since one or another instrument was missing for 16 subjects.
† = Significant at .01 level.   ° = Significant at .05 level.

TABLE 3

Correlations Between Rating-Factor Variables and
California Psychological Inventory Scales

Scale	Meaning	Factor Variables I	II	III	IV
Do	Dominance	235°	315†	184	308†
Cs	Capacity for status	094	220°	035	393†
Sy	Sociability	137	210°	264†	436†
Sp	Social presence	—043	138	055	236°
Sa	Self-acceptance	—034	216°	156	324†
Wb	Sense of well-being	402†	—021	118	112
Re	Responsibility	369†	221	082	028
So	Socialization	540†	—018	256†	236°
Sc	Self-control	411†	—007	—029	027
To	Tolerance	385†	145	062	122
Gi	Good impression	380†	—025	153	141
Cm	Communality	220°	—013	234°	083
Ac	Achievement via conformance	388†	055	064	251†
Ai	Achievement via independence	170	157	034	—010
Ie	Intellectual efficiency	274†	230°	060	137
Py	Psychological-mindedness	130	258†	—113	082
Fx	Flexibility	—115	—003	103	—034
Fe	Femininity	137	006	148	—027

N = 112.   ° = Significant at .05 level.   † = Significant at .01 level.

ROBERT F. PECK

TABLE 4

Correlations of Rating-Factors with Cattell 16PF Second-Order Factors

Cattell 16 PF	Rating Factor			
	I	II	III	IV
Anxiety Second-order Factor	—351†	—096	—161	—325†
Introversion Second-order Factor	080	153	—289†	—335†
Scholastic Performance Prediction	427†	021	038	086
N = 90.				

Some Questions Submitted In Advance of the Symposium

How have other colleges and universities studied themselves to discover something of their institutional self-concept? What are some of the outcomes which have been attained through efforts to evolve new self-concepts?

How can a college effectively study itself? What have other institutions done along this line?

Is pre-admission testing for emotional stability a justifiable procedure in college? To what extent is the college responsible for identifying emotionally disturbed students? Admitting them? Treating them?

How does the organizational structure of the college and also its self-concept affect the personality development of students?

PART III

Chapter 10

STUDENT CULTURES AND ADMINISTRATIVE ACTION

I

College administrators and sociologists of higher education have much in common these days. For one thing, we are both trying to understand and grapple with the enormous demands that are being placed on American higher education. And foremost among these is the demand that within the next decade it provide places for roughly twice as many college students as are currently enrolled and three times as many as were enrolled in 1950. Now, I do not mean to add to the mountain of literature about the growth of the college population. We all know the figures, at least approximately, and we all experience their meaning daily in our offices and classrooms. But while we may avoid speaking directly about the expansion of higher education in America, the brute fact is always in the background, as a force and movement which influences everything we say or do about our colleges.

Perhaps most significantly, the facts of institutional growth tend to dominate our attention, absorb our energies and our capacities to plan and thus to control the future of our institutions. This is most evident in our public colleges and universities, which are absorbing the bulk—over three-quarters—of the increased enrollments. In a state like California, and I suspect this is true here in Texas as well, the sheer provision of facilities—the problems of building, faculty recruitment, fi-

* Paper read at the Southwest Institute on Institutional Research, sponsored by the Southern Regional Education Board, Austin, Texas, July 19–22, 1961. A large portion of this paper is drawn from a chapter in *The Study of College Peer Groups, Problems and Prospects for Research*, edited by T. M. Newcomb and E. K. Wilson. Social Science Research Council, forthcoming.

MARTIN TROW

nancing, and organization—are so pressing that most of the time and energies of educational planners are enlisted in meeting them.

Now, the primacy of problems flowing directly from the expansion of higher education—the growth of plant, the provision of facilities and services, the recruitment of faculty, and the raising of money—is wholly understandable. And if somewhat more subtle, or at least less immediately pressing, problems and issues in higher education get less than adequate attention, that also is understandable. It is hard to design an irrigation system, or worry about soil erosion, in the middle of a flood.

And here is where social scientists may be of some use, and for precisely the reason that makes us so often irritating to educational administrators. It is that we are essentially observers rather than actors, that in our ivory towers the sound of the flood is audible but not deafening, that we experience it as an idea rather than as an immediate problem, and that we are thus more able to think about its implications for the present and the future. It is somewhat risky for a bystander to interrupt a group of men who are piling sandbags on a levee with some observations on the circumstances of climate and terrain that make for floods, and some reflections on their long range consequences for the fertility of the land and the beauty of the region. But I think that the Southern Regional Education Board is to be praised for arranging such periodic interruptions and for its steady commitment to the dialogue between social scientists and administrators in higher education.

This morning I would like to talk about two things: about the life of students in college, and about the ways student life influences and is influenced by the nature of the institutions in which they are pursuing (or passively enduring) their higher education. I would like first to describe and characterize some broad patterns of student culture on American college campuses, and next draw some implications from this description for the planning and organization of higher education. In these remarks I will be drawing on research currently in progress at

MARTIN TROW

the Center for the Study of Higher Education at Berkeley.

II

Let us look first at the dominant forms that student subcultures take on American campuses. As a first approximation, we can distinguish four broad patterns of orientation toward college which give content and meaning to the informal relations of students. When these patterns of orientation define patterns of behavior, sentiment, and relationship, we can usefully think of them as subcultures. The names we have given to them are the collegiate, the academic, the vocational, and the nonconformist.

Collegiate Culture

The most widely held stereotype of college life pictures the "collegiate culture," a world of football, fraternities and sororities, dates, cars and drinking, and campus fun. And a good deal of student life on many campuses revolves around the collegiate culture; it both provides substance for the stereotypes of movies and cartoons and models itself on those stereotypes. In content, this system of values and activities is not hostile to the college, to which, in fact, it generates strong loyalties and attachments. It is, however, indifferent and resistent to *serious* demands emanating from the faculty, or parts of it, for an involvement with ideas and issues over and above that required to gain the diploma. This culture is characteristically middle and upper middle class—it takes money and leisure to pursue the busy round of social activities—and flourishes on, though is by no means confined to, the resident campuses of big state universities. Part-time work, intense vocational interests, an urban location, commuter students, all work *against* the full flowering of a collegiate subculture, as do student aspirations for graduate or professional school, or more generally, serious intellectual or professional interests on the part of students and faculty.

Vocational Culture

The countervailing forces of student poverty and vocationalism, on the one hand, and serious intellectual or academic interests on the other, are strong enough on many American campuses which differ in many other respects, to make the collegiate culture relatively weak. In the urban colleges which recruit the ambitious, mobility oriented sons and daughters of working and lower middle class homes, there is simply not enough time or money to support the expensive frivolities of the collegiate culture. To these students, many of them married, most of them working anywhere from 20 to 40 hours a week, college is largely "off-the-job training," an organization of courses and credits leading to a diploma and a better job than they could otherwise command. These students have very little attachment to the college where they buy their education somewhat as one buys groceries. But like the collegiate culture, these students, for whom college is an adjunct to the world of jobs, are also resistant to intellectual demands on them beyond what is required to pass the course. To many of these hard-driven students, ideas and scholarship are as much a luxury (and distraction) as are sports and fraternities. If the symbol of the collegiate culture is the football and fraternity weekend, the symbol of this vocationally oriented college culture is the student placement office.

Academic Culture

Present on every college campus, although dominant on some while marginal and almost invisible on others, is the subculture of serious students, the academic culture. The essence of this system of values is its identification with the intellectual concerns of the serious faculty members. Where the collegiates pursue fun, and the job-oriented pursue skills and a diploma, these students pursue knowledge; their symbols are the library and laboratory and seminar. For these students, their attachment to the college, which may be as strong as among the collegiate crowd, is to the institution which

MARTIN TROW

supports intellectual values and opportunities for learning; the emotional tie is through the faculty to the college, and through the friends of similar mind and temper made in college. These students are often oriented toward vocations, but not so directly or narrowly as are the lower and lower middle class commuters who hold the "consumer-vocational" values described above: in any case, it is not necessary to decide whether they are concerned with their studies more because of their career ambitions or for the sake of learning. The distinctive qualities of this group are (a) they are seriously involved in their course work *beyond* the minimum required for passing and graduation, and (b) they identify themselves with their college and its faculty.

Nonconformist Culture

It is in this latter respect, identification with the college, that "non-conformist," "intellectual," "alienated" students differ from their serious academic classmates. Some kind of self-consciously non-conformist student subculture exists in many of the best small liberal arts colleges, and among the undergraduates in the leading universities. These students are often deeply involved with ideas, both the ideas they encounter in their classrooms, and those that are current in the wider society of adult art, literature, and politics. To a much greater degree than their academically oriented classmates, these students use off-campus groups and currents of thought as points of reference over against the official college culture in their strategy of independence and criticism. The distinctive quality of this student style is a rather aggressive nonconformism, a critical detachment from the college they attend and its faculty (though this often conceals a strong ambivalence), and a generalized hostility to the college administration. The forms this style takes vary from campus to campus, but where it exists it has a visibility and influence far beyond its usually tiny and fluid "membership." Its chief significance is that it offers a genuine alternative, if only a temporary one, to the rebellious student seeking a distinctive identity in keeping with his own temperament and experience; in a sense it provides some intellectual content and meaning to the idealism and rebelliousness generated in adolescence in some parts of American society. Where the preceding three types of students pursue fun, a diploma, and knowledge, respectively, these students pursue an identity, not as a by-product, but as the primary and often self-conscious aim of their education. And their symbol is a distinctive *style*—of dress, speech, attitude—that itself represents the identity they seek.

The types of student value systems and subcultures we have been describing emerge from the combination of two variables: (a) the degree students are involved with ideas, and (b) the extent to which students identify with their college. If we dichotomize these variables, the above four types of student orientations (which, as we noted, provide the *content* of the most important and distinguishable student subcultures) emerge thus:

Involved with ideas

		+	—
Identify with their college	+	1	2
	—	3	4

1. The academic subculture
2. The collegiate subculture
3. The nonconformist subculture
4. The vocational subculture

I want to emphasize that these are types of subcultures and not types of students, despite the fact that we often describe these subcultures by characterizing their members. An individual student may well participate in more than one of the subcultures available on his campus, though in most cases one of them will embody his dominant orientation—will be, so to speak, his normative home on campus. These subcultures are fluid systems of norms and values which overlap and flow into one another on any particular campus in ways that challenge the effort to distinguish them analytically. Yet that effort, for all the violence it does to the complexity of social life, appears justified by the congruence of these types with observed reality, and by the light it sheds not only on student subcultures themselves, but on colleges as social organizations embedded in a larger social structure.

This elementary typology of student subcultures allows us to raise a number of questions relevant both to basic research and knowledge about higher education, and also to educational practice and planning.

1. In what strengths and combinations are these orientations found in different types of colleges? Among the 9000 undergraduates on the Berkeley campus of the University of California, all these systems of values are represented, and in some strength with perhaps the collegiate dominant; while among the equally large number at San Francisco State College, the collegiate subculture is almost wholly absent and the academic and nonconformist subcultures are weak as compared with the dominant "consumer-vocational" orientations of the great majority. At academically elite schools such as Reed and Swarthmore, the academic subculture is clearly dominant, with nonconformist values represented, while both the consumer-vocational and the collegiate are less strong and visible. And we can think without difficulty of schools where the older collegiate values still reign supreme, tempered perhaps by an academically oriented minority, with the leaven of nonconformists almost wholly absent.

2. What are the social characteristics of the typical members of these different subcultures; where in the social structure do they come from, and what are the links between their shared life experience and their college styles and orientations? There are distinctive patterns of life experience that heavily condition the qualities and characteristics that students bring with them to college; the question is, *what* are the important qualities, and what are their sources? Behind the patterns of life experiences lie social class, parental occupation and education, racial and ethnic ties, and religious identi-

fications; it is the subcultures in the general population, with *their* values and orientations and aspirations, that shape the orientations most students initially assume toward college.

3. How do these biographical linkages differ in different kinds of colleges? We have already suggested the connections between lower and lower middle class origins, strong mobility aspirations, and the consumer-vocational orientation. But some students thus oriented will find themselves in a minority, in an Ivy League college for example, while others will find themselves among the majority in, say, a municipal college. How do these similar students deal with their college experience in these quite different situations?

4. What are the historical and structural characteristics of colleges that affect the character of their "cultural mix?" The purpose of an institution, its historical traditions, its size and rate of growth, its sources of funds and faculty, its physical location, the images of it held in different parts of the population—these and other factors shape the character of student life within a college. The task we are grappling with is to specify *how* these forces operate, in conjunction with the forces in the larger society that shape the college's raw material and receive its products.

As I suggested, those are essentially research questions, questions which are of interest largely independent of the educational values of those who ask them. It is when we ask the question most relevant to immediate educational policy and practice that value positions cannot be avoided. That question can be put this way: how may a college attempt purposefully to affect the relative strengths of the various student subcultures represented on its campus? This question presupposes first that the college have some sense of its own educational purposes, have some idea of what kinds of cultural environments it wishes to provide for its students, and is prepared to act in the service of those purposes. Not every college has such purposes or is prepared to act on them. There is a strong tradition, especially in some parts of public higher education in America, which prescribes that the central function of the college is to *serve* the community, rather than "impose" some conception of education on those who come to it.

This conception of service is variously interpreted, but in most cases where it is strong, it tends to reduce the autonomy of the institution, its freedom to define its own goals and to act on them, and to assign to the students, that is, the clients or customers, the chief role in defining the nature of their own experience in college. And where a college defines its function as the provision of expert educational *services* to a body of clients or customers, it is not able to formulate educational purposes, independent of and even at variance with the purposes and interests of its students, their parents, and adult representatives.

Now, I do not wish to debate these alternative educational philosophies; moreover, even to state them in this way is to exaggerate their polarity. I have suggested that the doctrine of "community service" can be and is variously interpreted—and where it is interpreted as a service to the broader and more long-range interests of the commonweal, it is perfectly compatible with the formulation and pursuit of autonomous educational purposes at variance with the immediate wishes of the students and the community. Nevertheless, whatever the relative merits of these different educational philosophies, my remarks now presuppose some measure of institutional autonomy, the ability and readiness of an institution to pursue its own purposes and shape its own character. If that is not present to a significant degree, then the "cultural mix" within a student body may certainly be a matter of *interest* to faculty and administration, but its character will be shaped by forces in the community and the larger society over which the institution will exert little control.

Moreover, my remarks are also predicated on the assumption that American colleges and universities, even technical colleges and professional schools, want to do more than equip students with salable vocational skills or social graces, but wish to contribute in some degree to their liberal education—to the extension of their intellectual horizons and the strengthening of their capacities for independent judgment. This means that we are interested in encouraging students to take an active and lively interest in ideas (in the broadest sense of the word), and to learn something of the intrinsic rewards of the intellectual life. And this in turn means that as educators we have a special concern for student cultures that contribute to and support such interests. We do not have to encourage vocational or collegiate subcultures on our campuses—there are many other forces in the society that do that most effectively. But we do have to concern ourselves with the existence and strength of the academic, and to some extent with the nonconformist, subcultures among our students, for it is in them that *our* interests in the students' intellectual growth link with and are supported by the values and interests of the students themselves. Half a century ago, Woodrow Wilson, then President of Princeton University, observed that:

The real intellectual life of a body of undergraduates, if there be any, manifests itself, not in the classrooms, but in what they do and talk of and set before themselves as their favorite objects between classes and lectures. You will see the true life of a college . . . where youths get together and let themselves go upon their favorite themes—in the effect their studies have upon them when no compulsion of any kind is on them, and they are not thinking to be called to a reckoning of what they know.

But it is not enough for us to be concerned with the character of the informal life of students—in Wilson's words, "what they do and talk of and set before themselves as their favorite objects between classes and lectures," in their several subcultures. We must also be alert to the *conditions* within institutions which encourage those student subcultures that promote an interest in ideas and learning, and conversely, with the conditions which undercut and weaken those fruitful informal groupings and relationships.

There are many forces that affect student life, and what I have called the "cultural mix," on a given campus. Some of these, perhaps the most important, lie outside the institution and are beyond its influence. For example, there is considerable evidence that the collegiate subculture is on the decline in American colleges as a result of long-range trends in the society at large. Three of these changes in the society, which we can summarize as the professionalization of occupations, the bureaucratization of organizations, and the democratization of higher education, all work against the playful irresponsibility, the youthfulness, of the collegiate culture. Increasing numbers of undergraduates go on to graduate and professional schools or to jobs in large organizations, as higher education becomes increasingly closely linked to the occupational structure, and thus a prerequisite to social mobility. And both graduate schools and the personnel offices of large organizations take an active interest in the students' academic records, an interest that tends to encourage a more sober tone among students, increases their concern both with their grades and with the acquisition of useful skills and knowledge, and thus strengthens the vocational at the expense of the collegiate orientations. And these trends are reinforced by the larger numbers of students from lower social and economic strata who cannot afford the luxury of collegiate playfulness, and who are especially concerned with social advancement.

But while the educational orientations of college students across the country are heavily influenced by broad social and economic trends of the kind I've mentioned, the situation on any *given* campus can be influenced by the institution, its administration, and faculty. I would like now to speak of just one of the ways that an institution can deal with the character of student life on its campus—specifically, through how it deals with the educational influence of its own size and complexity. (And we can see, in the not very distant background, the relevance of my earlier remarks about the college population explosion.)

III

To anticipate briefly what I shall be saying: rapid growth and large scale in higher education tend to work against the development and maintenance of informal student cultures which are seriously interested in ideas and learning for their own sakes. What can be done about that?

The trend in western society toward increasing size and complexity in formal organization is nowhere more apparent than in American higher education: a large college before the Civil War had 600 students and most were much smaller, while today central campuses of state universities run to 20,000. Large scale in college organization is permanently with us, campuses of over several thousand students will soon accommodate the overwhelming majority of college students. For the form and content of student life, nothing appears to be of greater consequence.

In almost any large organization that works on people rather than on products, thousands of individuals must be routinely admitted, classified, treated, and ejected. This is generally done by routinizing procedures and processing people in batches; in the large college or university, impersonal processing is reflected in the registration line, the objective test, and the mass graduation. With increasing size, there is also a general tendency for the faculty member to work on more students in the classroom than ever before, and to interact less with the individual student outside the classroom; with the TV camera and taped lecture, students may need a special appointment in order to meet the man. This mass processing does not seem to encourage a serious concern with ideas on the part of most students. Routinized class work, for example, can be done without serious thought. The tendency for increasing size to weaken social ties, turning groups into aggregations, promotes the atomized vocational subcultures. And, conversely, vocationalism encourages growth in the size and complexity of colleges and universities. Business associations, professional bodies, and other interest groups that see the college as a training center encourage them to proliferate vocational courses; parents and students aiming for upward mobility seek broad admissions and occupational preparation in a host of fields. Occupational training in a complex society is indeed efficiently handled by large enterprises tooled to train large numbers in diverse fields; liberal education fares less well.

If increasing scale primarily promotes vocational subcultures in the student body, it secondarily supports the continuation of the collegiate life, this principally through a weakened connection between the academic curriculum and the students' social life. Large scale tends to separate work from nonwork, teaching and learning from what goes on outside the lecture hall. Student life then develops aside from the academic structures, its content filled in by student interests. In a society where intellectual values have a marginal existence, it is not to be expected that the interests of the majority of entering students are intellectual; and many of those so inclined seek the small schools that have a liberal arts image. Those finding their way to the large institutions have predominantly a vocational interest; but some will be additionally inclined to have fun, college-style, before work and marriage. The collegiate world, in its less rah-rah forms, will continue to receive some administrative support in the very large places if for no other reason than that it helps the administration to handle the overwhelming problems of student housing and social life. The collegiate life also helps to soften the harsh contours of vocationalism, offering some leisurely play around the edges of the campus, and making the large college appear more like its smaller, historical antecedents.

There is less of this impersonal processing of students in smaller colleges, which are more likely to resemble communities. Size and student residence appear to be the most important determinants of where colleges fall along a continuum from community to bureaucracy. At the extreme of community, approached principally through small size and residential facilities, the interaction of students, faculty, and administration is intense and informal; faculty and students respond to one another as personalities. The individual is known across the system; for example, a death is a campus event. Importantly, *social and academic activity are integrated.* Here the faculty has some chance to shape student culture and educate liberally through personal influence and example. But for occupational training in a complex society, such colleges are expensive, inappropriately oriented, and relatively unspecialized.

The bureaucratic end of the continuum is reached chiefly through large size and off-campus living. Here relationships are formal and segmented, and academic activity is separated from social relationships. Teaching and studying are jobs, the personality of the student is little involved, and death is an announcement in the newspaper. These conditions are not usually as favorable for liberal education as for occupational training, although such a college *can* offer expert instruction and service in a large number of fields.

IV

Up to this point, I have been distinguishing between large and small institutions. The absolute size of colleges and universities may be a seriously misleading factor, however, because its effect on interpersonal relations and student cultures changes markedly with the nature of the *organization substructure.* Harvard's House system clearly "reduces" its size, and some state universities are psychologically and socially smaller than others of similar size because of the way that campus subunits ("colleges," "houses" and the like) substructure an otherwise loose aggregation. An effective substructure provides groups small enough to encourage networks of face-to-face relationships, and to prevent the "we-they" dichotomy between the students and the faculty that we find typically in large scale institutions. It offers systems of action that are within the human scale of observation and understanding, especially the limited scale of the adolescent and inexperienced adult. At the same time, when the smaller units are part of a large college, the larger setting may also offer a rich and varied environment in which students can explore a wide range of experiences.

In the main, colleges and universities whose size and impersonality threaten the existence of student cultures, especially the academic, have attempted little substructuring along any lines. Faculties have not been markedly interested, their attention diverted by other commitments, while college managements and outside supporters have held to logics of economy and efficiency that favor standardized procedures. College comptrollers, for example, simply do not like to work with diversely organized subunits. At the same time, many small colleges worry about the consequences of large size every time they contemplate expanding by one or two hundred students, concerned that the character of the campus, especially the closeness of personal relations, will be changed. One answer now being offered to the problem of how to grow and yet stay small is a federation of colleges—essentially a multiplication of small, distinct units rather than the continued growth of one. The five colleges of the Pomona-Claremont complex in Southern California are one such example; Wesleyan University's new "College Plan" is another.* Wesleyan is attempting a reorganization that will allow the enterprise as a whole to grow larger, while newly established "colleges" involve the student in smaller systems of activity focused on a set of related disciplines. Of course, all universities have units called colleges, but in most cases these are largely paper assignments for students. Substructuring makes a difference when it changes the nature of the student's relationships, both with other students and with faculty. A set of sub-colleges on a comprehensive campus may enable students and faculty to keep one another in view and to share some academic interests, and these are important conditions for the maintenance of academic student cultures in a society where collegiate fun and vocationalism come naturally.

The organization of the college as a community has

* See *The College Plan*, a Report of the Subcommittee of the Educational Policy Committee of the Faculty, Wesleyan University, 1958. (Mimeo.)

profound effects on student life in ways that have been given too little consideration by administrators and too little study by scholars. The possibilities in this respect vary with circumstances; a residential college can purposefully shape its own internal organization in ways that a commuter college cannot; a college of ten thousand has problems unknown to the college with a thousand students. Nevertheless, what we have said about the effects of size and impersonality, of the dilution of intellectual interests among great numbers of students and their neglect by a faculty which deals with students fleetingly and in the mass, suggests that structural innovations working against these anti-intellectual forces might contribute to the growth and maintenance of academic and intellectual subcultures among at least a significant minority of students. The main thing is to get such students together so that they can stimulate and support one another's often precarious commitments, and to provide direct and personal encouragement and rewards for such commitments by similarly committed faculty members. This requires serious effort by the administration and at least a part of the faculty to minimize the "people processing" aspects of mass higher education. I have suggested that the effective size of an institution can be reduced, even without a reduction of its absolute enrollment, by creating what are in effect distinctive smaller communities within the larger organization, communities which include both students and faculty, which have a sense of identity, and above all whose members share interests and commitments which can be supported and furthered, rather than diluted and discouraged, through the ordinary ongoing relations of the members of the community. Such communities cannot be called into being by proclamation; they have to have structural definition and support, formal membership, physical place for meeting and working, and insulation against distracting and competitive interests and appeals. They must be small enough to allow members to know one another personally and as wholes; they must be stable enough to allow patterns of sentiment, identi-

MARTIN TROW

fication, interaction, and intellectual support to develop; they must be reasonably homogeneous with respect to the values and interests represented so that members can center their relationships around these shared and developing interests, rather than, as in the collegiate cultures, around the static interests in pop tunes, automobiles, and dates which comprise the lowest common denominator of student life. In short, these have to be genuine intellectual communities, rooted in residence halls and groups of departments, or in some other combination of structured interactions and shared intellectual interests. In colleges like Swarthmore and Reed, where the academic subcultures pervade the entire student body, the residence halls themselves come to define these academic communities, especially after self-selection has increased the homogeneity of interest and temperament within them. In colleges and universities where the academic values are by no means predominant, but compete with vigorous collegiate and vocational orientations, the division of a student body in the residence halls may simply reproduce the heterogeneous and atomized mass of students in smaller units: the structural definition of a community is present, but not the essential sharing of interests and values. That, at least, seems to be the case on most large state university campuses.

Residence halls may or may not take on the characteristics of a genuine community; the bigger they are, the faster the turnover of students in them, the more heterogeneous the students' interests and fields of study, the less likely they are to be anything but dormitories where students are linked to one another through the lowest common denominators of the collegiate culture. But where residence units are smaller, where students have greater freedom to select their hall, where the hall acquires a distinctive image and character and thus attracts students of similar interests and values, and above all where the intellectual life of the campus penetrates the residence halls, through such devices as having faculty fellows attached to the halls, and libraries, meetings, and seminars inside them, there we are more likely to find genuine student communities in which intellectual and social life are intermixed and mutually supportive.

But residence halls are by no means the only basis for substructing a large campus. We tend to forget that only about a third of American college students live in college-provided housing. On many non-residential campuses, departments and divisions can provide the structural support for intellectual and academic subcultures. At San Francisco State College, a very large non-residential institution, the Creative Arts Division, which includes the departments of theater, art, music and the like, provides an illustration of this. Students majoring in these fields have strong common bonds of interest, and they are continually involved with one another and with their work; moreover, within this division there is a good deal of direct relationship of faculty to student, and the creation of a genuine cultural community with its strong involvements, at considerable variance with the impersonal and fleeting relationships typical of much of mass higher education. Moreover, this division has strong ties with the cultural life of San Francisco, and there is thus an additional link between the students' lives on and off campus.

It is neither possible nor necessary for all of us to move our colleges to San Francisco, for lively student cultures can be found on campuses remote from any city. There is certainly more to be known of the nature and determinants of student communities and of the role which administrative action can play in the creation of the best of them. But I do not think it necessary to wait on more research, however helpful that may be, before attempting to think through, in the special and different circumstances of one's own institution, how administrative and faculty action might create the conditions in which such intellectually live student communities might flourish. Moreover, it is certain that this kind of thinking has gone on in many places; it might be of great value now to develop some machinery for sharing ideas, and for assessing and analyzing those administrative arrangements which seem to have the best results.

A good deal of educational planning in this area is now done by architects, and especially so at a time of rapid expansion of physical plant for higher education all over the country. And that is because the subcultures I have been speaking of exist in places and spaces. Students eat together here under these physical arrangements, they have coffee there, they get together informally (if possible) in this corridor or that study hall or the other lounge. And the architect is concerned with spaces, what they look like, what they are shaped like, where they are located. Now the existence of places for meeting is not the only factor which affects student subcultures: students who are deeply involved in their own education will find places in which to pursue it in company with their peers almost regardless of the obstacles we place in their way. But such students, I need scarcely say, are rare; there are many more whose emerging interests in ideas can be encouraged or discouraged, reinforced by their fellows or punished by them. And such students will be involved in intellectual life under some conditions but not under others—in other words, they are provisional members of academic subcultures which are fragile, and which can be destroyed or prevented from coming to life if they find little structural and physical support. When architects, often in consultation with faculty and college administrators, design a dormitory or library or commons building, they are, in their provision and arrangement of spaces, affecting the probabilities that subcultures of the kind we are speaking of will flourish in that environment.

To some extent, architects are aware of this; the best of them know, often I suspect on the basis of their own experience in college, that an important part of the life of the institution goes on outside the classrooms and during "leisure" hours, and it is customary to provide lounges, coffee shops and the like where students can get together informally. My point is that the provision and arrangement of these spaces does not customarily get nearly the thought and study that they deserve, nor does it get the right kind of thought and study. For example, one major university recently built a number of large student dormitories. These are eight stories high, handsome, well furnished buildings in the international style. Each has a very large lounge, two walls of which are glass, full of bright modern furniture, a large fireplace, and so forth. On another level a large open recreation room links pairs of these dormitories, and this is available for parties, dances, and the like. Now these dormitories are handsome buildings, and the large lounges in each are attractive places shown with pride to parents and visitors. The only trouble is that they are not used very much. Despite, perhaps because of, their openness and brightness they are not warm places; they do not invite small groups to wander in to talk or read. The space is there, the furniture is there; it is not difficult to see how designers could *assume* that the students would fill the room with life. But this was all based on assumptions about how students live, and live together, or how they ought to. To my knowledge, these important decisions were not based on any observations of how students do use spaces, when they use them, and for what purposes. It seems evident to me now that the large lounges should be a cluster of small spaces, which encourage small groups to use them and for different purposes—one with phonograph equipment, some with books and magazines, another with a piano, another with a hot plate. But my point is not that my hunches are better than someone else's—which is at least questionable—but rather that decisions with such lasting consequences and of such clear importance for the intellectual life of the institution ought to be based on something more than hunches. I am not suggesting controlled experiments involving space use, but something much simpler: that our experience in each institution with how the existing spaces are actually used by students informally may well give us clues to the design of new spaces. And we might well strengthen our experience in this respect by actually observing the uses of space, by really paying attention to the informal life of students, with the question in our minds—how can we create conditions which will especially encourage those patterns of student life which are linked to their education, that is, the conditions which will support academic subcultures. I am quite aware that there are many considerations other than those I am speaking of that enter into new construction; I submit, however, that the informal life of students—when "youths get together and let themselves go upon their favorite themes," in Woodrow Wilson's words—ought not be the least of our considerations when we are providing the physical structures in which our colleges will be living over the next 50 or a 100 years.

While thinking of this sort need not wait on more research in higher education, there are kinds of useful research which can be carried out by faculty and administrators in institutions which are engaged in planning. There are many good reasons for doing research within your own institution. For some purposes you need detailed records; for other purposes you may want to learn more about your students through questionnaires and psychological inventories. But for the study of student cultures in your own institutions, you don't have to be a sociologist or psychologist or statistician. What is needed are the skills, and perhaps more important, the temperament, of an anthropologist. This is because what we are concerned with here is the character of the social life, not of an exotic tribe in the South Pacific or the Andes, but of the students in our own colleges. And I submit that much of student life, especially the large part of it that doesn't cause us trouble, lies outside our knowledge and attention; and that what we know of it derives more than we suspect from our recollections of our own student lives.

To learn more in this area we do not need detailed information about individuals, because here we are not studying individuals, but rather the character of their informal social environments. For this we need actually to watch what goes on around campus, to listen to what students talk about informally, and to talk with them about how they spend their leisure time, and to do this with the combination of passivity, patience, and alertness of the anthropologist in the field. This actually doesn't take any more time than collecting records and administering and processing tests. But people in colleges are less likely to do it at all systematically because it is harder to justify; it is less busy and purposeful (or seems so), and you don't have a folder of statistics to show for it when you are done. But, on the other hand, you *are* likely to have a much more detailed sense of the varieties of student life and culture on campus: how spaces are used, how time is filled, what brings students together, and where and when.

But there are differences as well as similarities between what I am describing and anthropological field work. From the anthropologist's point of view, all the subcultures on a campus are equally interesting; he is not likely to make value judgments among different patterns of behavior. But as educators, we are likely to be more interested in, and sympathetic to, some subcultures than others. And this can simplify our task. For this means that we don't have to observe with equal attention all aspects of students' informal and social life; quite a lot of it simply doesn't have much relevance for their education, or at least, the part of their education that we are concerned with. But if we are patient and sensitive, we may learn more about where the students' informal life is infused with intellectual and cultural interests. We will probably find that happening for only a minority of the students—though if we define intellectual interests more broadly than merely as the content of the curriculum, we may find it happening at least some of the time for a larger proportion of the students than we suspect. In any case, whatever the numbers involved, it is the conditions under which that happens that are of special interest and relevance to us. And if we learn where and how intellectual interests enter the informal life of at least some of the students, then we have at least some empirical basis for planning—in curriculum, organizational structure, building, and the like —so as to strengthen and extend those conditions on our campuses. And some empirical basis for making these decisions is preferable to the unsupported assumptions and hunches which are in fact the basis on which these decisions are frequently made today in even the greatest universities.

I am sorry to have to deal with this matter in such general terms. The topic clearly deserves more time and discussion that I can give it now. My purpose is chiefly to illustrate one of the ways in which a concern with the cultural life of students is of direct relevance to, and can be influenced by, administrative decisions and actions. Let us be modest; I do not think we can create these cultures among students, we cannot impose our interests and purposes on them, and especially on their informal life and relationships with one another. The more managed, the less spontaneous that life is, the less likely it is really to engage the students' own interests and motivations, and the more likely they will remove their social life even further beyond our sight and influence. But if we cannot create an informal intellectual life among students, we can in modest and indirect ways strengthen the conditions which support and encourage it. How can we do this? By resisting the pressures toward the mass, impersonal processing of students; by encouraging and structuring high levels of student-faculty interaction outside of class; by creating administrative units of small enough size so that students and faculty with shared interests interact with one another frequently and informally and over reasonably long periods of time; and by giving some thought and attention, and even empirical study, to the ways in which the college can provide the setting for a genuine liberal education that is not restricted to the classroom, the kind that under the best circumstances students and faculty give to one another in the course of living with one another.

OTHER STUDIES—WHERE TO FIND THEM

Adorno, T., Frenkel-Brunswik, E., Levinson, D., and Sanford, N., *The Authoritarian Personality*. Harper, New York, 1950.

American Council on Education, Problems and Policies Committee, *Spotlight on the College Student*, Habein, Margaret L., editor, Washington, D.C., 1959.

American Educational Research Association, *The Coming Crisis in the Selection of Students for College Entrance*, Washington, D.C., 1960.

Appleby, Thomas L., and Haner, Charles F., "MMPI Profiles of a College Faculty Group," *Proceedings of the Iowa Academy of Science for 1956*, 63:605–609, 1956.

Atkinson, Byron H., and Brugger, A. T., "Do College Students Drink Too Much?" *Journal of Higher Education*, 30:305–312, 1959.

Axt, Richard G. and Sprague, Hall T., *College Self Study*, Lectures on Institutional Research, Western Interstate Commission for Higher Education, Boulder, Colorado, 1959.

Barton, Allen H., *Studying the Effects of College Education*, Edward W. Hazen Foundation, New Haven, 1959.

Berdie, Ralph F., and Others, *After High School What?* University of Minnesota Press, Minneapolis, 1954.

Bidwell, C. E., editor, *The American College and Student Personality: A Survey of Research Progress and Problems*, Social Science Research Council, New York, 1960.

Birney, Robert, and Taylor, Marc, "Scholastic Behavior and Orientation in College," *Journal of Educational Psychology*, 50:266–274, 1959.

Borg, Walter, "Personality and Interest Measures as Related to Criteria of Instructor Effectiveness," *Journal of Educational Research*, 50:701–709, 1957.

Boroff, David, "California's Five-College Experiment," *Harper's Magazine*, 219:70–78, 1959.

Brown, Donald R., "Non-intellective Qualities and the Perception of the Ideal Student by College Faculty," *Journal of Educational Sociology*, 33:269–278, 1960.

Brumbaugh, A. J., *Research Designed to Improve Institutions of Higher Learning*, American Council on Education, Washington, D.C., 1960.

Bushnell, John, "What Are the Changing Characteristics of the

Undergraduate and What Do These Changes Mean for Programs of General Education?" *Current Issues in Higher Education, 1959, Proceedings of the Fourteenth Annual National Conference on Higher Education,* 137–144, Association for Higher Education, National Education Association, Washington, D.C., 1959.

Caplow, Theodore, and McGee, Reece J., *The Academic Marketplace,* Basic Books, New York, 1958.

Center for the Study of Higher Education, *Selection and Educational Differentiation,* Report of Conference, University of California, Berkeley, 1959.

Clark, Burton R., "College Image and Student Selection," *Selection and Educational Differentiation,* 155–168, The Center for Study of Higher Education, Berkeley, California, 1960.

Clark, Burton R., "The 'Cooling-Out' Function in Higher Education," *American Journal of Sociology,* 65:569–576, 1960.

Clark, Burton R., *The Open Door College: A Case Study,* McGraw-Hill, New York, 1960.

Coffman, William E., "Determining Students' Concepts of Effective Teaching from Their Ratings of Instructors," *Journal of Educational Psychology,* 45:277–286, 1954.

Commager, Henry S., "Is Ivy Necessary?" *Saturday Review of Literature,* 43:69ff, 1960.

Crannell, Clarke W., "A Preliminary Attempt to Identify the Factors in Student-Instructor Evaluation," *Journal of Psychology,* 36:417–422, 1953.

David, Opal D., editor, *The Education of Women—Signs for the Future,* American Council on Education, Washington, D.C., 1959.

Donaldson, Robert S., *Fortifying Higher Education: A Story of College Self Studies,* The Fund for the Advancement of Education, New York, 1959.

Dressel, Paul L., and Mayhew, Lewis B., *General Education—Explorations in Evaluation,* Final Report of a Cooperative Study of Evaluation in General Education, American Council on Education, Washington, D.C., c1954.

Eckert, Ruth E. and Keller, Robert J., editors, *A University Looks at Its Program,* University of Minnesota Press, Minneapolis, 1954.

Eddy, Edward D., Jr., *The College Influence on Student Character,* American Council on Education, Washington, D.C., 1959.

Educational Testing Service, *Background Factors Relating to College Plans and College Enrollment Among Public High School Students,* Princeton, 1957.

Eells, Walter Crosby, *College Teachers and College Teaching, An Annotated Bibliography on College and University Faculty Members and Instructional Methods,* Southern Regional Education Board, Atlanta, 1957.

Erickson, E. H., "Growth and Crises of the Healthy Personality," *Symposium on the Healthy Personality,* Josiah Macy, Jr. Foundation, New York, 1950.

Farnsworth, Dana L., "Emotions and Learning," *Harvard Educational Review,* 25:95–104, 1955.

Farnsworth, Dana L., *Mental Health in College and University,* Harvard University Press, Cambridge, 1957.

Farnsworth, Dana L., "Motivation for Learning—The Community's Responsibility," *Rhode Island College Journal,* 1:55–64, 1960.

Farnsworth, Dana L., "Some Non-Academic Causes of Success and Failure in College Students," in College Entrance Examination Board, *College Admissions,* No. 2, 72–78, Princeton, 1955.

Farnsworth, Dana L., "What is Mental Health in a University?" *Mental Hygiene,* 38:34–48, 1954.

Festinger, Leon L. and Schachter, Stanley, *Social Pressures in Informal Groups: A Study of Human Factors in Housing,* Harper, New York, 1950.

Festinger, L. and Others, *Theory and Experiment in Social Communication,* Institute for Social Research, University of Michigan, Ann Arbor, 1950.

Fishman, Joshua A., "Non-Intellective Factors as Predictions, as Criteria, and as Contingencies in Selection and Guidance of College Students: a Socio-Psychological Analysis," *Selection and Educational Differentiation,* 55–73, The Center for the Study of Higher Education, Berkeley, 1960.

Fishman, Joshua A., "Unsolved Criterion Problems in the Selection of College Students," *Harvard Educational Review,* 28: 340–349, 1958.

Fishman, Joshua A., "The Use of Tests for Admission to College: the Next Fifty Years," in Educational Conference, 1957, *Long-Range Planning for Education,* 74–79, American Council on Education, Washington D.C., 1958.

Freedman, Mervin B., *Impact of College,* U.S. Office of Education, *New Dimensions in Higher Education,* No. 4, Washington, D.C., 1960.

Freedman, Mervin B., "The Passage Through College, "Personality Development During the College Years," *Journal of Social Issues,* 12:13–28, 1956.

229

Freedman, Mervin B., "What Does Research Show About the Effects of the Total Institutional Program on Student Values?" *Current Issues in Higher Education, 1958, Proceedings of the Thirteenth Annual National Conference on Higher Education,* 102–107, Association for Higher Education, National Education Association, Washington, D.C., 1958.

Freedman, M., Sanford, N., and Webster, H., "A New Instrument for Studying Authoritarianism in Personality," *Journal of Psychology,* 40:73–84, 1955.

Fricke, Benno G., "How Colleges Should Check Their Students," *College Board Review,* 34:17–22, 1958.

Fricke, Benno G., "Prediction, Selection, Mortality and Quality Control," *College and University,* 32:34–52, 1956.

Funkenstein, Daniel H., "What Does Higher Education Need to Know About the Student in Today's Changing Society?" *Current Issues in Higher Education, 1960, Proceedings of the Fifteenth Annual National Conference on Higher Education,* 160–164, Association for Higher Education, National Education Association, Washington, D.C., 1960.

Funkenstein, Daniel H., and Wilkie, George H., *Student Mental Health: An Annotated Bibliography, 1936–1955.* Prepared for an International Conference on Student Mental Health, Princeton, September 5–15, 1956.

Gardner, Eric F., and Thompson, George G., *Social Relations and Morale in Small Groups,* Appleton-Century-Crofts, New York, 1956.

Gee, Helen H., "Differential Characteristics of Student Bodies— Implications for the Study of Medical Education," *Selection and Educational Differentiation,* 125–154, The Center for the Study of Higher Education, Berkeley, 1959.

Gillespie, J. M. and Allport, G. W., *Youth's Outlook on the Future,* Doubleday, Garden City, New York, 1955.

Gladstein, Gerald A., "Study Behavior of Gifted Stereotype and Non-stereotype College Students," *Personnel and Guidance Journal,* 38:470–474, 1960.

Glenny, Lyman A., *Autonomy of Public Colleges, The Challenge of Coordination,* McGraw-Hill, New York, 1959.

Glass, Bentley, "The Academic Scientist: 1940–1960," *American Association of University Professors Bulletin,* 46:149–155, 1960.

Goldsen, Rose K., and Others, *What College Students Think,* Van Nostrand, Princeton, 1960.

Griffiths, Daniel Edward, *Research in Educational Administration,* Teachers College, Columbia University, New York, 1959

Guetzkow, Harold, Kelly, E. Lowell, and McKeachie, W. J., "An Experimental Comparison of Recitation, Discussion, and Tutorial Methods in College Teaching," *Journal of Educational Psychology*, 45:193–207, 1954.

Gustad, John W., "The Career Decisions of College Teachers," *Research Monograph Series No. 2*, Southern Regional Education Board, Atlanta, 1960.

Gustad, John W., editor, *Faculty Preparation and Orientation*, Proceedings of a Regional Conference, Sponsored by the New England Board of Higher Education, Winchester, Massachusetts, 1960.

Gustad, John W., editor, *Faculty Supply, Demand, and Recruitment*, Proceedings of a Regional Conference, Sponsored by the New England Board of Higher Education, Winchester, Massachusetts, 1959.

Gustad, John W., editor, *Faculty Utilization and Retention*, Proceedings of a Regional Conference, Sponsored by the New England Board of Higher Education, Winchester, Massachusetts, 1960.

Gustad, John W., "They March to a Different Drummer: Another Look at College Teachers," *Educational Record*, 40:204–211, 1959.

Hall, Thomas, S., "In What Ways Can the College Best Assist the Student in Developing His Basic Pattern of Values?" *Current Issues in Higher Education, 1960, Proceedings of the Fifteenth Annual National Conference on Higher Education*, 157–159, Association for Higher Education, National Education Association, Washington, D.C., 1960.

Hamlin, Wilfrid G., "A College Faculty Looks at Itself," *Journal of Higher Education*, 28:202–206, 1957.

Hare, A.P., Borgatta, E. F., and Bales, R. F., editors, *Small Groups: Studies in Social Interaction*, Knopf, 1955.

Heath, S. Roy, "Personality and Student Development," in *New Dimensions of Learning in a Free Society*, 225–245, University of Pittsburgh Press, Pittsburgh, 1958.

Heilman, Robert B., "Fashions in Melodrama," *American Association of University Professors Bulletin*, 45:250–373, 1959.

Heist, Paul, and Webster, Harold, "Differential Characteristics of Student Bodies—Implications for Selection and Study of Undergraduates," *Selection and Educational Differentiation*, 91–106, The Center for the Study of Higher Education, Berkeley, 1960.

Heist, Paul, "Diversity in College Student Characteristics," *Journal of Educational Sociology*, 33:279–291, 1960.

Heist, Paul, and Williams, Phoebe, *Variation in Achievement Within a Select and Homogeneous Student Body*, Research

Report for the Center for the Study of Higher Education, Berkeley, 1959.

Hilgard, Ernest R. and Spalding, W. B., editors, *Mental Hygiene in Teaching*, Harcourt, Brace, New York, 1951.

Hobson, Robert L., "Some Psychological Dimensions of Academic Administrators," in *Purdue University Studies in Higher Education*, No. 73, 7–64, Purdue University, Division of Education, Lafayette, Indiana, 1950.

Holland, John L., "Undergraduate Origins of American Scientists," *Science*, 126:433–437, 1957.

Hollinshead, Byron S., *Who Should Go To College*, Columbia University Press, New York, 1952.

Hollis, E. V., *Factors Related to Application, Admission, Registration, and Persistence in College*, Cooperative Research Project No. 166, Division of Higher Education, U.S. Office of Education, Washington, D.C., n.d.

Holmes, Charles H., "Why They Left College; A Study of Voluntary Freshman Withdrawals from the College of Liberal Arts at Syracuse University," *College and University*, 34:295–300, 1959.

Holtzman, W. H., and Others, *Inkblot Perception and Personality-Holtzman Inkblot Technique*, The University of Texas Press, Austin, Texas, 1961.

Holtzman, W. H., Iscoe, I., and Calvin, A. D., "Rorschach Color Responses and Manifest Anxiety in College Women," *Journal of Consulting Psychology*, 18:317–324, 1954.

Holtzman, W. H., "A Study-attitudes Questionnaire for Predicting Academic Success," *Journal of Educational Psychology*, 46:75–84, 1955.

Holtzman, W. H., Brown, W. F., and Farquhar, W. G., "A Survey of Study Habits and Attitudes: A New Instrument for the Prediction of Academic Success," *Educational and Psychological Measurement*, 14:726–732, 1954.

Hoopes, Robert, and Marshall, Hubert, *The Undergraduate in the University*, Stanford University Press, Stanford, 1957.

Horn, Francis H., "Who Should Go To College?" *Current Issues in Higher Education, 1955, Proceedings of the Tenth Annual National Conference on Higher Education*, 38–46, Association For Higher Education, National Education Association, Washington, D.C., 1955.

Iffert, Robert E., "Drop-Outs: Nature and Causes, Effects on Student, Family and Society," *Current Issues in Higher Education, 1956, Proceedings of the Eleventh Annual National Conference on Higher Education*, 94–102, Association for Higher Education, National Education Association, Washington, D.C., 1956.

Iffert, Robert E., *Retention and Withdrawal of College Students, Bulletin No. 1,* Office of Education, U.S. Department of Health, Education and Welfare, Washington, D.C., 1958.

Iffert, Robert E., "Study of College Student Retention and Withdrawal," *College and University,* 31:435–447, 1956.

Western Interstate Commission for Higher Education and Center for the Study of Higher Education, *Institutional Research on Students,* Report on Institute for College and University Administrators, University of California, Berkeley, July 26–30, 1960.

Jacob, Philip E., *Changing Values in College,* Harper, New York, 1957.

Jacob, Philip E., "Does Higher Education Influence Student Values," *National Education Association Journal,* 47:35–58, 1958.

Jahoda, Marie, *Current Concepts of Positive Mental Health,* Basic Books, New York, 1958.

Jex, Frank B., and Merrill, Reed M., "Intellectual and Personality Characteristics of University of Utah Students," *Journal of Educational Research,* 53:118–120, 1959.

Johnson, Burges, *Campus Versus Classroom,* Ives Washburn, New York, 1946.

Kahl, Joseph A., "Educational and Occupational Aspirations of 'Common Man' Boys," *Harvard Educational Review,* 23:186–203, 1953.

Knapp, Robert Henry, and Goodrich, H. B., *Origins of American Scientists,* University of Chicago Press, Chicago, 1952.

Knapp, Robert Henry, and Greenbaum, Joseph J., *The Younger American Scholar: His Collegiate Origins,* University of Chicago Press, Chicago, 1953.

Koile, Earl A., "Faculty and the University Counseling Center," *Journal of Counseling Psychology,* 7:293–297, 1960.

Koile, Earl A., "A Measure of Interest for Selecting Faculty Counselors," *Educational and Psychological Measurement,* 15:47–57, 1955.

Koile, Earl A., "Characteristics of College Teachers Interested in Faculty Counseling," *Journal of Counseling Psychology,* 2:32–34, 1955.

Kosa, John, Rachiele, Leo D., and Schommer, Cyril O., "Psychological Characteristics of Ethnic Groups in a College Population," *Journal of Psychology,* 46:265–275, 1958.

Lazarsfeld, Paul Felix, and Thielens, Wagner, Jr., *The Academic Mind,* The Free Press, Glencoe, Illinois, 1958.

Lerner, Max, "Education and the Image of Man," *National Parent-Teacher,* 54:7–9, 1959.

Little, J. Kenneth, "College Scholarships in Wisconsin," *Educational Record*, 40:348–352, 1959.

Little, J. Kenneth, *Explorations Into the College Plans and Experiences of High School Graduates*, University of Wisconsin, Madison, 1959.

Little, J. Kenneth, "The Wisconsin Study of High School Graduates," *Educational Record*, 40:123–128, 1959.

Lunn, Harry H., Jr., *The Student's Role in College Policy Making*, American Council on Education, Washington, D.C., 1957.

MacKinnon, Donald W., "Identifying and Developing Creativity," *Selection and Educational Differentiation*, 75–89, The Center for the Study of Higher Education, Berkeley, 1959.

MacMinn, Paul, Miller, Carroll H., and Wellman, Frank E., *Research in School and College Personnel Services: Summaries of Unpublished Studies, September 1956–September 1958*, Bulletin No. 10, U.S. Office of Education, Washington, D.C., 1960.

McConnell, T. R., "The Diversification of American Higher Education: A Research Program," *Educational Record*, 38:300–315, 1957.

McConnell, T. R., and Heist, Paul, "Do Students Make the College?" *College and University*, 34:442–452, 1959.

McConnell, T. R., "A Look at the Total Educational Scene," *The Changing University*, Daigneault, G. H., editor, Center for the Study of Liberal Education for Adults, Chicago, 1959.

McConnell, T. R., *The Rediscovery of the Gifted Student*, Center for the Study of Higher Education, Berkeley, California, 1959.

McGee, Reece J., "The Function of Institutional Inbreeding," *American Journal of Sociology*, 65:483–88, 1960.

McGee, Reece J., "The State University: A Prolegomenon," *The Graduate Journal*, 2:223–238, 1959.

McGuire, Carson, "Factors Influencing Individual Mental Health, *Review of Educational Research*, 26:451–478, 1956.

McGuire, Carson, "Personality," *Encyclopedia of Educational Research*, 945–957, 3rd Edition, Macmillan, New York, 1960.

Maslow, A. H., and Zimmerman, W. A., "College Teaching Ability, Scholarly Activity and Personality," *Journal of Educational Psychology*, 47:185–189, 1956.

Medsker, Leland L., "Cooperative Action Among Two-Year and Four-Year Colleges: Opportunities and Obstacles," *The Educational Record*, 39:114–121, 1958.

Merton, R. K., Reader, G., and Kendall, Patricia, editors, *The Student Physician: Introductory Studies in the Sociology of Medical Education*, Harvard University Press, Cambridge, 1957.

Mitchell, James V., and Pierce-Jones, John, "A Factor Analysis of Gough's California Psychological Inventory," *Journal of Consulting Psychology*, 24:453–456, 1960.

Mitchell, James V., "Goal-Setting Behavior as a Function of Self-Acceptance, Over- and Underachievement, and Related Personality Variables," *Journal of Educational Psychology*, 50:93–104, 1959.

Morsh, Joseph E., and Wilder, Eleanor W., *Identifying the Effective Instructor: A Review of the Quantitative Studies 1900–1952*, U.S. Air Force Personnel and Training Research Center, Research Bulletin, No. AFPTRC–TR–54–44, 1954.

Mueller, Kate Hevner, "The Married Student on the Campus," *College and University*, 35:155–163, 1960.

Murphy, Gardner, *Human Potentialities*, Basic Books, New York, 1958.

Neugeboren, Bernard, "Clinical Study of Academic Underachievers," *Psychosocial Problems of College Men*, Wedge, Bryant M., editor, Yale University Press, New Haven, 1958.

Newcomb, T. M., *The Acquaintance Process*, Holt, Rinehart, and Winston, New York, 1961.

Newcomb, T. M., *Personality and Social Change: Attitude Formation in a Student Community*, Dryden Press, New York, 1957.

Newcomb, T. M., and Wilson, E. K., editors, *The Study of College Peer Groups: Problems and Prospects for Research*, Social Science Research Council, New York, in press.

Pace, C. Robert, and Stern, George G., "An Approach to the Measurement of Psychological Characteristics of College Environments," *Journal of Educational Psychology*, 49:269–277, 1958.

Pace, C. Robert, and Stern, George G., *A Criterion Study of College Environment*, Psychological Research Center, Syracuse, New York, 1958.

Pace, C. Robert, "Evaluation of Institutional Programs," *Review of Educational Research*, 24:341–350, 1954.

Pace, C. Robert, "Five College Environments," *College Board Review*, 41:24–28, 1960.

Peck, Robert F., and McGuire, Carson, "Measuring Changes in Mental Health with the Sentence Completion Technique," *Psychological Reports*, 5:151–160, 1959.

Peck, Robert F., "Measuring the Mental Health of Normal Adults," *Genetic Psychology Monographs*, 60:197–255, 1959.

Peck, Robert F., "Personality Patterns of Prospective Teachers," *Journal of Experimental Education*, 29:2, 1960.

Peck, Robert F., and Others, *The Psychology of Character Development,* Wiley, New York, 1960.

Pitkin, Royce, S., "Should Colleges Reflect or Help Change Value Systems of Society?" *Current Issues in Higher Education, 1960, Proceedings of the Fifteenth Annual National Conference on Higher Education,* 213–215, Association for Higher Education, National Education Association, Washington, D.C., 1960.

Rettig, Salomon, Rawson, Harve E., and Pasamanick, Benjamin, "Changes in Moral Values Over Three Decades," *Social Problems,* 6:320–328, 1959.

Rettig, Salomon, Rawson, Harve E., and Pasamanick, Benjamin, "Differences in the Structure of Moral Values of Students and Alumni," *American Sociological Review,* 25:550–555, 1960.

Rettig, Salomon and Pasamanick, Benjamin, "Moral Codes of American and Foreign Academic Intellectuals in an American University," *Journal of Social Psychology,* 51:229–244, 1960.

Riesman, David, "The Academic Career; Notes on Recruitment and Colleagueship," *Daedalus,* 88:147–169, 1959.

Riesman, David, *Constraint and Variety in American Education,* Doubleday Anchor Books, New York, 1958.

Riesman, David, "The Influence of Student Culture and Faculty Values in the American College," *The Year Book of Education 1959: Higher Education,* Bereday, George Z. F., and Lauwerys, Joseph A., editors, 386–404, World Book, Yonkers-on-Hudson, New York, 1959.

Riesman, David, "Student Culture and Faculty Values," in Habien, Margaret L., editor, *Spotlight on the College Student,* American Council on Education, Washington, D.C., 1959.

Riesman, David, "Where is the College Generation Headed?" *The Atlantic,* 207–39–45, 1961.

Rust, Ralph M., "Personality and Academic Achievement," in *Psychosocial Problems of College Men,* Wedge, Bryant M., editor, Yale University Press, New Haven, 1958.

Ryans, David G., *Characteristics of Teachers,* American Council on Education, Washington, D.C., 1960.

Sanford, R. Nevitt, editor, *The American College,* Wiley, New York, in press.

Sanford, R. Nevitt, "The Development of Maturity of Personality in College," *Selection and Educational Differentiation,* 169–187, The Center for the Study of Higher Education, Berkeley, 1959.

Sanford, R. Nevitt, "The Professor Looks at the Student," *The Two Ends of the Log—Learning and Teaching in Today's College,* 3–25, Cooper, Russell M., editor, University of Minnesota Press, Minneapolis, 1958.

Sanford, R. Nevitt, "Uncertain Senior," *Journal of the National Association of Women Deans and Counselors,* 21:9–15, 1957.

Sanford, R. Nevitt, editor, "Personality Development During the College Years," *Journal of Social Issues,* 12:3–72, 1956.

Schachter, S., *The Psychology of Affiliation,* Stanford University Press, Stanford, 1959.

Schommer, Cyril O., Rachiele, Leo D., and Kosa, John, "Socioeconomic Background and Religious Attitudes of Catholic College Students," *American Catholic Sociological Review,* 21: 229–237, 1960.

Sherif, Muzafer, and Sherif, Carolyn W., *An Outline of Social Psychology,* Harper, New York, 1956.

Slater, John Marlowe, "Perception; a Context for the Consideration of Persistence and Attrition Among College Men," *Personnel and Guidance Journal,* 35:435–440, 1957.

Smith, John E., *Value Conviction and Higher Education,* Edward W. Hazen Foundation, New Haven, 1958.

Sprague, Hall T., *Institutional Research in the West,* Western Interstate Commission for Higher Education, Boulder, Colorado, 1959.

Stecklein, John E. and Edkert, Ruth E., *An Exploratory Study of Factors Influencing the Choice of College Teaching as a Career,* U.S. Office of Education, Cooperative Research Program, Washington, D.C., 1958.

Stern, George G., "Congruence and Dissonance in the Ecology of College Students," *Student Medicine,* 8:304–339, 1960.

Stern, George G., *Preliminary Manual: for the Activities Index and College Characteristics Index,* Psychological Research Center, New York, 1958, mim.

Stern, George G., "Environments for Learning," *Social Science and Higher Education,* Sanford, R. N., editor, Society for the Psychological Study of Social Issues, New York, in press.

Stern, George, Stein, Morris I., and Bloom, Benjamin S., *Methods in Personality Assessment,* The Free Press, Glencoe, Illinois, 1956.

Sutherland, Robert L., *Can An Adult Change?* The Hogg Foundation for Mental Health, The University of Texas, Austin, 1957.

Sutherland, Robert L., "Conformity and the Inner Self," *Journal of the National Association of Women Deans and Counselors,* 21:162–165, 1958.

Sutherland, Robert L., "Some Aspects of the Culture of a Campus," *Trends in Student Personnel Work,* 350–355, Williamson, E. G., editor, The University of Minnesota Press, Minneapolis, 1949.

Sutherland, Robert L., and Others, "Students and Staff in a Social Context," in American Council on Education, *Student Personnel Work*, Series VI, No. 18, Washington, D.C., 1953.

Tagiuri, R., and Petrullo, L., editors, *Person Perception and Interpersonal Behavior*, Stanford University Press, Stanford, 1958.

Taylor, Harold, "The American Idea," *Current Issues in Higher Education, 1960, Proceedings of the Fifteenth Annual National Conference on Higher Education*, 43–46, Association for Higher Education, National Education Asociation, Washington, D.C., 1960.

Taylor, Harold, "World of the American Student," *Current Issues In Higher Education, 1956, Proceedings of the Eleventh Annual National Conference on Higher Education*, 21–28, Association for Higher Education, National Education Association, Washington, D.C., 1956.

Taylor, Harold, "Let's Give Our Colleges Back to the Students," *Journal of the National Education Association*, 45:367–368, 1956.

Thibaut, J. S., and Kelley, H. H., *The Social Psychology of Groups*, Wiley, New York, 1959.

Thistlethwaite, Donald L., "College Environments and the Development of Talent," *Science* 130:71–76, 1959.

Thistlethwaite, Donald L., "College Press and Student Achievement," *Journal of Educational Psychology*, 50:183–191, 1959.

Townsend, Agatha, *College Freshmen Speak Out*, Harper, New York, 1956.

Trabue, Marion R., "College Teachers at Work," *Review of Educational Research*, 22:233–237, 1952.

Troller, A. E., editor, *Long Range Planning for Education*, American Council on Education, Washington, D.C., 1958.

Trow, Martin, "Cultural Sophistication and Higher Education," *Selection and Educational Differentiation*, 107–123, The Center for the Study of Higher Education, Berkeley, 1959.

Trow, Martin, "Reflections on the Recruitment to College Teaching," *Faculty Supply, Demand, and Recruitment*, Gustad, John W., editor, New England Board of Higher Education, Winchester, Massachusetts, 1959.

Tyler, Ralph W., "Place of the Social Sciences in the Liberal Arts Curriculum," *Journal of General Education*, 10:114–120, 1957.

Tyler, Ralph W., "What Will Be the Emerging Curricular Implications for Colleges and Universities of the New Social and Technological Concepts?" *Current Issues in Higher Education, 1957, Proceedings of the Twelfth Annual National Conference on Higher Education*, pp. 78–80, Association for Higher Education, National Education Association, Washington, D.C., 1957.

Ulich, Robert, "The Contemporary Academic Scene in the United States," *The Year Book of Education 1959: Higher Education*, Bereday, George Z. F., and Lauwerys, Joseph A., editors, 122–130, World Book, Yonkers-on-Hudson, New York, 1959.

Warren, Jonathan R. and Heist, Paul A., "Personality Attributes of Gifted College Students," *Science*, 132:330–337, 1960.

Webb, Sam C., "Comparative Validity of Two Biographical Inventory Keys," *Journal of Applied Psychology*, 44:173–183, 1960.

Weber, C. A., "Some Characteristics of College Teachers," *Journal of Educational Research*, 46:685–692, 1953.

Webster, Harold, "Changes in Attitudes During College," *Journal of Educational Psychology*, 49:109–117, 1958.

Webster, Harold, Freedman, Mervin, and Heist, Paul, "Changes in Personality During College," *The American College*, Sanford, R. N., editor, Wiley, New York, in press.

Webster, Harold, and Heist, Paul, *Construction of a Multiple Trait Personality Test for Use With College Populations*, Center for the Study of Higher Education, Berkeley, California, n.d.

Webster, Harold, *On Measuring Change*, Research Report of the Center for the Study of Higher Education, University of California, Berkeley, 1959, mim.

Wedge, Bryant M., "Mental Health in Universities," *World Mental Health*, 11:149–154, 1959.

Wedge, Bryant M., editor, *Psychosocial Problems of College Men*, Yale University Press, New Haven, 1958.

Wise, William Max, *They Come for the Best of Reasons*, American Council on Education, Washington, D.C., 1958.

Wolfle, Dael, *America's Resources of Specialized Talent*, Harper, New York, 1954.

Wolfle, Dael, "Diversity of Talent," *The American Psychologist*, 15:535–545, 1960.

Woodburne, L. S., "The Qualifications of Superior Faculty Members," *Journal of Higher Education*, 23:377–382, 1952.